THE SANTA CLAUS MAN

*The Rise and Fall of a Jazz Age Con Man and the
Invention of Christmas in New York*

ALEX PALMER

Guilford, Connecticut

To Mom for her reading. To Dad for his storytelling.

An imprint of Rowman & Littlefield

Distributed by NATIONAL BOOK NETWORK

Copyright © 2016 by Alex Palmer

British Library Cataloguing in Publication Information Available

Library of Congress Cataloging-in-Publication Data

Palmer, Alex.
  The Santa Claus man : the rise and fall of a Jazz Age con man and the invention of Christmas in New York / Alex Palmer.
    pages cm
  Includes bibliographical references and index.
  ISBN 978-1-4930-0844-5 (hardcover) — ISBN 978-1-4930-1890-1 (e-book) 1. Gluck, John Duval, 1878-1951. 2. Santa Claus Association, Inc. (New York, N.Y.)—History. 3. Santa Claus—New York (State)—New York. 4. Christmas—New York (State)—New York—History—20th century. 5. United States. Post Office Department—History—20th century. 6. Charities—New York (State)—New York—History—20th century. 7. Swindlers and swindling—New York (State)—New York—Biography. 8. New York (N.Y.)—Social life and customs—20th century. 9. New York (N.Y.)—Biography. I. Title. II. Title: Rise and fall of a Jazz Age con man and the invention of Christmas in New York.
  GT4986.N7P35 2015
  394.2663097471—dc23

                              2015011994

♾™ The paper used in this publication meets the minimum requirements of American National Standard for Information Sciences—Permanence of Paper for Printed Library Materials, ANSI/ NISO Z39.48-1992.

Contents

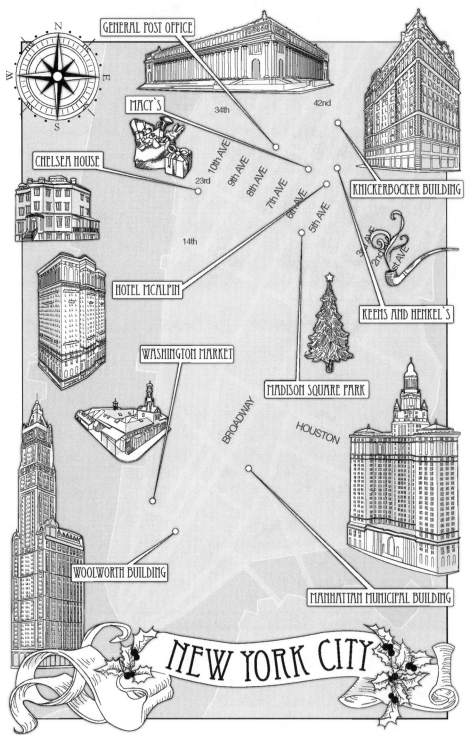

GENERAL POST OFFICE

MACY'S

CHELSEA HOUSE

KNICKERBOCKER BUILDING

HOTEL MCALPIN

KEENS AND HENKEL'S

WASHINGTON MARKET

MADISON SQUARE PARK

WOOLWORTH BUILDING

MANHATTAN MUNICIPAL BUILDING

NEW YORK CITY

34th

42nd

23rd

14th

10th AVE

9th AVE

8th AVE

7th AVE

6th AVE

5th AVE

3rd AVE

2nd AVE

1st AVE

Broadway

HOUSTON

N
W   E
S

MARA SHAUGHNESSY

Author's Note

I first heard about John Duval Gluck on Christmas Eve. As my family sat around the Christmas tree after opening gifts, my uncle Dan mentioned a great-granduncle of mine who had been New York's Santa Claus. My brothers and I peppered him with questions, and he told us what he knew. He was fuzzy on the details but dug up a few photos and an old Seagram's V.O. holiday print ad that featured Gluck as a man who'd "helped save Christmas" once upon a time. How had I never heard of this guy? A quick Google search pulled up little. But my curiosity was piqued—I wanted to know more about this long-lost relative of mine. It turned out there was much more.

With the few leads from Uncle Dan, I scoured newspaper archives, the New York Public Library, and Ancestry.com. I found that Gluck, in fact, had been the toast of New York a century before—a regular presence in the newspapers, a widely quoted expert on philanthropy, and a man friendly with many of the era's biggest stars and politicians. It came thanks to his founding of the Santa Claus Association, which for fifteen years answered every letter a New York City kid sent to St. Nick. Without Gluck and his group, these hopeful missives would be sent to the Dead Letter Office and destroyed. He made Santa real for thousands of New Yorkers.

Under this glowing tale, however, a more illicit story line swirled—suspicions of thievery, blackmail, and espionage; an arrest; and eventual exposure as a huckster. Who was the real John Gluck?

My search to uncover his true story took me to Florida, Texas, Washington, DC, and the far corners of Gotham. I connected with experts on Christmas, the US Postal Service, and New York City. I met with relatives I hadn't known existed. Frances, a widow of Gluck's nephew, recalled John fondly; after some digging, she found several storage boxes full of his papers. She sent a fifty-five-pound trove of John's personal correspondences, official Santa Claus Association documents, and original Santa letters that served as the backbone of the story you are about to read.

Among the papers was a letter from Muriel, the daughter of another of John's brothers. Muriel proved a wonderful resource on John's personality and checkered history, and she remembered her uncle warmly, if also as a bit peculiar.

Through their invaluable input, loads of research, and luck, the rest of the pieces—a riveting Bureau of Investigation (the precursor to the FBI) report on Gluck's schemes, a Supreme Court case against the Boy Scouts of America, and lots of Santa letters—fell into place. They revealed a man who yearned for escape from a mundane life but who lost his bearings once he broke free. He was a fitting man for his time—from World War I to the Great Depression—when civic engagement and optimism were at a high point and could be easily exploited by a man with a touching cause and a good story. This was when Christmas became the garish, commercial, spectacular holiday we celebrate today, with Gluck himself playing a key role in its transformation. But it was also a time when the whole party was about to come to a crashing end.

This may be a story about Santa Claus, but all of it is true. Anything in quotes comes verbatim from the original letter, testimony, or report. In some cases I have adjusted the formatting for consistency, but I have left any misspellings or grammatical quirks intact. In a few cases I have used italics to indicate exchanges that took place but where the exact wording was not documented. Where firsthand accounts could not be found, I have noted what combination of sources I drew on in order to render the scene. Telling the true story of a fabulist presents challenges, but I verified Gluck's claims with additional sources whenever possible.

I like to think Gluck embodies the myth-making spirit of America—combining ambition, charm, and a healthy share of bull, when it suited him. He wanted not just a good life but greatness, and his story can be a cautionary tale or an inspiration, depending how you look at it.

Alex Palmer
Brooklyn, New York
February 2015

Alas! how dreary would be the world if there were no Santa Claus. It would be as dreary as if there were no Virginias. There would be no childlike faith then, no poetry, no romance to make tolerable this existence.

—FRANCIS P. CHURCH, *NEW YORK SUN*, 1897

PROLOGUE

An Arrest in Coney Island

How quickly fortunes reversed.

At 9:30 p.m. on the cool evening of September 9, 1913, John Duval Gluck Jr., dressed in his best suit and bowler, his mustache carefully groomed, basked in the excitement of a stadium full of his fellow New Yorkers. A light breeze carried the scent of salt water and stale food over the hundreds of onlookers packed into their seats. They whooped at what they saw before them: In the flesh, ambling around the arena, was something they had only heard about in stories and seen in picture books.

But just moments after this marvelous spectacle appeared, delighting and thrilling the audience, it all came crashing down. By 10:30 p.m., Gluck sat handcuffed and humiliated in the Coney Island Police Station.

It was New York City's first bullfight and the headline event of Coney Island Mardi Gras week. George Tilyou, creator of the beloved Steeplechase Park, took a chance and hired the untested Gluck to publicize it. Though a novice publicity man, the thirty-five-year-old Gluck proved adept at sparking interest. By taking out newspaper ads alongside those for Broadway shows, promising "three ferocious bulls each performance," and talking up the showdown to his press contacts, Gluck elevated the bullfight into one of the most talked-about draws of the festival. Running two times each day, almost all of the tickets had been sold by the time the bacchanal began. Although it remained true to the spirit of the more familiar Louisiana festival, Coney Island's Mardi Gras was held not before Lent but after Labor Day, marking the end of summer days spent lying on the beach and eating hot dogs on Surf Avenue.

Gluck hoped this new gig might give him a fresh start. He'd followed his father into the family business at age twenty-four and dedicated himself to customs work, as vice president and then president of the customs brokerage firm John D. Gluck & Son. But a decade on, he yearned for escape. He'd spent his entire adult life immersed in the nuances of importing and exporting, excise tax and tariffs. Now he wanted his hours to go to something more meaningful. At such an exhilarating time, it seemed a shame to just watch the thrills of New York City from the outside, like the poor children he often saw on the sidewalk, faces pressed against the windows of Gotham's proliferating shops, lobster palaces, and hotel lobbies. Gluck wanted inside.

He possessed a natural gift for storytelling and had accumulated plenty of business associates from his brokerage work, so he decided to try his hand at publicity. His well-connected friend, the restaurateur Paul Henkel, connected Gluck with the Mardi Gras opportunity. Henkel sold tickets to the event from his newly opened steakhouse, helping bring in business as he supported his friend's efforts to move into a new line of work.

But now the day had finally arrived. Gluck joined the delighted crowd as New York's eleventh annual Mardi Gras launched in the large ballroom of Luna Park with the crowning of the festival's king and queen—tubby silent-film star John Bunny and actress Lillian Walker. They led a great parade atop their royal float, covered in garlands and incandescent bulbs, marching from Ocean Parkway and Neptune Avenue all the way to West Twenty-Second Street. Behind them traveled floats representing far-flung countries while costumed mummers and brass bands rounded out the procession. Bringing in the rear was the Coney Island float—a giant electric-lighted lobster ridden by a bevy of young beauties. Gluck could barely make out the floats through the blizzard of confetti and paper streamers.

For Gluck and the other spectators, the dancing crowds and colors seemed like a kaleidoscopic dream. Among the audience that evening, Italian-born painter Joseph Stella described the "hectic mood the surging crowd and the revolving machines generating for the first time, not anguish and pain, but violent, dangerous pleasures." The swirling lights and colossal rides he saw that night inspired his first masterpiece—the hallucinogenic oil painting *Battle of Lights, Coney Island, Mardi Gras*. Coney was a place where New Yorkers could forget everyday obligations and social codes—cuddling in the Barrel of Love and laughing as clowns zapped men with electric stingers and hidden air jets blew up girls' skirts in the Blowhole Theater. One of the most popular attractions was a booth with fake china dishes that customers paid to destroy. "If you can't break up your own home, break up ours!" read the sign. And at Mardi Gras, Coney Island got wilder than usual.

The crowd was especially lively thanks to acting mayor Adolph Kline's decision to provide twenty-five all-night licenses to local cafes and hotels, supplying drinks to all who wanted them, as late, or early, as they liked. It fueled the horde, which made its way past Steeplechase's Ferris wheel and mechanical racecourse toward the large makeshift arena Tilyou had installed for the headline event. The shop girls, newsboys, and other revelers, who had each paid fifty cents to as much as five dollars per ticket, filled the seats overlooking an emptied swim tank, its water replaced by a foot of sand. Gluck had arrived early to ensure all the performers were ready and to provide a few interviews to reporters. *Was there any truth to the rumors the bullfight might be cancelled? What about the safety of the bull?* they asked. *Absolutely no truth to it,* Gluck assured them. *And there is no reason to worry about the safety of the bull—or the matador, for that matter.* As he had explained many times already, this would be a "bloodless bullfight"—a demonstration, not a violent confrontation. He could barely hide his annoyance and urged the reporters to stop speaking with the meddling Humane Society folks, who had been ginning up protests about the event the past week. *Just watch the show for yourself,* he urged. As the crowd of seven hundred settled, Gluck found a place on the sideline with a view of the action. He lit a cigarette to dissipate some of his nervous excitement as his watch struck 9:30. He would show these skeptics.

A thick, muscular man strolled into the arena, wearing colorful *traje de luces*, complete with wide-brimmed hat, short jacket, and snug tights. The clothing, aided by the lightness of his smooth movements, gave him a deceptively slender appearance. The crowd knew this man: famed Spanish matador Enrique Robles, whom Gluck had trumpeted as a daredevil, brindled with scars, who had nearly lost an eye during a recent scrap with a bull. Spectators whispered to one another the story of how Robles had defeated his first bull at age fifteen—how he'd sat in the audience just as they did today, but at a crucial moment jumped over the barrier, pulled from his pocket several sharp *banderillas*, and planted them deep in the beast's back. The bull threw him seventeen feet, and kicked off the teenager's death-defying career. Now Robles had brought his first show in the United States to Brooklyn, and these spectators were there to witness history.

Several picadors on horseback galloped onto the sand following the matador, each dressed in a short velvet jacket, silk shirt, and velvet stockings with a *pica* lance used to test the bull's strength and to signal Robles which side the creature favored. Over the loudspeaker, announcer Eugene Talrone described each step of the dance in excited tones, while assuring the onlookers this was only an exhibition. Robles and his retinue would not taunt, injure, or kill the bull but merely demonstrate what such a performance looked like in Spain. Gluck glanced at the reporters to ensure they jotted that last point. A pair of cowboys, ready to perform between Robles's demonstrations, waited nearby.

The introductions over, a side gate opened and the real star of the evening appeared: a hulking Andalusian bull, brought from Spain on the same ship as Robles. It trudged around the ring, ignoring the riotous crowd that called to it. Few in the audience had ever seen such a creature in action, and their cheers validated Gluck's promises that this would be an event New York would not soon forget.

Gluck drummed up a packed house, partly because bullfighting remained a divisive sport. The last high-profile show had taken place almost a decade earlier, at the 1904 World's Fair in St. Louis. When the authorities had tried to halt the event, a mob of almost seven thousand stormed the arena, destroyed the furnishings, and burned it to the ground. A 1911 letter to the editor of the *New York Times* urged that the international community condemn bullfighting or "in some way lift the Spanish people to a more enlightened form of amusement."

At least five men in the audience shared this distaste for the sport. They bought seats not for their own entertainment but because they distrusted Gluck's assurances that this fight would be nonviolent. Three were

New York veterinarians: Edward Leary, Thomas Childs, and Philip Finn. Next to them sat Thomas Archer, a representative of the Humane Society, and Thomas Freel, superintendent of the Society for the Prevention of Cruelty to Animals (SPCA).

They watched hawk-eyed as Robles delicately approached the bull. The creature moved slowly and seemed hardly the furious animal the crowd expected. The matador placed a tissue streamer between the animal's horns. No reaction. The announcer attempted to add excitement to the proceedings, describing how fierce and dangerous the creature could get, but the somnambulant bull took little notice of the strutting matador. Sensing the dissipating energy, with a showman's desire to give the people what they paid for, and flouting all of Gluck's assurances and New York City law, Robles smacked the bull on the nose. Gluck's throat tightened. The bull's gloominess vanished. Snapping to furious attention, the animal charged. It ran at Robles, who dodged the beast. And then it kept running—straight at the crowd.

Without slowing down, the bull slammed headlong into the wooden barricade separating it from the audience. Members of the crowd shrieked and dove from their seats, frightened he would charge again or crash through the barricade altogether.

While many ran for their lives, the veterinarians jumped from their seats and sprinted toward the bull, which now lay on its side. Upon striking the arena wall, the creature had knocked itself unconscious. The crowd and the doctors had little to fear from the beast now. The reporters on the sidelines began gunning questions at Gluck, but he could only stare silently as Leary, Childs, and Finn examined the bull from hoof to horns and found its nose badly cut. An animal lover himself, Gluck pitied the poor bull—but more distressful at that moment was that the gore pouring from the creature's face made Gluck's "bloodless" claim a lie. That was not only embarrassing, it was illegal. The doctors signaled to the men from the SPCA and the Humane Society. In the past, the two organizations had traded barbs about each other's effectiveness but set aside their differences for such a high-profile gathering. Freel and Archer worked together in arranging for the veterinarians to be on hand and—as Gluck was about to learn—in securing the involvement of several cops.

As if in slow motion, Gluck watched as uniformed police officers consulted with the animal-rights men and then moved on Robles's six picadors and the two cowboys, corralling and cuffing the costumed figures. Next they went after announcer Talrone and, amidst his protests and in view of the reporters he had tried so hard to impress, handcuffed Gluck himself. The papers the next day would gleefully recount the event's meltdown and arrest of its press agent, much to Gluck's ire. Fleet-footed Robles managed to escape. Though reports differed whether the collision with the fence or the strike from the matador caused the bull's bloody nose, the fracas provided the police with enough to charge the event's organizers with breaking sections 181 and 185 of the New York City penal code—baiting animals and animal cruelty, respectively. The officers frog-marched the motley band of men to the Coney Island Police Station.

It was the last bullfight Coney Island hosted, bloodless or otherwise, and the organizers took a loss on the rest of the week's shows. The police eventually charged Gluck and the others with fines and released them. But while seated in the jail cell, his carefully pressed suit now disheveled, the wild party continuing outside without him, Gluck faced the failure of his first serious attempt to break out of his life's mundane routine.

He could have reasonably accepted defeat and returned to the tedious world of taxes and tariffs he understood. But the brief taste of the excited crowd, of having brought something to New York that it had never seen before, left Gluck intoxicated. And as it happened, he knew of another way to enchant New Yorkers and bring joy to his own humdrum life. He had been toying with an idea for a couple of years after reading about a change in Post Office Department policy and a need that it produced for a creative individual to step forward. It began as a frivolous thought, but as the months passed, Gluck grew convinced that he alone qualified for the assignment. It required a playful imagination but also an instinct for efficiency, a knack for attracting attention but for causes worthier than base entertainment, plenty of business connections and the ambition to make new ones. On all counts, Gluck felt certain he fit the bill.

That's it, Gluck decided. This Christmas, he would bring Santa Claus to New York City.

Part I

CHAPTER 1

The Adventurers' Club

Santa has a new scheme. He has appointed a personal representative to take charge of his New York children, to learn their hearts' desires and to make their wishes come true.

—*The Evening Telegram*

The postman charged with delivering Santa's first batch of mail pushed through a difficult shift. In addition to his usual heavy load, he struggled with hundreds of additional letters as he trudged east from the General Post Office on Thirty-Third Street and Eighth Avenue. Somehow he made room for these in an already cramped canvas bag. The grind of automobile motors mingled with the clopping of horse hooves, hollers of newsboys, and chugging of the Sixth Avenue Elevated train as it left the Thirty-Third Street station. But more than the city noise and extra weight, the postman fought the wretched weather, especially the wind, as he strove to get this pack of wishes to its rightful recipient.

This was no ordinary breeze. Off the southern tip of Manhattan, the gusts of December 8, 1913, kept Mayor-elect John Purroy Mitchel from returning to his city. After a three-week vacation through the sunny climes of Jamaica, Panama, and Costa Rica, the thirty-four-year-old "Boy Mayor" and his fellow passengers aboard the liner *Tenadores* found themselves stuck at the New York Quarantine Station on Staten Island. It would be two hours of waiting for the weather to calm before the group at last got approval to continue on to the East River pier to disembark.

Near the island's western tip, the gales shook the dilapidated Wash- · ington Market where merchants hawked their fruits and meats and attempted to keep their stalls from blowing out from under them. Towering above the sellers was the brand-new Woolworth Building's neo-Gothic façade and exemplary structure—able to withstand wind pressure as high as 250 miles per hour, with a lightning-deflection system on its spire. It seemed to mock the rickety hundred-year-old market below.

The winds rushed so fast that a young woman, rounding the corner across from Madison Square Park where city officials prepared Gotham's second annual Christmas-tree lighting, was thrown into the path of a westbound automobile. The chauffer behind the wheel stopped his car and rushed to her side against the battering breeze. He proved of little assistance, fainting upon seeing the woman's bloodied face. A doctor nearby proved steelier and sent the young woman away in an ambulance before reviving the overwhelmed driver. Excluding the girl's fractured jaw and chauffer's wounded pride, both would fully recover by the time Madison Square Park's "Tree of Light" lit up on Christmas Eve.

Eleven blocks north of the averted tragedy, the wind blew against Macy's Herald Square storefront, rattling the windows of the new fifth-floor "Toyland." In the toasty interior, a man dressed in the red fur robe and cotton-white beard of Santa Claus greeted children in front of a thatched cottage made up like his home. For fifty-one years Macy's had brought the jolly character into its stores and helped inspire every other department-store chain to do the same. But this year, surrounded by thousands of toys—wooden swing horses, magic lanterns, doll carriages, and ducks on wheels—Santa presided over his most opulent Christmas yet.

The postman trudged not to Toyland but a block north of it and a few doors east. When he arrived, windswept and soaking wet, at St. Nick's headquarters at 58 West Thirty-Sixth Street, he felt grateful for two reasons. For one, he was unloading more than five hundred letters of his cargo and lightening his bag for the rest of the day's rounds. But it also allowed him, for at least a moment, to indulge in the hospitable surroundings of Paul Henkel's Chop House.

The hearty scents of steak, roasting lamb, and whiskey, along with the ever-present undercurrent of tobacco smoke, beguiled the postman's nose as he took in the cozy scene. The restaurant, all dark wood and leather, sat at the center of the Herald Square theater district, steps from the Garrick Theatre's back entrance. Paul Henkel, the restaurant's proprietor and namesake, was a gregarious, industrious man respected in the New York dining scene. "Paul Henkel knows everybody worth while in New York," read one of his print ads, and he likely did. The postman would of course know Henkel from his daily deliveries to the restaurant, though probably not from having enjoyed a meal there—a pleasure too pricey for someone on his postman's salary. No, Henkel's Café (another name by which it was known) played host to characters like the Adventurers' Club, which held monthly meetings at the restaurant for well-heeled members to tell stories of escapes from South African cannibals and the daring apprehension of jewel thieves. At a recent gathering, the host even read a letter from that most famous of New York City adventurers, Theodore Roosevelt:

> *I claim to be a little of an adventurer myself, in the proper sense of the term, that is, in the sense of a willingness to run risks and incur hardships for an adequate cause. I am sorry that all I can do is to wish you a most pleasant dinner.*

Santa's mailman, incurring his share of hardships, no doubt looked forward to ending this day's adventure. He passed through Henkel's front dining room, up a set of stairs, and into a back office where he encountered a burst of activity and cacophony of laughter, rustling papers, and typewriter keys. Wooden chairs were scattered throughout the room, papers covered the tables, and framed photographs filled the walls. A couple of men hauled a desk into the already rather full space, trying to find somewhere to cram another surface. At the sight of the postman, the sharply dressed crowd moving about the room cheered. One man in particular seemed very happy to see him. Stepping forward in a brown three-piece suit, with stiff collar and tie, and a hand outstretched, the fellow wore a wide smile accented by his well-maintained mustache. He shook the postman's hand and introduced himself: John Duval Gluck Jr., the founder and president of the Santa Claus Association and, as of that day, the one man in New York City authorized to receive Santa's mail.

As he helped the postman deposit the letters on a wooden desk in the corner, Gluck's ebullient energy seemed to fill the small room. While his balding head, short stature, and suit gave him little resemblance to the mythical saint, his twinkling eyes and easy laugh certainly fit the character. Gluck, all chattiness and charm, cracked a joke to help the postman appreciate both the humor and the significance of the mail drop he just made. They had been waiting for him.

With his big delivery complete, the postman left Santa's warm, crowded workshop. Now it was up to Gluck to do something about this pile of North Pole mail. Even with the letters in front of him, disbelief must have passed over the man the papers would soon be calling "Santa's Secretary." Gluck had asked for them less than a week earlier, the sting of his Coney Island arrest still aching, and learned within three days that his request would be granted. The morning had been spent rushing to prepare the office for the letters' arrival, addressing envelopes, and setting up workstations. Now, as if by magic, Santa's mailbag had actually arrived. *Where to even begin?* He picked up one of the envelopes, tore it open, and read aloud to the others, the child's ungrammatical words taking on an odd weightiness in Gluck's baritone voice:

My dear Santa
I am 7 year have two siter and brother Mother said you will not call
to our house, as she has no money but try and come Margie is sending
a letter to she cant write good by try and give me skates and a cow boy
suit and margie a doll.
—Edward Lennan

Its return address was Amsterdam Avenue at 141st Street. That was Washington Heights, a scrappy neighborhood of Italian and Irish immigrants. A week earlier, ten minutes before midnight, a mafioso gang, the Black Hand Society, had detonated a bomb inside the shoe shop of a man named Joseph Forno just seven blocks north of Edward's home. It blew out hundreds of nearby windows. Though it was the first such bombing in the neighborhood, Washington Heights residents knew crime and destitution well.

Despite these conditions, even as his own mother assured him they were too poor for a visit from Santa, Edward held out enough hope to drop this letter in the mail. In an earlier year, Edward's mother would have been proven right by Christmas Day. The boy's scribbled expression of faith in the face of hardship would have ended up where it always had: the city's Dead Letter Office, where it would soon be destroyed along with any envelopes lacking a legitimate address.

But this year, the postmen had Santa's address. This year, because of Gluck, Edward would hear back from Santa.

Gluck lit a cigarette and pulled another letter from the pile, reading it aloud.

Dear Santa Claus

I am a little girl eleven years old. I have one little brother and three little sister beside myself. My papa is sick with Rheumatism and cannot work. So dear Santa I am writing this letter to you. I hope dear Santa you will not forget us on Christmas.

Loretta Giblin of 328 Avenue A, at Fourteenth Street, wrote this one. She lived on the northern edge of the Lower East Side (it would not become the "East Village" until half a century later), an area near enough to the city's garment factories to draw Eastern European, Jewish, Irish, and Italian immigrant families seeking work. The 1910s were the tail end of the "new immigration" wave that brought millions of European immigrants to Gotham as they found the journey faster, easier, and cheaper than ever. These newcomers crammed into dumbbell-style tenements, with pairs of apartments separated by a narrow corridor and most rooms receiving no direct light or air. A day like December 8, 1913, tormented the tenement dwellers with bursts of wind through the broken plaster in the walls and rain through leaky roofs.

Getting enough to eat when parents made meager factory wages was difficult. Doing so with an unemployed and enfeebled father would be near impossible. The Santa Claus Association could not find little Loretta's dad a job, but they could prove to her that Santa remembered her, and brighten her Christmas in a small way.

A back office in Henkel's Chop House, the Santa Claus Association's headquarters in its first year. GLUCK SCRAPBOOKS.

Hundreds of these appeals covered the desk in this cramped back room. Fortunately, Gluck did not dig through the pile alone. About a dozen secretaries assisted Santa's Secretary in his mission—young women "on loan" from their sympathetic employers, as well as a few retired matrons with the time to dedicate to nonpaying enterprises. The proceedings had the warm bustle of friends preparing an elaborate holiday party. Each person provided help wherever he or she could—opening envelopes, typing addresses, logging each letter received. Volunteers sat in the scattered wooden chairs or just stood as they worked, pausing often to ask a question of Gluck or to share a funny or touching note.

Several of the association's newly appointed "directors" joined in the work. These men of affairs and society ladies included Paul Henkel and his wife, and the wives of Frederick Goodwin and architect Robert T. Rasmussen (her husband could not spare the time, as he was in the midst of building the new Flatbush Theatre, southeast of Prospect Park). Dr. William Edward Fitch, a medical man specializing in metabolic diseases

7

Volunteer Gertrude Whitaker and Gluck, manning one of the group's tables.
GLUCK SCRAPBOOKS.

and dietotherapy, joined the group. Editor of the journal *Pediatrics* at the time, he possessed a professional interest in the well-being of the city's children. Although a man of science, he also appreciated the power of childish faith. Gluck knew them all through business and social dealings, and had charmed them with his pitch about this project.

This group made up its own motley Adventurers' Club, with a quest before it: five hundred wishes—and the promise of many more to come. They were to be opened, categorized, investigated, and answered, following an elaborate system devised by Gluck—not just to make the children of New York City happy but also to protect the association from mistakes that had destroyed similar operations elsewhere in the country. It was "an adequate cause," in Roosevelt's words, and one as clear as the name "Santa Claus" at the top of Loretta Giblin's letter.

But as the founding members of the Santa Claus Association dug into their first delivery, much cloudier to them was the other half of Roosevelt's formula for adventure: the "risks" to be run and the "hardships" endured in pursuit of this cause. It would take fifteen more Christmases, thousands more letters, a kidnapping, investigations by the Bureau of Investigation and the New York City district attorney, a world war, and finally the crusade of a Scrooge-like charity commissioner before the risks of answering Santa's mail would fully reveal themselves.

So who was John Gluck? A strange candidate for Santa Claus, for one thing. Although he had made it his mission to answer letters from New York City children, Gluck had no children of his own. He was a bachelor, since his marriage to Baltimore native Katherine Wheeler ended in divorce five years earlier, just shy of their fifth anniversary. Though a member of St. Mark's Episcopal Church, Gluck was not particularly religious either.

The oldest of five brothers, Gluck had lived for two years in the Bedford-Stuyvesant neighborhood of Brooklyn before his family moved to Westfield, New Jersey. He described it as a happy home with few wants and where every holiday was a huge deal, especially Christmas, and where elaborate decorations, feasting, and kind gestures both within the family and toward less-fortunate outsiders were a tradition. Third-generation German Americans, their grandfather Johann Baptiste Carl Glück had emigrated from Stuttgart to Baltimore in 1838 to take a position with the US Coast Survey, helping to produce nautical charts that firmly established the young country's borders. His son, John Duval Gluck Sr., inherited Johann Baptiste's interest in national boundaries, parlaying it into a successful customs brokerage that brought him, his wife Emilie, and their growing family to Brooklyn and then New Jersey.

Although he was the eldest, John Jr. was the most playful of his brothers, always pulling pranks or telling tales to entertain others. His niece

John's playful personality made him a favorite among his nieces and younger brothers.
COURTESY OF DAN PALMER.

Muriel recalled plotting a Halloween scheme with Uncle John when she
was a young girl: They spent several days turning an old stuffed animal
into a moon-faced monster and devising a pulley system to lower the
creature from her second-floor bedroom window to startle those down
below. Gluck seemed to have even more fun than his niece as they created
the elaborate prank. "He was just a great guy—full of fun," said Muriel.
In family photos, John Jr. is reliably mugging for the camera, striking a
silly pose or eliciting laughs from younger family members. There is little
question of who was the favorite uncle.

He stood out from his four brothers in other ways. At five feet six, he
was the shortest by several inches and also the only one losing his hair, for
which he began to compensate with a lustrous mustache, maintained with
an assortment of combs, brushes, and clippers. He seemed more comfortable in the role of jester than mentor and got along well with his brothers.

Gluck's imagination and abundant energy added a sense of whimsy to
his days, but it also made him restless and hungry to do something important with his life. He looked up to his father, who had found considerable

success in New York City and skillfully connected with others, professionally and socially. When John Sr. died suddenly on Halloween 1907, his son, then age twenty-nine, reluctantly took over the brokerage. But John Jr. did not share his father's passion for customs work.

While John Sr. had taken part in a few high-profile customs cases during his career—overseeing the transport of an antique machine gun, serving as manager of the American-Asiatio Steamship Company—John Jr. actively sought press coverage for himself and the firm. Gluck's customs work put him in contact with a number of business leaders, and reporters occasionally reached out to him for comment. But he began sending his own tips to the press to applaud a customs ruling in his favor or disagree with a decision made against him. When a wealthy British executive of Dick Car Works learned that his daughter had run off to New York to elope with one of his employees, he called Gluck to ask that the couple be detained upon their arrival. Gluck called the newspapers, which reported how he woke up early on April 24 and headed to the Battery, boarding the *Etruria* ship on which they arrived, and "lost no time in ferreting out" the young lovers. He let the twenty-three-year-old bride know of her father's displeasure, but since both were consenting adults, he could do little more. It nonetheless pleased him to see his name in the *New York Times*. Gluck continued to run the brokerage, but bylines in *American Carpet and Upholstery Journal* did not satisfy his hunger for bigger things.

As it happened, a man with a sharp sense of storytelling, a network of business connections, and access to the press could tap into a fast-growing trade in these years: publicity. At the turn of the twentieth century, the cost of printing dropped, newspapers lowered prices, and they drew an expanding base of readers and advertisers. New York City alone boasted eighty-five dailies by 1910. As mass media grew, the idea that enterprises needed to present their work to the public in a particular way grew alongside it. The field provided a new type of brokering for Gluck—mediating between client and public—that allowed him to manage more interesting subjects on a grander scale. Gluck was soon dedicating more of his time to a mix of freelance and short-term contract assignments, from legal consulting to publicity gigs for organizations as disparate as the Republican League, the Merchant Marine Committee, and a charity group known as the Good Fellows movement. The successful years at the helm of John D. Gluck & Son allowed John Jr. a high degree of financial independence to grow his nascent publicity career, with an office at 50 Church Street in downtown Manhattan, half a block south of St. Paul's Churchyard.

Then in December 1911, sitting at the desk in his small brokerage office, he read in the papers about a change in the US Post Office Department policy. After years of debate, they had finally decided to allow Santa letters to be answered by any group the city's postmaster deemed worthy. The idea appealed to Gluck's imaginative side and fondness for elaborate Christmas celebration. Santa had been a familiar presence in the Gluck household. Without a qualified person to answer them, the fact that the Santa letters would simply be thrown out seemed a callous, unnecessary cruelty to him. He could picture what joy it would be to play New York's Santa Claus, to introduce poor kids to the sort of holiday cheer he had known growing up.

It would also provide him with the exciting, higher-profile work for which he longed. Picking up any day's newspaper or stopping in at one of the movie theaters proliferating throughout Manhattan, one encountered thrilling stories of heroes, self-made men, and adventurers. Gluck sensed he was destined for great things too, to bring delight to the city, help his fellow New Yorkers, and garner himself some public esteem in the process. Santa might offer just the route.

It also appealed to his political leanings. In his work liaising between governments and private businesses, Gluck had become convinced that overregulation hindered his clients' ability to get things done. He believed the same was true of government relief efforts, conducted by the city's Public Charities Commission, and the work of established groups like the Association for Improving the Condition of the Poor and the Charity Organization Society. These traditional agencies spent "too much on officials who are overhead and too little upon sufferers who are underfoot," as Gluck was fond of saying. He knew from speaking to friends and business associates that they hesitated to donate to these causes, not because they were unworthy but out of concern that the money would go mostly to administrative costs. "There are people in New York who will gladly give a $50 note to a poor family who would grudge a fifty-cent piece to an organized charity," he said.

He was sure that a man with his business background could devise an efficient, cost-effective, and fun way to play Santa—one that emphasized red ribbons, not red tape. Gluck knew a few things about fund-raising and a lot about investigating claims and running an office. Directing gifts from donors to recipients would be just another type of importing and exporting.

But while Gluck mulled these ideas in 1911, his other clients and assignments demanded his attention. He let the notion pass. Christmas came and went again the following year, and the New York Post Office Department again called for someone to step up and take charge of the Santa letters. He ignored the pleas for a second year. After all, he had an exciting opportunity coming up in the Coney Island Mardi Gras festival; who knew where that might lead? It turned out to lead only to an injured bull and Gluck in handcuffs.

But unlike those who might be cowed by failure, Gluck's determination only intensified after humiliation. In December 1913 he sensed it was now or never. He sent a letter to the postmaster general volunteering for the job of New York's Santa Claus. His friend Paul Henkel happily offered up space for Gluck to test out his idea and readily signed up friends and associates to assist. By the time he got word he could play Santa, his ragtag association was ready. With Henkel and the others, Gluck spoke of the association as an entertaining holiday diversion for all those involved—donors, volunteers, and especially the little letter writers. But he harbored far loftier dreams for this Santa Claus experiment. Though Gluck kept these hopes to himself in these early days of the group, he believed success could prove his foresight in running a new kind of charity, garner attention in the press, and bring in more publicity clients, while allowing him to engage in the fun, imaginative work to which he felt naturally suited. It could mean respect from the city elite and escape from the drudgery of customs work. It could mean a new life.

Eager for a firsthand look at how Santa answered his mail, Zoe Beckley, a reporter for the *Evening Mail*, dropped in on Henkel's Chop House a couple of days into the group's operations. After winding her way to the back office, squeezing past a few well-dressed men and young secretaries, through a maze of small tables, Beckley reached Gluck's desk. He popped up from a pile of envelopes, wishing her a hearty welcome and offering to walk her through each step of the association's process.

Gluck was a natural showboat, and in the first days of the association's operations, he had proven adept at delighting the handful of reporters who dropped by the headquarters. But he may have been grandstanding a bit more than usual under Beckley's attention. She had recently joined the *Mail* after working as a secretary on Wall Street and was by all accounts an attractive, flirtatious, and artful conversationalist. A colleague who worked with her at the time described Beckley as "buxom, apple-cheeked, with a zest for life and an infectious laugh," who brightened the often dull newsroom. This vivacious spirit had helped her move swiftly from "sob-sister sub," writing overtly sentimental takes on the news of the day, to producing more prominent features bearing her byline. Getting one's name in print was still a rare distinction at the time, reserved only for those whom the editors felt could attract regular readers. She had Gluck's attention.

Before they got into the details of how these letters got answered, Beckley had to know: *What were the kids asking for?* "Well, the boys seem to have a run on Boy Scout suits," said Gluck. "Another one of their particular joys is a sled. The girls ask mostly for dolls. Just to prove they do not change much, when they grow up, you will find almost every little girl asking for candy. Lots of them want roller skates." Some peculiar requests came in as well. "Please Mr. Santa," one boy wrote, "will you send me a glass eye? Mine is broke." Another asked for a new suit to wear when meeting his father, who was soon due to leave prison.

As Beckley let out sympathetic sighs and spirited laughs, Gluck described how basic necessities like food and soap often came up. Several writers even asked for coal; so cold and desperate were these letter writers, they would consider it a blessing, rather than a punishment for naughtiness, to receive coal in their stockings. Writers addressed letters to Ice Street, Cloudville, and Behind the Moon (it would be a few more years before the North Pole was definitely set as Santa's home). Some kids were more creative in their correspondences. Gluck grabbed

Envelopes from Santa letters, saved in GLUCK SCRAPBOOKS.

up an envelope from his desk he had just been reviewing, from a young boy who had drawn a pair of images on the front, asking that if Santa thought they were "done good" perhaps he would send the burgeoning artist a box of paints.

Of course, they also received appeals of a more lavish sort, Gluck explained as he walked with Beckley to a neighboring desk where the group had stacked letters marked for further investigation. A few asked for expensive toy pianos. A pair "bearing fashionable addresses" were written on gilt-crested paper, one requesting electric railway equipment and another toy automobiles—both very pricey items. These letters and a number of others were to be personally investigated by an association volunteer. They would confer with the writer's parents to see if they really needed Santa's support.

So now Beckley knew what was to happen to this stack of letters awaiting investigation. But what about all the others? Looking about the room she saw so many other piles—some opened and neatly assembled, some in disorderly heaps. *What is your method for them all?* Gluck's eyes lit up at the question. The process he had devised, drawing on years of exacting customs work, was what really made the Santa Claus Association special.

He moved swiftly through the room as Beckley tried to keep up, arriving at the envelope-scanning table covered with unopened Santa letters, many stamped Insufficient Address by the Post Office Department. A young woman sat at the desk going through the pile. It was here that each day the postman dropped the new mail, and it was up to this volunteer to ensure that each letter explicitly read "Santa Claus." The 1910 Census listed at least three people with the name "S. Claus" living in Brooklyn alone, not to mention several families of Kringles. Opening their mail, or that of any other nonmythical recipient, would put the association in violation of federal postal law. Gluck didn't want anyone going to jail on Santa's behalf, he joked.

Next to this station was the letter-opening table, where a pair of young ladies methodically slit open every approved envelope, giving each letter a quick review to confirm that the request and return address were legible enough to answer. They also checked that none included any money, which legally went back to the sender or the Post Office Department (in the first eight hundred letters examined, just two pennies turned up). For each letter she could discern, the volunteer wrote the child's name on a card and assigned it a number to be filed. If she found the child's name already on file, the letter would be flagged; no clever kids should be taking advantage of Santa's generosity.

Next Gluck walked Beckley, dazzled by how many steps were involved, to the letter-reading table, where several older volunteers sat. These women thoroughly reviewed each missive. They determined the number of children for whom each writer requested gifts, jotting this number on the paper's top right corner. If the child described starvation, homelessness, or abuse, the volunteer set it in a special stack, which was forwarded to the Public Charities Commission for further investigation. If the writer asked for excessive gifts or gave some other indication of not *really* needing Santa's help, it was put in the investigation stack. If the missive passed all these tests—Gluck estimated 70 percent of them did—the letter was finally ready for a response.

All these steps for every single envelope? It struck Beckley as very time-consuming. But Gluck explained that such precision was necessary. In years past, groups in other cities had created more lackluster operations to answer Santa's mail and it had not only caused waste and inefficiency but had driven the Post Office Department to revoke the privilege. He would not allow the Santa Claus Association to suffer a similar fate.

And that is also why, Gluck explained, he and the association members did not actually touch the gifts these children would receive. *So Santa does not send them gifts?* Beckley asked. Far from it, replied Gluck. Each approved letter was sent out to a potential donor—drawn from a list of names and addresses he compiled from his own business along with suggestions made by the association's directors and volunteers. The catalog ran to several thousand names, and Gluck proudly declared that he added to it every day.

He pointed to a table right next to his own desk, where several young typists busily tapped away. They were preparing letters that asked, "Will you play Santa Claus to poor little kiddies?" and would be sent to each name on the list, along with one of the approved Santa letters. Each recipient could return the letter if they did not want to play Santa, or ask for more Santa letters as they liked (so far few had declined a letter, perhaps 5 percent, Gluck estimated). But once they agreed to answer, it left the association's hands—the donor tracked down the item requested, wrapped it up, mailed it to the child, or personally delivered it if he or she wanted to see the look of joy on the little one's face. The donor decided whether to sign the letter with his or her own name, or Santa's. The association only asked that they handwrite their responses to each appeal, to maintain the personal touch.

In the midst of Gluck and Beckley's lively exchange, a volunteer interrupted to drop a batch of letters onto a nearby desk.

"Have you enough helpers to take care of these letters?" asked Beckley.

"More than enough," assured Gluck. "There are thousands of folk willing and anxious to help make the Yuletide happy for children, but they do not know exactly how to proceed. They want to be sure the money they give reaches its destination." In the association's first two days, New Yorkers responded to the question "Will you play Santa to the poor little kiddies?" with a spirited "Yes."

Gluck listed off for Beckley several of these early givers. The broker W. E. Smith and paper manufacturer Henry Langstadter both said they would assist in any way they could. Lawrence P. Goldstone, a wealthy tin mine owner living near Battery Park, volunteered to cover the cost of five hundred letters. Tower Manufacturing and Novelty Co. president James H. Einstein did the same.

The socialite H. M. Joralmon said he would pay for the postage of one thousand letters. It was a lavish offer but one the man could certainly afford. The year before, he left his wallet at William Hammerstein's Roof Garden club, stuffed with $616 (about $14,000 today). Hammerstein sent an usher to the rich man's Manhattan Hotel to return it, but on three separate trips Joralmon refused to allow him up, explaining each time he was in the midst of more pressing engagements than getting his money back. Annoyed, Hammerstein took out an ad in the paper asking the busy man, at his convenience, to please collect his wallet at the box office. At least coordinating with the Santa Claus Association gave Joralmon a way to give his money to a noble cause.

Gluck told of "a prominent drug manufacturer" who also agreed to cover the cost of one thousand responses. He likely referred to Paul O. Jadwin or Palmer H. Jadwin, a pair of brothers and the heads of New York drug firm O. H. Jadwin & Sons. They had recently taken over the firm from their father and would answer letters for the Santa Claus Association in future years. They had good reason to seek out positive publicity, after a recent tragedy gave their family name a ghastly public image. Donald, the third Jadwin brother, and his twenty-year-old debutante wife Minna Van Bergen, were the toast of San Francisco, throwing frequent parties and a celebrated wedding that drew all the local blue bloods. But months into their marriage, the dark side of Donald's partying revealed itself as his drinking worsened and he grew more violent and abusive. Deciding she could take no more, Minna left him. On the night of January 13, 1913, as Minna dined with her grandmother, brother, and mother, they were startled to look up and see Donald standing in the entryway, drunk. He'd snuck in through the servants' entrance but assured the guests that he dropped by only for a kiss from his wife. Before the shocked Minna could answer, he calmly approached her and leaned in, placing his lips on her forehead and a pair of revolvers into her chest. He pulled both triggers, killing the young beauty as her family watched. He then placed one of the guns to his left temple and ended his own life. The murder-suicide, with its grisly details and high-society intrigue, had made national news; almost a year later, few could hear the name "Jadwin" without picturing the crime. Maybe Santa could help restore the family reputation.

"Anybody can join. There are no initiation fees," Gluck explained. "The applicants simply express a desire to help Santa find gifts for his children, and are admitted to membership."

Gluck's tour delighted Beckley. She adored the whole idea and was impressed by the meticulousness of the association's process. But a question lingered: *Why Santa Claus?* Gluck seemed clever and passionate enough to apply his skills to a whole range of endeavors. But he'd thrown himself full force into this rather whimsical project. Why? Gluck explained that since he'd been a child, he'd loved Christmas—that for his family, who took every holiday seriously, it was the most important day of them all. His sadness at the idea of all those letters sitting unanswered, combined with his interest in creative problem solving as a customs broker, compelled him to create the organization.

But he revealed to Beckley something unmentioned to other reporters, a credential that made him almost cosmically qualified to play New York City's Santa Claus: Gluck had been born on Christmas Day. "[Gluck] never had a birthday," Beckley would write after her tour. "He had one of course, in a way. But nobody noticed it because it fell upon the twenty-fifth of December. Deeply Master Gluck pondered on this left-handed compliment of fate. He finally decided that while it was tough luck to be done out of birthdays, it would be tougher yet to be done out of Christmas."

"Christmas should be a thrilling day in the year for children," Gluck said, attempting a dramatic finale to the office tour as Beckley gathered her belongings. "That's all we're trying to do. There's no charity about it. We are purveyors of Christmas spirit!"

This was a point Gluck would return to again and again in the first years of the association: Its business was not to distribute necessities, but to spread Christmas cheer; not to rescue poor children, but to protect their belief in Santa Claus. The idea that the holiday spirit was in danger and needed protection went back to the earliest days of Santa Claus in

America. The first known depiction of St. Nicholas in the United States had been created a century earlier out of concern that the figure might be forgotten altogether if he were not somehow preserved. At that time, few New Yorkers, except perhaps dedicated seminary students or Dutch grandmothers, thought much of St. Nick at all.

This concerned John Pintard, a civic-minded merchant and cofounder of the New-York Historical Society. In 1810, he personally paid an engraver to create a woodcut of the character along with a poem about the "good holy man." Thin as a rail, in ecclesiastical robes, a halo hovering above his bald head, the illustration hardly resembled the Santa Claus we know today. This was the Saint Nicholas venerated by the Dutch who first colonized New York (then called New Amsterdam), and Pintard hoped to return the figure to his former glory. He was a "dear good friend" who brought gifts to children, but the switch held in his hand, along with an accompanying image of a crying young boy next to a smiling young girl, made the point clear: While Saint Nicholas rewards, he also punishes.

Like Gluck fearing in 1913 that children's faith in Santa would flicker out if his mail went unanswered, in early nineteenth-century New York, Pintard worried St. Nicholas's moral example would be forgotten without tributes to him and his virtues. Pintard passed out broadsides of the illustration to members of the New-York Historical Society at their inaugural St. Nicholas Day celebration on December 6 that he helped organize—an event distinct from Christmas, held in honor of the figure reputed to have saved sailors from famine, and children from pirates. "To the memory of Saint Nicholas," a fellow society member toasted, in a typical tribute. "May the virtuous habits and simple manners of our Dutch ancestors not be lost in the luxuries and refinements of the present time." Pintard hoped the society would lead by example, turning St. Nicholas Day into a citywide or even national holiday, and he campaigned to appoint St. Nick the patron saint of New York City.

In many ways, his efforts failed. St. Nicholas never became Gotham's patron saint, and St. Nicholas Day never caught on outside the upper-crust membership of the New-York Historical Society. But in other ways, Pintard's work to preserve and spread the spirit of St. Nick in the city proved far more durable. Versions of the poem he commissioned and the moralizing figure he promoted would be reprinted in newspapers as well as children's books, beginning the character's march toward national and global omnipresence. As historian Stephen Nissenbaum puts it, Pintard was "John the Baptist to the figure of Santa Claus," and his efforts were key in saving St. Nicholas from oblivion.

But by 1913, Gluck was striving to protect a very different sort of St. Nicholas—and to further transform him from the character of "virtuous habits and simple manners," Pintard introduced to New York a century earlier.

—◆—

After Beckley left and Gluck and the volunteers put in a few more hours addressing, stamping, and sending letters, the association called it a day. Gluck headed downstairs for one of Henkel's mutton chops and cheery conversation in the dining room. The youthful, sleek-haired Henkel, a constant presence in his restaurant, joined in the conviviality along with a few of the cafe's usual clientele. The clatter of silverware on dishes and reds pouring into wineglasses added to the cheery clamor. Gluck talked up the day's work, perhaps recruiting some new donors or volunteers over puffs from the restaurant's clay churchwarden pipes.

Before starting this establishment, Henkel had worked a few doors west, managing the famous Keens Chophouse. He left after its proprietor's financial mismanagement threatened to ruin the restaurant frequented by the city's actors, playwrights, and visitors with theatrical personalities, if not professions. But Henkel took with him many of the offerings that made Keens so popular: setting up shop practically next door, promoting his own "famous English mutton chop" when that was Keens's signature dish, and, most crucially, providing churchwarden pipes. Hundreds of the individually numbered vessels hung from Keens's ceiling, retrieved upon the request of card-carrying members of the restaurant's "Pipe Club"—which claimed such members as J. P. Morgan, Buffalo Bill Cody, and Teddy Roosevelt. The long-stemmed pipes (measuring up to thirteen inches) were a throwback—like Pintard's St. Nicholas—to New York's early Dutch era, when the colonists were believed to have smoked the elegant devices constantly.

Upon finishing his meal and smoke, Gluck was exhausted and knew the association had only made a slight dent in the pile of letters that was now its charge. The next day would be a busy one, but at least his commute home was short. Gluck lived upstairs.

Although he shared a stake in family property with his brother Carl in Asbury Park, New Jersey, he lived in a bachelor apartment above Henkel's restaurant next to the association's office. It was a comfortable setup. The apartments included "telephone, electric light, and running water in every room; reasonable; attractively furnished; bellboy," as one ad described.

As a bachelor, Gluck was living in the right place. A subculture of unmarried men flourished in New York City by 1913, during what historian Howard Chudacoff calls the "Age of the Bachelor" in America. Men's sense of responsibility to family diminished as the attractions of the wider world, particularly in bustling urban centers, proved more appealing than the sanctuary of domestic life. Cheap hotels, boardinghouses, and apartments like Henkel's provided men with the simulacrum of home—hot meals, friendly conversation, and clean laundry—without the obligations, and proliferated along Fifth Avenue and Broadway, south of Central Park down to Twenty-Third Street. This entertainment district offered plenty of diversions for single men, from innocent musicals to the nocturnal gratifications of billiard halls, saloons, and brothels.

But Gluck had little time for such things on this night. His mind would have been occupied by the challenges already weighing down his three-day-old association. As airtight as his system appeared, flaws in it had already surfaced. Gluck failed to predict that each letter would represent an average of two children, and sometimes as many as six or seven asking for presents, making it trickier to find willing donors. Even though the association stressed that no gifts should come through its headquarters, many donors misunderstood—a number of presents for needy children now arrived with the day's envelopes, leaving volunteers with little choice but to do the deliveries themselves. More concerning, the stack of letters to be investigated was getting out of hand. Gluck could not spare volunteers to go door-to-door and check in with letter-writers' parents when there was so much work to be done at Henkel's. But if they failed

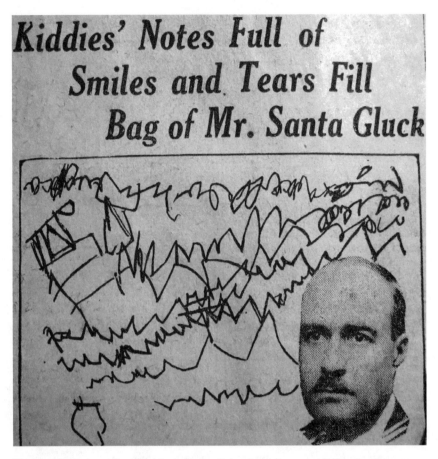

Kiddies' Notes Full of Smiles and Tears Fill Bag of Mr. Santa Gluck

Photo collage from Zoe Beckley's first article about the association for the *Evening Mail*. GLUCK SCRAPBOOKS.

to thoroughly vet the letters, the Post Office Department could yank its endorsement of the association.

An all-volunteer workforce presented other difficulties. Younger workers flitted in and out, working lunch breaks or dropping by after work, but could not be relied on for more than an hour or two. The older volunteers came in eager to help but quickly lost steam. The press attention brought additional aid: After Zoe Beckley's *Evening Mail* piece alone, more than twenty people stopped in to offer their assistance to Santa Claus. But the publicity also inspired more kids to write to Santa. The association had not only created a method to answer all the letters kids sent to St. Nick in any typical year—it had also created more demand.

～

The San Juan Hill district above Hell's Kitchen on the west side of Manhattan was a difficult place to grow up. When the New York Health Department investigated the city's rising infant mortality rate in the summer of 1910, it singled out San Juan Hill for suffering "particularly excessive" infant deaths. As one of the most predominately African-American neighborhoods on the island, the investigators drew the racist conclusions that the deaths were due to mothers who "do not care for their children properly, and will not readily follow advice, preferring to stick to the old mammy remedies and methods," and left the residents to fend for themselves.

Children who did survive navigated the impoverished, foul-smelling tenements. Leaving the dilapidated apartment buildings, they faced greater risks in the city streets, ruled by gangsters like John Painz and his One-Arm Gang. Riots, gunfights, and police raids occurred often, but like infant mortality, these troubles were dismissed as rooted in race. When New York City's leaders attempted to aid San Juan Hill, it was often to the exclusion of its majority African-American population. In 1911, when the park commissioner unveiled a playground on Fifty-Ninth Street between Tenth and Eleventh Avenues, with live music and celebratory speeches, the area's blacks watched the proceedings from a distance. "It was a gathering of the white population at the festivities," a reporter recounted. "The colored patrons are to have special hours appointed for them."

But after a San Juan Hill teacher read Beckley's article, she saw an opportunity to brighten her young students' dreary holidays. Each member of the class wrote to Santa, care of the *Evening Mail*.

Dear Mr. Santa Claus, Iceland:
My Teacher told me if I write you a letter you would be kind about sending me a Christmas present.

*I would like to have a pear of shoes sies twelev and a quarter sleigh
and a pear of skate and I would be very thankfel to you. Thanking you
again I am Your Friend,*
[UNSIGNED]

Dear Mr. Santa Claus, Iceland:
*I would be very thankful if you would send me a dolly. Thankful you
I am Your friend,*
LILLIE

Dear Santa:
*I would like if you could come to see me for Christmas. As my teacher
said write too you. I am a good boy 9 years old. I also have a sister 7
and a little brother 5. Would also like to hear from you. Good-by. Hop-
ing to hear from you*
JAMES

Gifts from Santa hardly compensated for the destitution and discrimination these children lived under—but how terrible it would be for
Gluck to give these hopeful kids one more disappointment when they
already had received far more than their fair share.

It was not just residents of San Juan Hill or Washington Heights
or the Lower East Side who wrote letters. The missives that poured into
the association office were as varied as the city itself—and by the end of
the group's first three days, seemingly as numerous. The first delivery of
five hundred letters amassed in the post office's Dead Letter Office over
several weeks quickly shot up to five hundred each day as reports of the
association spread. As Christmas Day approached, this was sure to grow,
perhaps to one thousand letters daily, if not more.

While Santa's mail was finally being answered in New York City, as
Gluck headed to his bedroom, taking one last glance in the association's
makeshift headquarters, he worried that the growing mountain of envelopes would become an avalanche, burying him and grounding his soaring ambitions. Gluck had kicked off the Santa Claus Association with
a burst of cheerful excitement and confidence in his ability to pull off

something to delight the city. But as he headed to bed, he felt a creeping sense that this latest venture might end up like the Coney Island bullfight. The time for grand theories of charity and talk of his innovative process was over. Gluck's miscalculations threatened to unravel the entire organization, taking the wishes of the city's children down with it.

For all the fanfare over the association's launch, by the end of its third day in operation, its first season looked like it might be its last.

CHAPTER 2

Appointed Rounds

To send these appeals to the Dead Letter Office, to be opened and returned to expectant children merely as an empty message, seemed to be a cold and heartless thing, and the Postmaster-General was unwilling to do it.
—JAMES BRITT, THIRD ASSISTANT POSTMASTER GENERAL

Gluck should have expected his Santa Claus scheme would run into trouble so soon. Although he had a charmed birthday, some clever ideas about charity, and a natural salesman's skill for telling stories, the Post Office Department gave Gluck the duty of answering Santa's mail for one reason only: Unlike any other, possibly more qualified, New Yorker, Gluck had asked for the position.

On December 2, 1913, Gluck sent a letter to US postmaster general Albert Burleson, outlining his idea for the association. Like a kid writing to Santa, Gluck's request brimmed with hope and a bit of naïveté, and its writer only half expected a response. Days later, William J. Satterfield, acting fourth assistant postmaster general, informed Gluck that city, not federal, officials decided who played Santa Claus. He assured Gluck that he had forwarded the request to New York City's postmaster, Edward M. Morgan, for consideration. What Gluck, and even Satterfield, may not have appreciated was that at the moment Morgan was dealing with some of the greatest difficulties the postal department had ever seen—concerns far greater than the junking of a few hundred Santa letters.

Morgan was a friendly but exacting man who had overseen New York City's postal system since 1907. He wore a bushy mustache that hid his upper lip, and a generous paunch jutted from below his vest. Morgan received Satterfield's call in his cramped office on the second floor of the city postal department's main headquarters, downtown at Park Row and Broadway, directly across the street from the months-old Woolworth Building.

The headquarters, which the organization had occupied for almost forty years, was an elegant Doric and Renaissance-style structure of light granite and iron, with domes up top modeled after Paris's Louvre Museum. But scanning the building's interior, Morgan's eyes took in the wear and dilapidation caused by decades of use. The number of workers and volume of mail had swelled with the city's population. The cramped office had become inadequate for the needs of the modern postal operation that Morgan was determined to lead into the twentieth century.

This inadequacy never felt more acute than in the first days of December 1913, as Morgan prepared for the largest volume of mail in the city's history. Eleven months earlier, the Post Office Department had introduced the parcel post, allowing not just envelopes and postcards but also packages and merchandise to be delivered through New York City's mail trucks and underground pneumatic tubes at lower rates than ever before. For Morgan, this meant rural and suburban residents flooded his offices with orders for medicines, clothing, and furniture from New York department stores. It meant his men delivered fresh eggs and produce to New Yorkers who now bought them from upstate farms. And, three weeks before Christmas Day, it meant an eye-popping mountain of presents.

"Mail Xmas Parcels Early" read the sign Morgan ordered hung in every post office in the city beginning November 8. A month later, he could see this public-awareness campaign only made a small impact on the flood of gifts filling his offices. This was not just a torrent but a tidal wave of letters and packages—double, even triple, the volume that the New York City postal department had processed just a year earlier.

Making Morgan's job no easier was the ongoing controversy surrounding his wagons. Only recently introduced, New York City's 250 mail trucks proved a godsend to the department, speeding up delivery times and reducing the wear on Morgan's men. They made rounds quickly because they obeyed no speed limits. Since mail trucks were government vehicles, the peculiar law of the time determined that, like fire engines and ambulances, they handled urgent business and should be exempt from the fifteen-miles-per-hour rule of the day. The illogic of giving mail trucks on their quotidian routes the same privileges as emergency vehicles took some time to reveal itself to the city's policymakers. But by late 1913, reports of accidents and deaths caused by careening mail wagons mounted, and a special committee on speed regulation was formed to investigate. The committee discovered that while one out of every 230 regular vehicles killed a New Yorker annually, one of every *eighteen* mail trucks proved lethal. Despite the pleas of the department, the city aldermen unanimously adopted on November 25 a resolution to remove mail trucks from the speed-limit exemption. Morgan's men had to slow their pace just as the Christmas rush struck.

Despite these challenges, looking about his office, Morgan could draw strength from tokens that testified to a long career of challenges met. A framed photograph of him and Postmaster General Frank Hitchcock—Burleson's predecessor—taken on September 23, 1911, showed the two men as they stood next to pilot Earle Lewis Ovington seated in his Biériot XI monoplane. Minutes after the camera shutter snapped, Ovington flew a sack of 640 letters and 1,280 postcards less than three miles—from Garden City to Mineola, Long Island—dropping his sacks of letters from sixteen feet in the air, thereby completing the country's first airmail delivery.

Near the photograph sat a small ladder of dried immortelle plants, a gift from his colleagues. It held ten rungs, one for each position Morgan had served since beginning at the postal department, as a letter carrier in 1873. He was the only New York City postmaster to begin at the bottom and work his way to the top, rather than simply receiving the appointment as a political favor. A few months before, after Woodrow Wilson beat out his three rivals for the presidency, the *New York Times* declared, "it is to be taken for granted that Mr. Morgan will continue to be Postmaster, because under him the office has been admirably administered." Indeed, here he remained.

His optimism could also be stoked by the fact that on the horizon lay a far more impressive home for Morgan's postal department than the cramped Park Row headquarters: the General Post Office, a grand beaux arts edifice under construction for more than two years. Once opened, it would be the largest, and by all accounts the most majestic, post office in the country, with two pavilions, connected by a row of twenty pillars rising two stories and stretching from Thirty-First to Thirty-Third Streets. The building set twenty-two feet above street level and far back from Eighth Avenue; visitors felt they approached not an administrative office but a venerable monument. It would be the third-largest building in New York City after the Pennsylvania and Grand Central Stations. It was far larger than his staff of 1,666 needed, and that was by design; Morgan wanted to ensure the congestion his postmen currently struggled under would not plague them in the decades ahead.

But solving these logistical puzzles was only part of the building's importance. It served as a lofty symbol not just of New York City's Post Office Department but of all letter carriers. It represented the universal value of delivering messages and conveying meaning—as much a simple post office as Grand Central was only a train station. William Mitchell Kendall, of the celebrated architectural firm McKim, Mead & White and the chief architect of the General Post Office, turned to ancient Greece to add a noble touch to the new headquarters. Across the cornice, he ordered engraved: "Neither snow nor rain nor heat nor gloom of night stays these couriers from the swift completion of their appointed rounds." Not the official motto of the Post Office Department, as popular belief holds today, the lines were just a borrowed flight of inspiration from the building's designer. The phrase captured the sense of universal importance this post office served. It elevated the work of Morgan's men to something more than a job—it was a calling. Like the Persian couriers to whom the quote from Herodotus's *Histories* originally referred, New York City's postmen were not just disciplined workers but also parts of the engine propelling this changing city.

And how the city was changing! The post office was just the latest in a series of impressive new buildings transforming New York's Midtown over the past couple years. All the mail going into and out of the city now traveled on trains through the newly transformed Grand Central Station. It had reopened ten months earlier after a decade of renovations, switching locomotives from steam to electric and introducing a soaring main terminal complete with special "kissing galleries" running along the inclined walks. The design maximized the efficiency of foot traffic as well as the majesty of the structure. The *New York Times* called it "Without exception . . . not only the greatest station in the United States, but the greatest station, of any type, in the world."

It sat just up the street from the New York Public Library's main branch building ("the greatest public library in the world," per the *Evening World*), which had opened just two years earlier, replacing the distributing reservoir of the Croton Aqueduct System. A few blocks southwest was the other beaux arts achievement of Pennsylvania Station ("the largest building in the world ever completed at one time," according to the *Times*), opened in August 1910. The Hudson tubes, North River tunnels, and East River tunnels, had all opened in the previous few years and made it easier than ever to enter and exit Manhattan. If one strolled Midtown in 1908 and visited again in 1913, it would feel as if the city had experienced not five years of change but fifty. All these great buildings shared another characteristic: They were open to the public. A poor man unable to afford a book about classical architecture could now stroll through structures as stunning as any ancient Roman temple or Greek theater.

Across the street from Pennsylvania Station, the General Post Office was scheduled to open to the public the next year, and in the meantime the postal department thankfully had use of some of its facilities for processing Christmas packages. Morgan and his staff had to prepare for the move sometime between January 1 and 15 of 1914, as soon as Postmaster General Burleson gave the order. Morgan had surely already begun to pack by the time he received Gluck's request to play Santa.

In addition to his photos and memorial ladder, Morgan would box up a large horseshoe bearing the words *Deo Gratias*, or "God be thanked." He had received the gift after surviving an attack from a paranoid lunatic five years before. The assailant, Eric Hugh Boyd Mackay, worked as a stenographer for a Wall Street law firm when he became convinced that the postmaster deliberately kept his mail from being delivered. "The

Postmaster withheld a registered letter addressed to me," Mackay wrote in a note left in his Upper West Side apartment. "I therefore, as he is the most prominent man who has antagonized me, selected him as my victim now that I have decided to kill myself."

On November 9, 1908, in a homicidal fury over missing mail he believed to be rightfully his, Mackay confronted Morgan as the postmaster walked to work with his young daughter. The stenographer shot Morgan in the abdomen, then shot himself in the head, dying instantly. Thanks to the quick response of his physician neighbor, Morgan survived, and kept the inscribed horseshoe given to him by his colleagues as he recovered, as a reminder of the precariousness of life and his own good fortune. Of course, Morgan had never hoarded Mackay's mail—these were the ravings of a madman. But during his time as New York City's beloved postmaster, Morgan had been guilty of systematically withholding and destroying thousands of letters belonging to another man: Santa Claus.

It's impossible to say who wrote the first Santa letter, but it was almost certainly *from* the mythical saint, not *to* him. From the earliest conception of Santa Claus in the United States, parents used the voice of St. Nicholas as a means of providing advice and encouraging good behavior in their children. The earliest reference to a Santa letter in America that I could find came from Theodore Ledyard Cuyler, recalling his childhood in 1820s western New York when he "once received an autograph letter from Santa Claus, full of good counsels." Fanny Longfellow (wife of poet Henry Wadsworth) regularly wrote her children Santa letters, commenting on their behavior over the preceding year. "I am sorry I sometimes hear you are not so kind to your little brother as I wish you were," she wrote to her son Charley on Christmas Eve 1851. A few years later she wryly scolded, "You have not been so obedient and gentle and kind and loving to your parents and little sister as I like to have you, and you have picked up some naughty words which I hope you will throw away as you would sour or bitter fruit." Soon enough, children started writing back, generally placing their letters on the fireplace, where they believed smoke would transport the message to St. Nick.

Having letters hand-delivered by postal workers, beginning for many urban areas in the midst of the Civil War, transformed how Americans viewed the mail—as a pleasant surprise arriving at one's door, rather than a burdensome errand. The *Chicago Tribune* captured this change in perception in an 1864 story about the introduction to the city of thirty-five deliverymen. "[W]e were strangers to the varying sensations produced by 'the postman's knock,'" the editors gushed. "Though we had often read of his journeyings and followed him in imagination through his daily round, as he dropped his gifts like a genuine Santa Claus into other households on his beat." It was only a matter of time before children began to view the post office as a direct conduit to the Christmas saint.

By the 1870s, scattered reports appeared of the receipt of Santa letters by local post offices. "The little folks are getting interested about Christmas," wrote a correspondent in the Columbia, South Carolina, *Daily Phoenix* in December 1873, describing a few Santa missives. "Several letters deposited in the Richmond Post Office, evidently written by children, plainly indicated that they, anticipating the annual visit of Santa Claus, wished to remind him of what they most desired," the *New York Times* reported the following year.

Each subsequent winter, as certain as snowflakes fell onto the city streets, a growing number of Santa letters ended up at post offices across the country, increasing every year. But with no actual fur-coated toymaker to receive his mail, each January, the department destroyed them. It was a depressing business. But, officials asked, if mailmen began delivering Santa's letters, to which other fictional characters would mail be shuttled?

By the turn of the century, the public and press complained about this destruction. "There are at present in the Post Office more than a bushel of letters to Santa Claus that the dear old mythical Saint will never receive," the *Times'* editors lamented in 1899.

When nothing changed, they raised the volume of their protests: "The Christmas season has no charm for the prosaic employes [*sic*] of the Dead Letter Office," the *Times* wrote in 1906. "So the letters remain undelivered and the requests unresponded to, and Saint Nick overlooks thousands of children just because he has not received their petitions."

Irked by the mounting negative press, then–postmaster general George von Lengerke Meyer announced on December 14, 1907, that he would allow the letters to be answered until the end of the year—for two weeks, give or take. For the first time ever, Santa would open his mail. Groups rushed to respond, and despite having little time to organize, that season saw the rise of organizations like one in Winchester, Kentucky, that began delivering Christmas goodies including nuts, fruits, and candy—as well as firecrackers and roman candles—to children. The Silver Belt Santa Claus Association dubbed Kris Kringle its "Chairman of the Board of Directors" and served the kids of Globe, Arizona.

But two weeks wasn't enough time to get a solid operation up and running. The groups had little time to properly investigate the letters, and many that did found a large number of dubious requests—children exaggerating their needs or seeking to take advantage of public generosity in some other way. In some cities, groups fought over who had the right to play Santa. Almost before the philanthropies began their work, Meyer, at the urging of a number of established charity groups, criticized these upstarts for their lack of oversight and the fact that few verified if the letter writers were actually in need. Citing this failure to investigate the letters and the generally unprofessional approach of the Santa groups, Meyer ruled that the experiment failed and would not be repeated. "That vicarious activity of Santa Claus which last Christmas removed from the minds of some children in the community the deep-seated notion that the Christmas saint was a snob who confined his presents to rich children, is not to be repeated this year," the *Times* morosely reported in 1908.

This was sad news for many, but perhaps no one was as devastated as Elizabeth A. Phillips. Prior to Gluck, she was the most famous Santa surrogate, affectionately known in the press as "Miss Santa Claus." The former schoolteacher transformed into a local hero in her Philadelphia neighborhood when she brought small gifts to ill children in the local hospitals during the holidays. Phillips expanded her efforts in subsequent years, as she hosted a Christmas dinner for several hundred destitute children at Philadelphia's grand Bellevue-Stratford Hotel. She even opened a seasonal Santa Claus store—with proceeds going to the needy, of course.

In 1907, when she learned that local Santa letters could finally be answered, Phillips claimed them, putting out calls to donors and recruiting what volunteers she could. Phillips herself delivered most of the gifts, in a borrowed automobile stuffed with presents that she drove through the city's poorer neighborhoods. It was a warmhearted effort, but a disorganized one far cruder than the sophisticated operation Gluck would introduce six years later.

While she threw herself into helping Philadelphia's children, Phillips herself needed help. She put everything into assisting those needier than she, which she found alleviated a chronic sense of depression that afflicted her. Meyer's demand that Santa letters be returned to the Dead Letter Office ended Phillips's work as Miss Santa Claus. Her Santa Claus store did not bring in enough donations to cover rent. On the morning of August 11, 1909, alone in her small apartment, Phillips stuffed old rags under the door and around the cracks of her window. She connected a plastic tube to the room's gas furnace and gripped it in her teeth as she turned the valve, steadily inhaling the fumes. The proprietress, smelling gas and fearing a leak, burst into Phillips's locked room. She was shocked to find Miss Santa Claus's lifeless body on the floor covered in quilts, plastic tube still held between her teeth. On Phillips's dress was pinned a notebook page:

> *No one knows my suffering. I cannot explain. I feel my mind growing weaker each day. I have pleaded with them to send me to an institution, but they would not. I have been in failing health for some time. I have always tried to do my best for mankind.*

The death of Miss Santa Claus saddened the public and renewed calls for the unfeeling postal department to free Santa's mail for good. Finally, in 1911, Postmaster General Hitchcock, a bit more of a romantic than his predecessor, decided that releasing the letters, in a limited and cautious manner, would pose few serious threats to the department's operations, and ordered that the letters could be answered the final two weeks of the year. The consequences could hardly be worse than the negative attention they had already been receiving for the current policy. Two years later, the

Post Office Department made the ruling permanent—every year, for the entire month of December, any organization approved by the local postmaster could answer Santa's mail.

It was a triumph for those who sought to protect the hopes of New York children. But after Hitchcock's ruling went into effect, Morgan was surprised to learn that nobody wanted the job. "Santa Claus Is Tardy Saint," read the front page of the *Sun*. "Mail Men Disown Santa," read the *Tribune*. Morgan entreated the public, asking that someone take these letters, but the only New Yorker to step forward was a clothier offering kid-sized suits and caps. "If Santa Claus doesn't call soon for his mail, which is piling up at the main New York post office, many of his small correspondents who are confiding to him what they would like for Christmas will be forced to believe that there isn't any Santa Claus," bemoaned the *Sun*. After all the calls for the release of the letters, when the change was finally made, Santa Claus decided not to show up in New York City.

As the days of 1913's final month ticked away, and Morgan rushed through his office managing the parcel post's first holiday season, he likely assumed that this year Santa would again be a no-show. But on December 8, with so much else on Morgan's list of tasks, Assistant Postmaster General Satterfield's call about a clever customs broker with a well-conceived system for receiving, verifying, and responding to kids' wishes caught Morgan's attention. The postmaster wasted no time in granting Gluck's request.

The windy afternoon of December 8, he dispatched to Henkel's Chop House the extra load of envelopes from the Dead Letter Office. In addition to the city's mail—and, this year, tens of thousands of packages and Christmas gifts—Santa letters would now be part of Gotham postmen's appointed rounds.

———◆———

And now it was up to Gluck to see that the letters were answered. Compared to the volume of parcels Postmaster Morgan expected, Gluck's hundreds of correspondences were modest. But the Santa Claus Association did not have thousands of men or monumental new headquarters at its disposal. It had a few volunteers working frantically in the second floor of a Garment District restaurant.

Beyond the influx of letters to process, the volunteers faced the challenge of separating the worthy from the unworthy letters. Gluck would have been well aware that the main reason cited in 1908 for Santa letters returning to the Dead Letter Office was the lack of investigation into whether the recipients were actually needy. If the Santa Claus Association could not prove the worthiness of its recipients, or if the group seemed somehow unserious in its mission, the postmaster might revoke its right to answer the letters as fast as he had done to Elizabeth Phillips and the others.

Though it was easy enough to spot a "fashionable address" on gilded paper, not all letter writers of privilege were so easily identified. As Gluck had initially conceived it, a volunteer would go to any address in question and confirm with the child's parents that they couldn't afford to play Santa themselves. A few workers had done this. But by the group's fourth day in operation, the opening and responding to appeals back at headquarters took up all of the volunteers' limited time, and it became clear such investigations would not be feasible citywide.

Then, on the group's fourth day, as challenges and envelopes mounted, the association office's phone rang, with a call for Gluck. On the line was one of the city's wealthiest men, with a surprising solution for the group's troubles.

CHAPTER 3

To All a Good Night

And the Christ-Child spirit, divinely fair,
That illumined the manger cold and bare
Is born again in the City square!
　　　　　—"The Christ Child's Christmas Tree"

Four days after New Yorkers learned of the existence of the Santa Claus Association, Gluck picked up the office phone to find General Edwin Augustus McAlpin on the other end. The businessman and National Guard veteran had inherited a fortune from his father, the founder of tobacco manufacturer D. H. McAlpin & Co., for which Edwin had served as president before selling it in 1901 for $2.5 million (about $60 million today). At sixty-five years old, he had more money than he knew what to do with, and his voice still boomed with the commanding timbre of a longtime military man—although he had never seen combat.

At the age of seventeen, in the final year of the Civil War, McAlpin attempted twice to be drafted as a drummer boy. His father would not allow it and demanded that Edwin at least wait until his eighteenth birthday to join. By then the war had ended, so the tobacco heir became an officer in the National Guard, dedicating decades of his life to serving his country and rising to the rank of major general.

McAlpin owned real estate throughout the city—also mostly inherited from his father—and just under a year earlier, he and his siblings had celebrated the opening of the Hotel McAlpin. Blocks from Henkel's

Chop House and across the street from Macy's, at Thirty-Fourth Street and Broadway, the building rose twenty-five stories and boasted 1,500 guest rooms. Luxuries like a Turkish bath, basement bar (or "rathskeller" as it was commonly called), and grand ballroom drew excitement. It not only included a telephone in every room but also a fully equipped private sanitarium on the twenty-third floor and a "Sleepy Sixteenth" floor for night workers, where daylight and noise were strictly prohibited. But most of all it was recognized for its size: Upon opening its doors, the McAlpin became the largest hotel in the world, another spectacular building in a city suddenly full of them.

It may have occurred to Gluck that McAlpin was calling to offer the group space at his hotel. Henkel's was proving a tight fit for the dozens of volunteers and piles of paperwork. The Hotel McAlpin might provide more room and a more prestigious location. However, the general was not calling to offer space but manpower. Although his real estate interests were keeping him busy, McAlpin had some civic pursuits on the side. In particular, he served as chief scout of the United States Boy Scout (USBS), an organization dedicated to strengthening the character of American boys and training them in military drills, and a competitor organization to the nascent Boy Scouts of America (BSA). McAlpin believed an opportunity existed for his and Gluck's organizations to collaborate.

McAlpin got right to the point: How would Gluck like to have the assistance of a few hundred of his scouts to help get the gifts to the children? Perhaps the boys could sort letters or wrap gifts or something along those lines. Gluck was thrilled by the enormous offer and quickly accepted. After he thanked McAlpin and assured him he could find plenty for his scouts to do, a thought occurred to Gluck. With the extra manpower, these boys could go to the homes of the letter writers and confirm for themselves whether the child was actually in need. Young men in Boy Scout uniforms marching door-to-door, dropping in on parents to verify their children's honesty. It had a wonderful upstanding quality to it that fit right in with the image of the Santa Claus Association Gluck strove to project.

What inspired McAlpin to reach out? Perhaps it was Gluck's comment to the papers that the letter writers "have a run on Boy Scout suits," or maybe the latest cover of the scouting magazine *Boys' Life*. It featured an illustration of Santa lying on a snow-covered hillside, looking surprised and slightly embarrassed, with gifts strewn about and his sleigh caught in a nearby tree. Two scouts wearing khaki uniforms and serious expressions had each taken an arm and helped the stunned man to his feet. Scouts lending Santa a hand—a funny and fitting image, and McAlpin might even have recognized the illustration as the work of the same artist who drew the last three *Boys' Life* covers. What he would not have recognized was the name of the nineteen-year-old artist who had just joined the magazine as art director several months earlier, but who would go on to become one of the most popular artists in American history. Norman Rockwell would illustrate some of the most iconic images of Santa Claus ever created, but the December 1913 *Boys' Life* cover was his first published depiction of St. Nick.

But the most likely inspiration for the general's outreach was his desire to improve the US Boy Scout's reputation, which had taken a brutal beating of late.

The group sprouted from the competitive spirit—or perhaps spite—of William Randolph Hearst. The newspaper baron founded the scouting group in May 1910 (then called the American Boy Scout) as a challenge to Chicago publisher William Dickson Boyce, who had incorporated the Boy Scouts of America three months prior. The choice to give them the singular name of "Scout" rather than "Scouts" was in part an attempt to distinguish the two organizations. The boys in both groups went on outdoor trips, volunteered in the community, and read *Boys' Life*. But their practices differed in at least one significant way: Hearst's scouts carried guns. Partly because Hearst believed boys should cultivate skill with firearms, and also to help prepare members for eventual service in the US military, rifles became standard accessories for American Boy Scout (ABS) members.

The two scouting groups sniped at one another, with each claiming that the other should change its name. The ABS boasted it had more members, while the BSA claimed the endorsement of Sir Robert Baden-Powell, the founder of England's original Boy Scout organization.

At first the two seemed well matched, but the Hearst organization soon lost ground. The BSA leadership solidified power on the national level, chartered new councils around the country, and standardized membership rules. The ABS held public events and troop meetings, but its leaders spent more time fund-raising than building the organization, and Hearst himself soon abandoned the group. At this point, McAlpin took over as chief scout, declaring that "I am accepting this honor and this labor without any desire for red fire," but proved more than eager for a fight.

The general believed in a strong national defense and saw scouting as an effective way to strengthen it—teaching boys firearm skills and military discipline. "This I find is the only way to train boys," he explained. "They will be the pillar of this country in the years to come . . . and we are trying to instruct the youths of this land in the true discipline." He loved the trappings of armed combat and believed the Boy Scouts of America to be both too weak (having toned down the militarism of the original British Boy Scouts) and too religious (due to the early support it received from the YMCA, among other things). He summed up his opinion of the BSA as "a bunch of religious enthusiasts—outright pacifists" and delighted in his role as general leading an army against its enemy.

But just over six months into his tenure, the gun-toting militarism that pleased McAlpin most about the ABS created a crisis. On March 23, 1912, nine-year-old Henry Luckhardt, his ten-year-old brother William, and their neighbor John Lightner walked home after filling up a few bottles from a spring near their uptown home. As they crossed a hill on a vacant lot at 169th Street in the Bronx, they encountered five other boys. One of them wore the uniform of the American Boy Scout and carried a rifle.

The scout was twelve-year-old Russell Maitland Jarvis, considered the terror of the block by some in the neighborhood. He had just come from an afternoon hike with his troop and brought along the ABS-approved rifle. Playing police officer, Jarvis demanded the three boys put their hands in the air. William and John crouched behind a nearby wagon, but Henry made a crack about his scout uniform and dared him to shoot. Jarvis pulled the trigger, hitting the nine-year-old in the stomach. Henry died soon after.

The shooting caused an outcry that rifles, even unloaded ones, be banned from the organization. The Boy Scouts of America expressed some of the loudest criticism, shaming McAlpin and his scouts for their irresponsibility. "When boys wish to become a Boy Scout, parents said, 'All right,' not knowing there are different organizations," James E. West, the chief scout executive for the BSA told *Boys' Life* in May 1912. "That was the way with Mrs. Jarvis, mother of the boy who did the shooting." West declared that members of the BSA would not be allowed to carry firearms and troops would take no part in military drills. The same issue of *Boys' Life* included news of more than 1,300 members of the American Boy Scout in Los Angeles filing a petition to join the Boy Scouts of America.

Despite the bad press, the American Boy Scout solidified its militaristic stance in July 1913, when an Arms Selection Committee chose the .22 caliber Remington no. 4S rifle as "the Official Arm of the American Boy Scout." The single-shot, military-style gun, complete with leather sling strap and bayonet, costing the scout just eight dollars, would be known as the "Boy Scout Rifle" from that point on.

McAlpin feared that his group now teetered toward collapse, and he took some halfhearted steps to deflect the BSA's challenges and change public opinion. This began with a name change: In October 1913, the American Boy Scout became the United States Boy Scout. But McAlpin knew the best way to ensure the group's survival was involvement in some high-profile civic work. He could hardly choose a better project than helping out Santa Claus.

———

Members of the US Boy Scout, dressed in full uniforms, including hats, military-style jackets, and trousers, arrived at Henkel's Chop House the day after McAlpin's call to Gluck, and became a regular presence at Santa's headquarters. Not only did Gluck teach them to help with more basic clerical tasks, he also showed his new ground force how to conduct investigations (leaving their rifles at home) to verify which children were truly in need. Besides the practical assistance, the scouts provided valuable optics. The upstanding boys fit perfectly into the wholesome, hardworking tableau Gluck was cultivating for the group. He called reporters and told them of the new recruits. Zoe Beckley, now a regular presence at Henkel's, followed

A unit of United States Boy Scout, lined up with members of the association. GLUCK SCRAPBOOKS.

her first story on the association with one the next week, framed by a photo of uniformed scouts. "Among Santa Gluck's most trusty aids are five hundred Boy Scouts, who have offered to do anything to help, from feeding the reindeer to sliding down moonbeams as a sort of rapid transit gift delivery at the last minute," Beckley wrote, in her typically whimsical fashion.

The Santa Claus Association heard from *St. Nicholas Magazine*, a children's monthly that aimed to preserve the spirit of St. Nick—the pedagogic, New Amsterdam version of St. Nicholas introduced to the New-York Historical Society by John Pintard in 1810. Don M. Parker, the magazine's advertising manager, wrote Gluck to thank him for his "wonderful work" and added that "You are sitting in an enviable place, and I can easily understand what sincere satisfaction you are getting from your work, because it is doing something good and noble, and something which you can feel."

The association's original volunteers were joined by new helpers attracted by the positive press coverage in the final days of the Christmas season. One notable addition to the team was eighty-year-old Eleazer Ely, who had read about the association in the papers and showed up at Henkel's on December 16 to offer his help; he then averaged more than ten hours a day at the office.

With enough volunteers to handle the letters, responses, and now the investigations, Santa was on track to handle all his mail. The first week of operation had surprised Gluck with the huge volume of letters. But once the scouts joined the effort and the volunteers got proficient at every step of the process, the biggest surprise became how generous New Yorkers proved to be. "There are thousands of folk willing and anxious to help make the Yuletide happy for children," Gluck said in astonishment at the outpouring coming into the headquarters. He chalked up the rush of support not only to a pent-up eagerness by the public to play Santa but also to the particular way he had designed the organization. New Yorkers just wanted to be sure their donations were "flung wide with a generous hand rather than doled out with the smugness of self-satisfied benevolence," he said, taking a swipe at the more established charities. Gluck began to see long-term possibilities for this group, devising plans for when the postmaster released next year's Santa letters on December 1. *And why limit these ideas to New York?* Gluck wondered. He began to openly suggest that soon "every city in every country may have a Santa headquarters."

But one challenge remained for Gluck to overcome: the two cents his group had to pay for every response sent to a child, every letter sent to a donor or potential donor, and every letter a child sent to Santa without postage. Since the group encouraged donors to buy and deliver gifts to kids themselves, rather than send money to the association, this presented a conflict. So Gluck went to the press with a request for assistance in buying stamps. At the rate the letters came in, he expected that fifty thousand two-cent stamps—about one thousand dollars' worth—would fully fund the group's needs.

"Santa in Need of Stamps," read the headline in the *Times*. Gluck took pains to explain the exact costs and describe to the public why an association, run by volunteers out of a rent-free office, did in fact need some money to function. Not wanting to fall into the fund-raising habits of the bloated charities he often criticized, Gluck made sure donors knew exactly where their money would go. He needn't have worried. Donors quickly stepped forward to supply financial support, no questions asked. It was the first outright request Gluck made for money, but the generosity and speed New Yorkers showed assured him that it did not need to be the last.

As Gluck mastered his influx of mail, Postmaster Edward Morgan was also keeping his head above his own ocean of letters and packages. By December 13, the post office had sent 49,126 foreign parcels and 340,292 registered articles. "Small Army Is at Work," reported the *Times* about the additional clerks and mail sorters secured by Morgan. So large was the inpouring of mail that Postmaster General Burleson requested one million dollars in emergency appropriation from the federal government. Extra mail cars and eight thousand more men would be tapped to help with the effort nationwide.

While the explosion of Christmas generosity in 1913 was for Morgan and his men a logistical concern, for other New Yorkers, it was a moral one. The Society for the Prevention of Useless Giving, or SPUG, had launched the year before; they campaigned against the excessive giving that had become standard practice and the extravagant gifts going to those who did not need them. "Too many gifts are delivered on Christmas Day which do not carry with them anything nearer the holiday spirit than surrender to custom or foolish seeking for favor," read a *Tribune* editorial. Following his call for volunteers, the Committee for the Distribution of Christmas Gifts—a collection of society ladies similar to SPUG—paid Gluck's headquarters a visit, their arms loaded with toys. They explained that the committee was on a Robin Hood–like mission, taking extra gifts from rich children (usually their own) and giving them to the poor. These toys came from under Christmas trees already crowded with gifts; perhaps Gluck's letter writers would get more out of them than the pampered kids for whom they were originally intended. As he asked a volunteer to try to find requests to Santa that matched the toys the committee had brought, Gluck thanked the women for their generosity—though perhaps he should have thanked their children instead.

If the campaigning of these groups was having any effect, it was hard for Morgan to see it through the tens of thousands of additional packages his department sorted that year. But despite the overwhelming level of gifts traveling through the city, the postmaster's aggressive approach paid off. By December 21, Morgan confidently declared that "Everything is being cleaned up as fast as it comes in." He attributed this to the good weather and the fact that foreign holiday mail arrived early, but the press gave much of the credit to Morgan's leadership of his fast-growing Post Office Department.

Like Morgan, Gluck had also gotten control over the flow of letters and packages that newly became his charge, through a combination of fast action and creativity. But now the real test for the Santa Claus Association arrived: Christmas Eve was here.

———◆———

By December 24, the association had coordinated the delivery of gifts to 13,160 children in the city. But a final influx of last-minute notes came in with requests for Christmas Day. Gluck was ready.

The calls for postage funds brought in more than enough to cover the season's needs, with money left over for next year's operations. With the Christmas Eve mail, Gluck received a letter from the personal secretary of William Kissam Vanderbilt, inheritor of $55 million from his father, Grand Central Railroad owner William H. Vanderbilt. Gluck likely tore open the envelope with excitement, curious what the rich man might be offering the association. "Dear Sir," read the letter. "Mr. Vanderbilt requests me to send you the enclosed check amounting to $10, his contribution towards your Santa Claus fund." It might not be much from such a wealthy man, but it covered the cost of another five hundred stamps.

Donors continued to fulfill their duties. "I enclose letter of Theresa Telese and thank you for the opportunity you have afforded me of making one child happy this Xmas," wrote Edgar Dennis.

"I complied withe [sic] the request of Miss Mary Gilmartin, and trust the package reached her safely and properly," wrote William D. Ward, a publisher's representative working in the Tribune Building. "I feel sure the work of your Association has helped many unfortunate children, and am glad I was able to do my little bit."

E. C. Schoonmaker of The Embossing Company confirmed that the requests of young Allsworth Hefferan were given prompt attention. "Trusting that the boy's faith in Santa Claus will be strengthened," he added.

Every note brought a wave of warm satisfaction over Gluck. His idea had worked and pulled in responses from the sorts of men not typically susceptible to charity appeals. A well-worded circular might draw in the usual generous society ladies, but to get an actual letter from a child, smudged and scrawled, struck a nerve with a wider audience. Reuben Leslie Maynard, a lawyer with an office in downtown Manhattan, captured how the association stood out to men like him:

> *We business men receive in almost every mail, requests for contributions to various charities. Almost every man becomes hardened at last, and as soon as he discovers the nature of the communication, he tosses it, without further examination, into the waste basket. I came very near doing this with your circular letter, which accompanied the letter written by the little Gutsche girl to Santa Claus, but fortunately did not do so. . . . The Santa Claus Association is a very happy thought, and I hope that it will long continue to do the work for the little ones of this great City, in which it is now so happily engaged.*

Gluck could not have said it better himself. His idea appealed to those of rich and more modest means alike. "The job [is being] done by the big heart of New York—plain, ordinary, 'little old New York,'" Gluck exclaimed. "It [brings] them into contact with an opportunity to do real good." The volunteers' deadline for delivering all gifts received at headquarters arrived. Gluck reached out to a number of automobile manufacturers to secure the services of dozens of cars to help fulfill these final requests, and many spent their Christmas Eve zipping through city streets, dropping in on the homes of strangers.

On the late afternoon before Christmas Day, nine-year-old Alfred Briggs no doubt expected that this late in the season, gifts would not miraculously appear under his family's Christmas tree. Santa had never visited his home before—perhaps because the family didn't have a chimney, or because their doorbell didn't work, or because they lived on the third floor of a five-story tenement apartment on Sixty-Fourth Street, where few kids seemed to get visits from Santa. But as hopes for seeing St. Nick that Christmas Eve faded away, Alfred heard a knock at the door. When his aged mother answered, he heard a woman's voice ask, "Does Mrs. Briggs live here?"

"Yes," said his mother.

"Well, where's Alfred?" the woman replied in a cheery tone. As Alfred approached the door, he first saw the gift-wrapped boxes piled high in the visitor's arms, obscuring her face as she thrust them through the doorway, offering them to the boy's mother. He rushed to the door as his astonished mother took the presents, revealing an elegantly dressed young woman with large eyes and dark hair done in a stylish bob—she was as bizarre a sight in a gritty West Side tenement as Santa himself landing on the sidewalk outside. This was Gertrude Whitaker, assistant secretary of the Santa Claus Association. "Santa Claus received Alfred's letter, and when he learned that the little boy was so modest in his wishes, he decided to be very generous with Alfred," she said, smiling as the boy cautiously approached, then began to open his gifts. Santa had indeed been generous: the box included a top, a set of dominoes, a ring game, illustrated storybooks, and a pair of small gloves. One gift confused him, though—an embroidered garment for which he was sure he had not asked. A note pinned on the item explained that this was for Mrs. Briggs.

"Now, what do you think of that?" the boy's mother exclaimed, dumbfounded and moved by the generosity. "Who would have thought Santa Claus would answer my little boy's letter this way?"

At the bottom of the package was a handwritten note from Santa himself, which Alfred read aloud. It praised him for his modest requests and exclaimed how glad Santa was that the boy had been good to his mother. It included the name and address of a "very kind lady" who lived outside of New York and would be pleased to receive a letter from Alfred expressing his pleasure with the gifts.

This donor had sent an inquiry about the association and received Alfred's letter in response. Since she could not herself deliver the gifts, she sent them to its headquarters for the group's volunteers to sort and deliver. Thanks to Whitaker and the association's more than twenty other volunteers, including Gluck himself, who spent their Christmas Eve weaving through tenement hallways and climbing up dimly lit stairwells, about one hundred of these last-minute packages reached their destinations. (Though even among a group of hardworking volunteers, Whitaker stood out. Just prior to the holiday, she reportedly worked about twenty hours a day, sleeping on a cot in the office.)

Each package was sealed with a red sticker that read, "From Santa Claus, North Pole," followed by the child's name. The *Times* reporter who watched Alfred receive his gifts noted that below the name of the Santa Claus Association and the address of Henkel's Chop House, the association included the name of the man who made this exchange possible: "John D. Gluck, Secretary."

About the same time that Alfred Briggs was singled out as a worthy recipient of Christmas spirit, the powers that be chose another boy from a large crowd gathered in Madison Square Park. It was Christmas Eve, just minutes before 5:30 p.m., and the boy was pulled from the thousands who had congregated in the park over the past few hours, ushered to a special area, and instructed to press a button when he got the signal.

The onlookers, staying warm thanks to their coats and close quarters to one another (and sips of hot, earthy coffee supplied by the Salvation Army), turned their attention to the clock on the Metropolitan Life Insurance Company Tower, which rose over the park. Since 1909, the structure had been the tallest building in the world, until the opening of the Woolworth eight months earlier reduced it to second best. Yet it remained the heart of New York City and had been the obvious choice the year before when city officials devised the idea of a citywide public celebration of Christmas. It had been the first time any city held a formal Christmas gathering of this type—inviting citizens to get together around a large tree to sing songs and enjoy entertainment. This year, the city officials arranged for a seventy-foot-tall "Tree of Light" in Madison Square Park as the hub of the Christmas Eve celebration, accompanied by a seven-hour concert of carolers, folk musicians, and brass bands. Five hundred boy scouts (Boy Scouts of America, not United States Boy Scout, who were helping the Santa Claus Association) stood at the ready to assist with crowd control.

As the giant clock struck 5:30, the boy got the signal and pressed the button. A large light burst on top of the pine tree as the Star of Bethlehem ignited. The crowd let out a collective gasp as the rest of the tree—a gift of Isaac Homestead of Westbury, New York, that had taken two teams of horses to pull from Long Island—sparkled as thousands of tiny lights illuminated the clear night. The bells in the nearby churches and Metropolitan Tower chimed. As a squad of trumpeters stood and initiated the program of music in the park, the wide-eyed boy stepped away from the button and returned to his place in the crowd. No reporters caught his name.

At 6:30 the singers of the Oratorio Society performed "Holy Night" and the carol "The Christ Child's Christmas Tree," specially written for the event. Its lyrics described a civic celebration of the holiday, where everyone was welcome.

> Come, gather. Rich and poor are one,
> Parent and child, and the strange lone,
> For the heart of the city goes out tonight
> In a burst of music, a flood of light;
> And the Christ-Child spirit, divinely fair,
> That illumined the manger cold and bare
> Is born again in the City square!

As attendees drank coffee and snacked on free sausages, the celebration and twinkling lights continued until midnight, when the hundred-member Negro Choral Society closed out the proceedings. "So were lighted the Christmas trees for all those in New York who had no trees of their own," the *Times* reported. The celebration was "for all the homeless, the lonely, the folk of the hall bedrooms, the strangers in New York at Christmas time." Every man, woman, and child in the city could enjoy a glowing Christmas tree, whatever their station in life.

But this type of celebration did not appeal only to those without a tree or a home of their own. Since its launch the year before, the gathering seemed to fill a need for community and connection that many New Yorkers had not been aware they were missing. The *Times* noted in 1912 that "Many people in the city have given up house parties to go to see the big tree and help swell the choruses." No matter how many decorations and gifts were piled at home, the excitement of the city beckoned.

Nor was it just New Yorkers who felt this attraction. This civic celebration of Christmas spread throughout the country in 1913. "That the public out of doors Christmas tree is a success was shown again tonight," the *Chicago Tribune* commented about New York's Tree of Light. No wonder Chicago was hailing New York's Christmas tree—its success led the Second City to erect its own for the first time in 1913. It was a commanding seventy-five footer, lit to the chorus of Chicago's Grand Opera Company as some of its stars sang Christmas songs through megaphones.

Cincinnati introduced a forty-five-foot-high tree—a first for the city. It was accompanied by ringing chimes, carols from choirboys, and a full flourish of trumpets. Just across the water from Gotham, Jersey City introduced its first public Christmas tree—rising thirty-five feet high and towering over the southeast corner of City Hall. Its lights, which could be seen from blocks away, were lit every night from Christmas Eve to New Year's Eve. Detroit, Baltimore, and numerous other cities lit up their first municipal Christmas trees in 1913, all following New York's successful example from the year before. "In all, fifty cities have this year followed New York's community tree example," wrote the *Tribune*. More than any other, this was the year that Christmas went public.

And it stayed that way. The community Christmas celebration that originated in New York would spread not only through newspapers but also pamphlets and instruction books that offered detailed descriptions for a city of any size to introduce its own civic gathering. In 1923, President Calvin Coolidge would light up the United States' first National Christmas Tree in President's Park. But as the grand tree-lighting tradition proliferated, the city that did it first continued to do it biggest. The Tree of Light remained for two more decades in Madison Square Park before moving to Rockefeller Center in 1933, where it reigns today as the highest-profile Christmas tree lighting in the country.

It is fitting that the year that these public lightings sprouted up in major cities across the United States was the same year the Post Office Department permanently released Santa Claus's mail and authorized an organization to send perfect strangers into the homes of the poor. If Santa was involved, the lines between classes, ethnicities, and social groups became blurred. A sprinkling of the Christmas spirit and suddenly it did not seem odd that a society lady dropped in on a poor kid in a gritty tenement, or that New Yorkers of every class would gather together around a Tree of Light, or that a little-known customs broker could get on a first-name basis with the city's elite. Santa Claus opened doors and kicked down barriers, in 1913 more than ever.

———

After the US Boy Scout helped the Santa Claus Association with its last-minute deliveries, a patrol of fifteen of its members went camping on Christmas Day in a woody area of Peekskill, New York. A few of the boys had a campfire going and began preparations for a rustic Christmas feast.

But Monroe Kniskern, thirteen-year-old son of an Episcopal reverend, lost interest in the proceedings when he spotted a rifle leaning against a nearby tree. It belonged to a fellow scout who had gotten it as an early Christmas present and brought it on the outing to show off to the other boys. Kniskern's curiosity got the best of him, and he began to play with the weapon. Few paid any attention to him.

Then the gun went off in his hands.

The rifle report was followed by a scream, and the other scouts looked up to see fourteen-year-old Edward Webb facedown on the ground. The pastor's son had accidentally shot him in the back of the head, killing him. A doctor rushed to the scene, followed by the coroner. The Christmas entertainment that the nearby Peekskill Church had planned was cancelled in light of the tragedy.

———

"The help of the Boy Scouts was quite invaluable," Gluck told the reporter seated across from his desk in the John D. Gluck & Son brokerage office. "They were a splendid mobile force."

It was about two weeks after Christmas Day, and the *New York Times* was interviewing Gluck about the group's successful first season. Gluck beamed as he described how with just four weeks from start to finish, the association had delivered gifts to some seventeen thousand children, as much as $100,000 in value. This they managed without paying salaries and while spending just $1,200 for postage and other expenses—less than

2 percent of the total value of donations. But the reporter was not here to write just another news item describing the association's work. He was conducting an extensive interview for a profile on Gluck's charity philosophy that would run to a full page in the *New York Times*' magazine section, under the headline "Played Santa Claus and Solved an Economic Problem."

The man jotting down notes as Gluck held forth was not just any cub reporter, either. He was Edward Marshall, the well-known journalist who covered social issues and wrote profiles on prominent men such as Thomas Edison. Now he'd arranged a sit-down with Gluck. He wanted to know what the association's success might mean for the city's other charities, ideas that excited the reform-minded Marshall. His career had taken off two decades earlier, when his muckraking had exposed the unsanitary conditions of New York City cellar bakeries, fueling the Bakeshop Act of 1895. Now at the *Times*, he focused on public policy and social reformers.

Marshall had heard about the scrappy charity group that had accomplished so much and was eager to hear from Gluck firsthand not just how he had done it, but also how others could follow his lead. "How would you organize a more efficient general charitable machine?" the reporter asked, sitting back in his chair and likely resting his hands on his right leg—his only leg, as he had lost the left one while a war correspondent in Cuba covering Teddy Roosevelt's Rough Riders. Gluck took a drag from his cigarette, thought a moment, and exhaled dramatically. "We simply offered to the people of New York, in such a way that it could not be doubted, the assurance that what they gave would really reach the poor in its grand total," he explained. Rather than the "old-line charitable agencies," which spent huge portions of their funds on salaried workers and administration, the association "tolerated very little waste" and "indicates to me that radical change is probable in the general methods of charitable operation, in New York at least."

Once Gluck got going on this topic, it was hard for Marshall to slow him down. Gluck emphasized that he did not mean to imply that the established charities did not "mean well; but I have become convinced that they do not do well, and I know they might accomplish marvels—for we did." He did not stop there. Gluck called for the city's public and private charities to be "officially investigated. I should like to take a hand in it."

Marshall asked for specifics on how Gluck would improve public relief efforts. By way of answer, the Santa Claus Man, as the press had now taken to calling him, presented two cases. In the first, a destitute man with an ill child applies for relief to the city's commissioner of charities. The commissioner refers him to the Society for Improving the Condition of the Poor, which investigates the claim and determines it should be referred to the City Mission. By the time the case is handled, "his babe sleeps peacefully in Potter's Field." On the other hand, following Gluck's more direct plan, the man's application would be referred to the official who oversees that borough and who would immediately designate it to individuals in charge of the man's neighborhood. They would then determine whether it was worthy and send a request to one of a number of donors who had previously volunteered to help in such situations. "Within ten hours or less the worthy case would find relief, without lost motion, without expensive offices or clerk hired," said Gluck.

For those who might doubt whether such a system could work, Gluck simply pointed to his success the month before: "[T]he same people doubtless would have said the Santa Claus Association plan was quite impractical. Yet we handled thirteen thousand cases in two weeks without the slightest previous preparation." Marshall delighted in Gluck's ideas of a more privatized, personal kind of relief, even as Gluck got a bit carried away, declaring, "This thing can't be stopped. It is going to revolutionize, reform, improve the whole system of our charities."

The reporter had to ask: "What real flaw developed in the system?"

"None that I know of," Gluck replied. "Perhaps there may be one so big that in the long run it would ruin everything, but none of us have found a hint of it."

Marshall was as struck by the association's success as Gluck himself. After the interview, he spoke with charity experts and determined that this was the first time as far as he could tell that an effort of this scope had been conducted by asking donors to take on the work themselves, rather than hiring professional solicitors and other intermediaries. "It seems

Edward Marshall's profile of Gluck, running in the January 18, 1914, edition of the *New York Times Magazine*. SANTA CLAUS ANNUAL.

impossible not to regard this thing as an extraordinary manifestation of efficiency linked to goodwill," he editorialized in the piece, which ran with a pen-and-ink illustration of Gluck sitting in his chair, in a three-piece suit, pince-nez, and thoughtful expression, reading a stack of papers. The subheadline declared that the association's work "points to a revolution in methods of distributing charity."

Gluck was thrilled with the final result. The profile capped off a season that, despite a few bumps, went far better than he could have hoped. In just four weeks, he went from unknown to beloved and respected, as if Santa had reached into his sack and pulled out the life Gluck always wanted. He saw an escape hatch—a ripe chance to reinvent himself. When Marshall asked Gluck whether he should refer to him in the article as a customs broker, Gluck suggested instead he be called "a publicity man and efficiency engineer."

Santa's Secretary captured the imagination of New Yorkers at the same time he proved his skill at garnering publicity on a grand scale—a valuable accomplishment as he sought out additional gigs to replace his earnings in the customs business. He filled many column inches talking up his work, his views of charity, and the contributions of his volunteers—the scouts in particular. The attention the group received for being a "splendid mobile force" for the association was the best press the United States Boy Scout garnered that year, and perhaps in its entire existence.

But in dozens of interviews with Gluck, in which he outlined almost every aspect of the association's work, he deliberately left out a conflict of interest that would cast these scouts, and the association's leader, in a very different light. During the same three weeks of great coverage for the USBS, in which nobody praised the scouts more highly than Gluck himself, the Santa Claus Man had in fact been working for them.

CHAPTER 4

The Most Photographed Man in the World

Broadway, Fifth Avenue, the mansions, the lights, the beauty. A fever of living is in their blood. An unnatural hunger and thirst for excitement is burning them up. For this they labor. For this they endure a hard, unnatural existence.
—THEODORE DREISER, "CHRISTMAS IN THE TENEMENTS"

Gluck savored his newfound celebrity and sought to parlay it into business opportunities. Running a nonprofit group could not pay his rent, so he found work that did. It is hard to determine exactly when he hopped onto the US Boy Scout's payroll, but most likely he made the arrangement with General Edwin McAlpin at the time the chief scout first offered the voluntary assistance of his boys—the men had little reason to interact prior to this introduction. By early 1914, Gluck was an official solicitor for the group. On the surface, the work resembled that of the Santa Claus Association: Gluck made appeals to New Yorkers for their support in a noble cause. Instead of promoting the spirit of Christmas, he promoted a spirit of citizenship and patriotism among the youth of Gotham. Instead of asking for the donation of presents, he asked for money to buy equipment and uniforms. The kicker was that L. W. Amerman, the USBS treasurer who oversaw its fund-raising work, granted Gluck 40 percent of whatever he solicited. It must have seemed an excessive amount, but after working long days with minimal payment for more than a month, Gluck needed the money.

More questionable was the fact that by talking up the scouts in his role at the association, Gluck was thereby putting money in his own pockets. The more positive publicity the USBS received, the more generosity was shown by New Yorkers toward the group. No laws against this sort of logrolling existed in New York City, and in fact few charity regulations existed at all early in the twentieth century, so Gluck may have felt within his rights to play both sides to his benefit.

Joining McAlpin's team of fund-raisers not only provided him with much-needed cash, it also exposed him to an operation that had been bringing in big contributions for years. He learned some promotional strategies that could be applied to his own organization. Though the Santa Claus Association would not officially return until the annual release of Santa letters on December 1, Gluck sought to keep up the momentum of its outstanding first year. One of the ways he set out to accomplish this was by associating with more prominent figures in New York City, beyond those with whom he had business connections or who volunteered to join after hearing of the group in the press. Gluck saw how eagerly the press and volunteers responded to the mention of a famous name, whether as a donor or volunteer, and wanted to find some way to make these names more central to the group's publicity. The trick was to get important and busy people to lend their names to the association while requiring that they do minimal, if any, work. Upon familiarizing himself with the workings of the USBS, Gluck found just the answer: honorary vice presidents.

The fund-raisers for the US Boy Scout had come up with the idea of inviting prominent people to serve as "honorary vice presidents," with the assurance that "no demands whatsoever, will be made upon your time," as one mailer explained. Upon his acceptance, the individual's name was added to the organization's masthead and to the official letters sent out to potential donors.

Gluck sensed the value of the idea immediately.

"I am very glad to serve as one of the Honorary Vice-Presidents of the Santa Claus Association and wish you all good luck in your worthy work," wrote the broker Ralph E. Samuel to Gluck on January 28, 1914. The same day brought a response from Reverend Edward Gabler, minister of the St. Mark's Church House at Tenth Street and Avenue

A. "Gentlemen: I will be very glad to be numbered among the list of Honorary Vice Presidents, and will be happy to help you in your most interesting work; kindly let me know what [are] my duties as a member of Said Committee," he wrote. "You have no duties," Gluck could have easily responded.

Gluck was not shy in his outreach. On March 13, New York State governor Martin Glynn's assistant wrote that the governor "is very much interested in the object of the [association]" and that "it will give the Governor great pleasure to become an Honorary Vice President."

The same month, he took another major step to bolster the Santa Claus Association, incorporating it on March 25. Composing the group's mission statement, he used it as a chance to formalize what he had told Zoe Beckley and others: The group was not a charity organization. Rather, "its primary object is the fostering of the true Christmas spirit, to bring Christmas cheer into the homes of the poor." He moved the John D. Gluck & Son operation from downtown to the twelfth floor of 347 Fifth Avenue, at the corner of Thirty-Third Street (across from where the Empire State Building now stands), renaming his brokerage office "the Santa Claus Association executive office." From his new station, Gluck coordinated a number of off-season requests for the association in addition to his other publicity, fund-raising, and customs work, which provided him income throughout the year.

The association's mission charmed brothers William and Frederick Muschenheim, proprietors of the Hotel Astor. But instead of volunteering to serve as honorary vice presidents, they offered up something far more valuable: space in their hotel for the group's 1914 season. Bounded by Broadway, Astor Plaza, West Forty-Forth, and West Forty-Fifth Streets, the beaux arts building had opened less than a decade earlier, around the time Mayor George McClellan changed the name of its neighborhood from Longacre Square to Times Square. William Waldorf Astor owned the lease to the hotel that bore his name, but the Muschenheims served as proprietors.

The seven blocks up Broadway from Henkel's Chop House to the Hotel Astor felt like a major promotion to Gluck. The hotel took up an entire city block, with one thousand guest rooms, a massive Grand

Ballroom, an Old New York lobby, and the American Indian Hall, complete with baskets, garments, and other artifacts on loan from the American Museum of Natural History. It was built with the Johnson system of temperature regulation—cutting-edge at the time—as well as fire alarms and construction that made it "unquestionably *THE* fire-proof hotel of New York," according to a promotional brochure.

The association, however, would not work in these elaborate areas. The Muschenheims offered the group the hotel's wine cellar. But as Gluck toured the new space, he saw that "cellar" did not do it justice—the rathskeller carried its own kind of grandeur. Gluck's eyes bulged as he took in the large, gothic chandeliers hung from the vaulted ceiling. Along the wood-paneled side walls, desks were set just a few feet in front of the glass cases holding wine bottles and crystal ware. Two rows of squat columns dominated the room, with three large wine barrels set against the far wall. Anchoring the room was a massive dark wood table that ran through the center. Gluck could already picture how this space could serve the group. One of the volunteers on the tour dubbed it the "Santa Claus Cave." Gluck loved the sound of that and adopted the name on the spot.

On December 1, the Santa Claus Cave opened for its second year in business. Gluck strolled into his new headquarters with pride as work got underway. The rush of activity outdid the bustle of Henkel's back room. Dozens, sometimes as many as two hundred, volunteers lined up on either side of the huge wooden table to assist in the responses. Placards set on small wooden stands, reading "Fresh Mail," "Special Investigation," and "Miscellaneous" brought some order to the piles of letters. The "Immediate Aid" placard indicated cases of extreme poverty requiring fast assistance from the city. At one of the side desks sat the nameplate for "U.S. Boy Scout—Leaving 30 Min" where volunteers placed any letters that needed investigating. The USBS again assisted the association that year, dropping off letters and packages and investigating the needs of letter writers.

Alongside the main table Gluck placed a series of small tables, setting a Royal typewriter on each. Stenographers sat in the cellar's heavy wooden chairs, swiveling their bodies from reading a letter at the main table to typing a response on the small one. As busy as things were, Gluck

The deepening ranks of the association, including scouts, sailors, and society ladies, posing in the Hotel Astor's basement wine cellar. SANTA CLAUS ANNUAL.

encouraged anyone to come by and see the work they were doing: "Anyone visiting the metropolis is invited to drop in for a chat with Santa," the papers declared. About a week after the Cave opened, Gluck hosted a large photo op for the press. He set up volunteers on both sides of the table, with typewriters on their laps, Boy Scouts lined against one wall, and even a team of sailors he had recruited to help with the day's delivery. Gluck sat at the head of the table, completing the first full tableau of the organization's resources. "Children who thought Santa Claus a figure of fiction will come to realize that even story-book happenings are events of life," wrote a reporter for the *Tribune*.

Gluck's ambitions now expanded beyond New York City. The successful first year gave him the confidence to franchise the association. This second year, a group of charity-minded Canadians coordinated with Gluck to create their own association affiliate. Based in Toronto's

Several association directors, including H. B. Sommer (fourth from the left) in the Hotel Astor's "Santa Claus Cave." SANTA CLAUS ANNUAL.

luxurious King Edward Hotel, the Canadian extension of the group not only allowed Gluck to prove his approach could be applied to other cities but also elevated the group's title to "International Santa Claus Association."

With an eye toward expanding the group into other cities, Gluck devised ways to simplify the group's process so it could be more easily exported. He adjusted the system of investigations to lighten the investigators' workload—changes that unintentionally opened old wounds for one Isabelle M. Colwell. A member of a prominent family from Atlanta, she was suffering a painful Christmas in 1914.

Six months earlier, while Isabelle tidied up her apartment on West 135th Street, her husband James suggested that he take their two-year-old boy Jimmie for a walk. Isabelle watched from the window as the two strolled down the street; when they stopped at the corner, Jimmie abruptly turned and waved to her, a look of concern in his eyes, before the two turned the corner and disappeared. It was the last time she saw either of them. James had been having an affair, and evidence suggested that he left with his mistress and the three had headed who knew where, to seek out a new life. She alerted the police and press, but it was viewed as a domestic matter. She attempted her own investigation but came up empty-handed and ran out of funds.

After a half year of searching, Isabelle felt no closer to finding her curly haired, blue-eyed young Jimmie. She would spend the holiday season alone and in despair, with only scattered inanimate items to remind her of her boy. One of these objects was a letter to Santa that she had helped the child scrawl the previous Christmas, guiding her son's fingers to write to the old saint, with no plans of sending it. Now, as the first Christmas without her son approached, Isabelle found a small satisfaction in dropping the letter into the mail, sending it off to somewhere magical. She expected that would be the last she heard of it.

As with the rest of the letters, this one arrived at the now-open General Post Office and then was redirected to the Hotel Astor where it was received, logged, and responded to. Gluck went through several drafts of the letter he'd crafted, giving it a tone of good humor but with a sting for anyone taking advantage of the group's charity. For Isabelle, the group's reply to her uptown home as she grieved for her absent child was heartbreaking.

TO PARENT OR GUARDIAN:

We received a letter from your child asking Santa Claus to remember it this Christmas. You may give the enclosed letter or letters from Santa Claus to your child or children just before Christmas. We suggest that you let the children find them somewhere; in any event you may keep them.

It is assumed that you know your child has written such a letter and so as to facilitate our investigation bureau we will thank you to put an X in the square above just to the right of the square bearing a number, which is the number we have stamped on your child's letter now; then return it to us immediately.

It is further understood that in putting an X in the square above, that you are not in sufficient financial circumstances to yourself attend to

the Christmas wishes of your little children. We rely on your judg-
ment and integrity in the matter and beg to remind you that for every
unworthy case attended to, a worthy child must suffer.

With kind personal regards and best wishes for your future success and
a Merry Christmas, we are,

Cordially yours,

SANTA CLAUS ASSOCIATION OF NEW YORK

John D. Gluck, Secretary

A postscript at the bottom of the letter advised that unless the letter
was returned within four days from when it was mailed, the association
would halt any further response. Accompanying this business letter, Isabelle found a small envelope with an illustration of Santa Claus laughing and holding an envelope bearing her son's name. Inside was a note
for the child, with "From Santa Claus, North Pole, December," written
across the top.

Of course, Isabelle could not give the letter to little Jimmie. She
had not heard of the Santa Claus Association and actually receiving a
response from Saint Nick startled and upset her. Not wanting to check
the box but also uncomfortable doing nothing, Isabelle grabbed the letter and headed to the address of the Santa Claus Cave, typed on the
letterhead. She was taken to Gluck while secretary Fannie M. Baker sat
nearby, learning of her touching reasons for forwarding the letter and the
painful situation in which she found herself. Gluck promised to muster
the association's resources and do all it could to help her find the child. It
was hard to imagine how his efforts could yield any assistance, but Gluck
promised nonetheless.

The Hotel Astor proved ideal for running an operation more elaborate
than the year before, but it was also fortunate the Muschenheims had

The letter and envelope every child received from the association. It reads: "My dear little one: I have received your dear letter and am happy to know you have been such a good child. Santa cannot promise, but will do his very best to visit your home this Christmas." GLUCK SCRAPBOOKS.

offered up their hotel for another reason. Even if Gluck had wanted to return to Henkel's Chop House for another year, that was no longer an option. Henkel's bid to replace Keens as the street's chophouse of choice failed to generate the interest and customers he had hoped. On January 26, 1914, several creditors filed a petition against Henkel for more than $2,000. At the end of the month, the restaurant entered into receivership.

Less than a month later, on February 24, Henkel declared bankruptcy at the New York Southern District court. Henkel's would become Oscar and Billie's, and Gluck was suddenly out of a place to live. So he moved to the Hoffman House on Broadway at Madison Square. Once a glorious stop for business leaders, actors, and US presidents, by 1914 the property was having trouble competing with the new hotels sprouting up on Broadway and Fifth Avenue. In fact, by March 1915, Hoffman House would close its doors and be auctioned off, requiring Gluck to again pack his bags and seek housing elsewhere.

Part of Henkel's—and the Hoffman House's—troubles were that the pre- and post-theater audiences were moving north. Times Square quickly eclipsed Herald Square as the center of musicals and theater in the city. The Hoffman House had advertised itself in 1884 as "Central to All Principal Theatres and Points of Interest in the City." When Gluck moved there three decades later, the party had moved uptown. No wonder in 1914 Keens Chophouse's new owners bought an additional property on Forty-Forth Street, adjoining the Stuyvesant Theatre. Dozens of these new "Broadway" restaurants opened between 1899 and 1914, mixed in with the colorful lights of the theater and extravagant shop windows of high-end department stores like Lord & Taylor, Arnold Constable, and B. Altman's (all of which moved north around the same time).

This "helped make the life of conspicuous consumption available to a wider portion of the city and the nation," according to historian Lewis Erenberg. But as these luxurious goods and sumptuous meals became more accessible, there for any passerby to see through a plate-glass window, it made them that much more painfully out of reach for the city's poor, and their children in particular. They could see the baubles and sweets that other children enjoyed but had to settle with spectating through the windows of extravagant shops and movie palaces. Theodore Dreiser witnessed this while living in New York City at this time, and called this longing of the poor for what they watched the rich enjoy, "the indissoluble link which binds these weakest and most wretched elements of society to the best and most successful."

Along with the New York Times Building, for which the newly dubbed square was named, and the Hotel Knickerbocker, the twelve-story Hotel Astor anchored this burgeoning area. It drew in some of the biggest celebrities and hosted parties for film and theater stars, such as a recent Friars Club dinner in honor of English actor Cyril Maude. Gluck did all he could to attract these theater folk to his own efforts.

While the "honorary vice presidents" campaign helped the association to capitalize on recognized names in the political and business arenas, Gluck wanted to tap into the prominence and energy of the Great White Way. Working connections he built while at Henkel's Chop House, he visited Broadway producer Albert H. Woods at his office to see if he could take a few letters. Woods, a Hungarian who had immigrated to the United States decades earlier, had produced some thirty plays since beginning in theater a decade before (within just the previous four months, he'd opened five plays).

Gluck asked if there was any way Woods could promote the group to the theater crowd. He explained that the extra advertising would raise awareness of the effort and help keep the city from forgetting the association. But then Gluck went further, telling Woods that, in fact, his group faced a significant debt if it did not pull in some extra funds to cover postage. This was a blatant exaggeration. The previous year, about $1,000, covering fifty thousand stamps, had been more than sufficient for the group's needs over the entire season. They had ended the year with a surplus of funds and had been steadily bringing in checks throughout 1914, which ensured it would exceed the donations of the previous year. Just the week before, mining executive J. Parke Channing had alone provided the association with $500 for postage. But unaware of these numbers and touched by Gluck's plea for funds, the producer told him, "I am most willing to fall in line and cooperate in every way possible to relieve the needy and bring a small amount of Yuletide happiness to the poor of our city."

As for how to get Broadway to do its part, Woods had an idea. He was willing to donate a night's box office receipts from one of his shows to the group—promoting it in the press to help boost audience interest. Gluck loved the suggestion and they settled on the Tuesday, December 22, performance of the play *Kick In* at the Republic Theater. The twenty-second happened to be opening night for Woods's latest production, *The Song of Songs*, which was already expected to draw a large crowd. The Santa Claus promotion would help keep the Republic filled as well. Tickets ranged from twenty-five cents for balcony seats to as much as two dollars, so a full theater could bring in a significant donation. The two men shook on the plan and Gluck dashed to the executive office to start spreading the word that Broadway was going to "Kick In" to help Santa Claus.

A few days after meeting with Gluck, Woods arranged for *Kick In* cast members Josephine Victor and Maidel Turner to drop by the Santa Claus Cave to offer a hand with the letters and pose for photos. But while Turner had appeared in a handful of short films the year before and Victor would have been a familiar face to the New York media, the man who

Actors Josephine Victor, King Baggot, and Maidel Turner (from left to right), visiting the Santa Claus Cave. GLUCK SCRAPBOOKS.

accompanied them was the reason so many reporters came that day. He had been sent to the Cave care of the Universal Film Company as part of the promotion for his new movie *The Mill Stream*, released three days earlier. Seated between the actresses in his three-piece suit and bow tie was King Baggot, known in newspapers and fan magazines as "The Most Photographed Man in the World." A year earlier he had starred in the silent films *Ivanhoe* and *Dr. Jekyll and Mr. Hyde*, which would remain two of his best-known performances, even as he appeared in some 269 films over his five-decade career. *The Mill Stream* came just weeks after the success of another Baggot two-reeler, *Shadows*, in which he played ten roles, including a policeman, girl, mother, jailer, wayward son, and thief (and which he also wrote and produced). It was such a bravura performance that one paper declared him the "king of movieland." In these germinal years of film, Baggot was inventing the very concept of a leading man.

After the man—who was also known as the "Monarch of Hearts and Arts"—posed for another photo, Gluck took him aside. He thought it

Gluck and King Baggot (in Santa costume) visit the General Post Office to promote the association's benefit show. SANTA CLAUS ANNUAL.

might be fun to take this holiday publicity a bit further—if the actor would be willing to don a Santa costume. Baggot, happy to give an added boost of publicity to the association, agreed.

Reporters were directed to head to the new General Post Office. The association was going to pick up its mail today, accompanied by a very special guest. Eschewing the "time honored sleigh with reindeers," as one show-business trade magazine called it, the superstar Santa and his trusty sidekick, Gluck, arrived to the press event in high style in a high-end automobile. Baggot strolled up the steps of the front entrance and Gluck handed him an armful of Santa letters—freshly retrieved from one of Postmaster Morgan's men. Baggot's costume looked a bit threadbare, a bit too large for his frame. But the eyes peering out between the beard and wool cap were vibrant. As the photographers prepared their cameras,

Gluck made a quick decision and moved into the frame next to the movie star. Cameras fired away.

—⁀—

The publicity stunt did the trick. The night of the benefit show arrived, and to Gluck's delight almost all the tickets sold. This was no small feat. Not only was the premier of Woods's *Song of Songs* pulling away theatergoers, just two weeks earlier, a musical called *Watch Your Step* had opened at the New Amsterdam Theatre (where Florenz Ziegfeld usually held his *Follies*). Incorporating ragtime—a popular musical style considered too crass for the theater—the show was a novelty to New Yorkers and delighted crowds and critics. One reviewer called the melodies "born to be caught up and whistled at every street corner." It was the beginning of a 175-performance run and would launch the career of the man who had written its music and lyrics, a Russian immigrant going by the name Irving Berlin. It was a particularly thrilling time of possibility for the theater. The 1914–1915 season would produce a record-breaking 133 new productions in and around Times Square (by comparison, just forty-four plays opened on Broadway in the 2013–2014 season).

To help pull theatergoers to *Kick In*, Woods made it more than a typical benefit show: not only did audience members donate to the cause, but everyone involved in the play, from support staff to actors, also "bought" tickets to the show, making their own contribution to the Santa Claus Association. The play's star, John Barrymore, donated $100 to cover the cost of a "gallery seat" for his own performance.

Those who paid for a ticket took their seats by the 8:20 p.m. curtain time, and took in the lavish detail of the walls and cherubs playing lyres on the rim of the domed theater's ceiling. But once the play began, all attention went to Barrymore. Many would have been familiar with him as a comic actor, but this night he took the stage in a much more serious style. He portrayed Chick Hewes, an ex-convict who tries to stay on the right side of the law but is drawn into avenging the murder of a poor child struck down by the district attorney's son. The actor would later write that "People thought Woods was crazy to trust me with the part. His friends—perhaps they thought they were my friends too . . . flourished the usual theatrical measuring stick of 'personal limitations.'" It was a "crook melodrama" that explored the gray area between a bad person and a person driven to do bad things, and required a sophisticated actor to win the sympathy and applause of the audience. Barrymore won both.

As the play ended with Chick Hewes's exoneration, the crowd cheered. The show would continue at the Republic until spring 1915, and positioned Barrymore as a serious actor on the rise. He would star in a string of dramatic roles on Broadway over the coming years— *Justice, Richard III,* and *Hamlet,* as well as in a number of hugely successful films that would lay the foundation for one of the most outstanding acting careers of all time as well as an acting dynasty. But on this night, he served Santa Claus. Overall, the box office and the performers' donations brought in some $2,000 for the group (about $46,000 today). It was double the entire budget of the association's first year, in just one night.

But bursting coffers and rubbing shoulders with celebrities only made Gluck hungrier for more attention and esteem—and perhaps some additional funds too. While the country's most famous stars garnered headlines for the association, there was one story that continued to overshadow all others this season, with which even the Most Photographed Man in the World could hardly compete. The war being fought in Europe saturated the public's attention. The front pages covered little else.

For a publicity man like Gluck, breaking through this saturation was difficult. Answering Santa letters was now a familiar idea in the group's second year and hardly as interesting as the latest news of foreign hostilities. But if there was a way to connect the association's work to the war overseas, he considered, that might bring the group additional interest, and even confer a greater sense of importance on its mission. After considering a few possibilities, Gluck arrived at an idea that would do exactly that. First, he just had to tell a few lies.

CHAPTER 5

"Enemy, Death, and a Christmas Tree"

I expect you think this a bit of a yarn. In fact the regulars, who were in reserve here would not believe it. Some of them came up to see for themselves.

—OFFICER IN QUEEN'S WESTMINSTER RIFLES

To whom does Santa send *his* Christmas wishes? The president of the United States, of course.

That was Gluck's thinking as he watched the war unfold in Europe. On June 28, 1914, Austrian archduke Franz Ferdinand's assassination while visiting Bosnia set off the chain of events leading to Austria-Hungary declaring war on Serbia; Germany declaring war on Russia, then France, then Belgium; and Britain declaring war on Germany—all within the span of a week. By December, after gaining control of Belgium, Germany hit a stalemate with French and British troops at the Aisne valley, where both sides fortified the area with trenches. It formed part of a front line stretching from the North Sea to Switzerland, and the press covered with breathless urgency every attack, loss, and new infusion of troops. The papers carried daily maps of the active theaters with briefs on the latest troop movements and exchanges.

Although the United States remained a grim spectator of the ongoing bloodshed, it provided active assistance through its charities. News of destroyed villages, desperate refugees, and suffering soldiers aroused sympathy and calls for relief, and donations flooded in from concerned

Dear Santa Claus
Before the war we were all happy
and had a nice home. Now we are poor,
and have no milk for my baby brother
and sister. Please send me some.
With Kind regards
yours beloving Edward Feldman
730, E, 85 strut

Letter from a child, written in 1914. SANTA CLAUS ANNUAL.

Americans. The continuing worry that the United States might be drawn into combat hung over everything. "[W]hen there is fire all about us you cannot stop the contagion," Secretary of the Navy Josephus Daniels told the House Naval Committee on December 10, as they debated whether to build more ships or if such preparations would prove foolish should the foreign war reach a resolution in the next months or weeks.

The war also impacted the United States through its economic toll. The association saw a marked increase in financial woe among the letters it received, with a number of children specifically citing their own parents' job losses and referencing the war's impact.

But the quotidian difficulties of the poor in New York City now competed with the more dramatic demands of the Great War. Organizations like the Children's Aid Society and the Society for Improving the Condition of the Poor took out ads in the newspapers to remind readers that New Yorkers still needed assistance too.

"We should not permit foreign conditions to interfere with our attitude toward the poor in the United States and in Canada," Gluck told a

Times reporter. "We cannot, at a time like this, hide behind the war curtain and fail to send Christmas cheer into the homes of the poor." Gluck wanted the Santa Claus Association's mission to remain relevant to New Yorkers, so he had to speak to wider world events. But how to connect the Christmas spirit to its antithesis—death and destruction overseas?

Working away in his executive office, Gluck arrived at a plan. The children of New York already sent their hopeful wishes to Santa Claus. Perhaps the association could ask them to send something else: a call for peace. The group could gather the signatures of thousands of American parents and children requesting a "Christmas armistice" between the warring nations in Europe, a pause in fighting from the Thursday of Christmas Eve to the following Monday morning of December 28.

To give the plan any chance of actually working, Gluck needed to make his call for prayers from the loudest bullhorn he could find. Extending the "honorary vice president" approach to its logical endpoint, Gluck came to the idea of contacting the president himself. He sent a letter directly to Woodrow Wilson, requesting his official endorsement of the plan. It was a crazy idea, but so was answering Santa letters. And just three days after sending his letter, Gluck actually received a reply at the association's executive office.

After careful consideration of the suggestion, which you make as to a petition for a 'Christmas armistice,' I have reached the conclusion that any proposal of this sort to the nations at war at the present time would certainly fail of its purpose and might be misconstrued. . . .

While regretting that circumstances prevent the fulfillment of a desire inspired by humanitarian sentiments and the Christian principle of unselfish service for others, my conviction is that it would be unwise as well as futile to pursue further your generous purpose.

It did not come from President Wilson but from Robert Lansing, counselor to the State Department, and acting secretary of state. "Unwise as well as futile" were not the words Gluck hoped to hear. But Lansing's logic was hard to dispute. Spreading Christmas cheer worked fine for private charity groups but not as official US policy, where the belligerent countries might misconstrue a call for an armistice.

But Gluck refused to abandon the idea. If the United States declined to pledge support for a truce, the association, as Santa's official ambassador, would personally ask the hostile nations for a pause in the hostilities. Gluck sent a letter to the ambassadors of the countries at war. Then he called the press. Rather than signatures, the association now promised a "simple prayer of the children of America, born of a people of all races, for a Christmas armistice" (later this would become a more secular "Christmas carol"). "We believe if this is accomplished we will have executed a favorable step in the direction of peace," Gluck explained. Unlike his letter to President Wilson, which asked for an endorsement once the signatures were gathered, these requests informed the ambassadors that the peace prayers of America's children were a certainty. Not only that, children from forty cities would be providing their voices to the global Christmas wish, totaling not thousands or hundreds of thousands, but *one million* kids.

The reporters ran with the story, even with no way to verify Gluck's claim. The association had overseen gifts to about seventeen thousand kids the previous holiday season. Even tapping connections at charity groups and schools throughout the country, they could hardly expect to generate a number close to one million. Gluck of course knew this. But searching for a way to boost press attention, he decided the gesture itself would make an impact, rather than the actual facts. Learning that one million American kids supported a cease-fire, even if it was not the pure unvarnished truth, would garner headlines and might also nudge the nations' leaders and soldiers to seriously consider armistice.

So Gluck stretched the truth in the service of Santa Claus. Sometimes one had to take liberties with facts in order to get, and keep, people's attention, he reasoned. What was Santa Claus if not a friendly deception invented to delight and encourage better behavior?

In fact, if not for some well-told lies and manipulation of the press, St. Nicholas probably would never have caught on in the first place. The original staid, proper character promoted by John Pintard would likely have remained cloistered in the halls of the New-York Historical Society, if not for a comical book that satirized all their high-minded efforts and put a more delightful twist on the character.

⸻ ⸻

"Distressing," read the one-word headline in the *New York Evening Post* of October 26, 1809. The notice reported an elderly man had gone missing. He'd been staying at the Columbian Hotel on Mulberry Street but had walked out wearing a black coat and "cocked hat" and never returned. "[T]here are some reasons for believing he is not entirely in his right mind," the notice claimed. A few days later, the landlord of the Columbian Hotel wrote in to note that while the gentleman remained missing, he left behind "a curious kind of a written book" that the landlord intended to publish if he did not hear from the author.

As promised, on November 28, a literary notice appeared to announce that this book, "found in the chamber of Mr. Diedrich Knickerbocker, the gentleman whose sudden and mysterious disappearance has been noticed" would be published on December 6, 1809—St. Nicholas Day— "in order to discharge certain debts he has left behind." The book, titled *A History of New-York*, would relate the early decades of Manhattan, *From the Beginning of the World to the End of the Dutch Dynasty*, as its subtitle grandly declared. Of course, the whole missing-person report was a publicity stunt. The author cooked up the old man, his disappearance, and origin of the manuscript as a way to get attention for *A History*. The immediate interest and strong sales of the book proved the deftness of the strange advertising campaign and helped introduce its twenty-six-year-old author to a large new audience. Through his elaborate fabrications in the papers, Washington Irving quickly made a splash.

A History was itself something of a prank, supposedly written by the eccentric Diedrich Knickerbocker, who proved an inept historian. Irving cooked up the origin story of New York using a few facts, mixed together with exaggerated characters and goofy tangents to create a funny, and heavily fictional, read. Although he created satirical biographies for the leaders of early New York, Irving also gave St. Nicholas, a venerated figure to the Dutch settlers, the sly Knickerbocker treatment. The saint pops up throughout *A History*, blessing and protecting the first Manhattanites.

But Irving's is a funhouse-mirror version of the virtuous and noble bishop Pintard sought to install as Gotham's patron saint. He rides "jollily among the tree-tops, or over the roofs of the houses, now and then drawing forth magnificent presents from his breeches pockets." He smokes a long clay pipe like those offered at Keens and Henkel's, wears a broad hat, and lays his finger beside his nose while "winking hard with one eye." It is a St. Nick with some resemblance to the one who now presides over department stores each Christmas.

The revelation that Irving was the author of this burlesque history catapulted his career and brought him fame both in America and abroad. He remains known for inventions like Rip Van Winkle and Ichabod Crane, but Diedrich Knickerbocker and the jovial St. Nicholas were his first hits. "Without Irving there would be no Santa Claus," as Santa historian Charles W. Jones sums it up. "[A]fter 1809 the spritely SC spread like a plague." Or, as Irving biographer Andrew Burstein says, "[I]t was Washington Irving who first associated this figure with fun."

Pintard and Irving—the preservationist and the prankster—each brought his own peculiar obsessions and interests to the figure of Saint Nicholas, each infusing him with his own personality, in ways that would shape the character for decades to come. But perhaps few would have noticed *A History*, and the jolly sleigh-riding St. Nick would never have caught on, had it not been for Irving's publicity stunts and affable lies.

———

Gluck lied to the press and public about one million kids praying for peace, and the responses from the ambassadors of the belligerent countries seemed to bear out his decision. On December 6, 1914, British ambassador Cecil Spring-Rice sent a reply:

You are good enough to write me that one million children, in forty cities, will sing on Christmas a carol, praying that the fathers of the nations at war will declare a Christmas armistice.

I will take care that in accorde [sic] with your desire, my government is informed of this mighty petition from children of all nations who, under the American flag, have learned the great lesson of dwelling together in peace and greatness.

In an odd coincidence of timing (unless the Holy See took cues from public-relations stunts of New York City charities), the day after Gluck announced his peace prayer, Pope Benedict XV also put out a request that the warring nations arrange a truce during the Christmas holidays. He appealed to the German kaiser and Austrian emperor, perhaps with only a mild expectation it might succeed, considering hostile countries of the Orthodox Greek Church did not even celebrate Christmas on December 25—they followed the Julian calendar, which meant Christmas fell on January 6.

The Germans responded to Pope Benedict on December 10, agreeing to the truce—on the condition that all the other warring nations sign on as well. The same day, US senator William Kenyon of Iowa introduced a resolution that the nations cease war for twenty days over the Christmas holidays, with "the hope that such cessation of hostilities may stimulate reflection upon the part of such nations as to the meaning and spirit of the Christmas time."

While the association found itself among a growing chorus of peace advocates, it wasn't just the Wilson administration that looked skeptically at the call for truce. Andrew Carnegie said it would be un-Christian and immoral to stop, and then resume, the fighting. The armies' leaders scoffed at the idea as well. German captain Rudolf Binding wrote to his father that any Christmas celebration would be inappropriate during war, that "Enemy, death, and a Christmas tree—they cannot live so close together."

The London *Morning Post* mocked the suggestion of a truce. "[O]ur good friends, the Americans, would be wise not to play with such pretty notions as that war may be interrupted for a Christmas truce." The *New York Times*' editors responded that the *Post* was mistaken—not on the foolishness of a truce, but that the public supported any such cause. The editors wrote, "if any criticism of this silly kind has been made here we venture to say that not one in 50,000 of our readers has ever heard a whisper of it." They called support for armistice "emotional insanity," and that those calling for it were "amiable and well-meaning people without the faintest influence on public opinion."

Gluck no doubt felt irritated to see himself accused of "emotional insanity," though he could have been consoled that among those the *Times* accused of lacking the "faintest influence on public opinion" were not only he but also a US senator and the pope. Nonetheless, just as it seemed there might be some momentum behind the idea, Russia declined the pope's suggestion, leading Germany to back out as well. The campaign to demonstrate that the Christmas spirit could survive in the midst of war appeared dead.

—•—

While the association's potential impact on world events appeared slight at best, Gluck found other ways to promote the group's work throughout New York City. For the 1914 season, they premiered a series of ten special seals, imitating a strategy by the American Red Cross in which supporters made a donation to the cause (in the Red Cross's case, the fight against tuberculosis), and received the seals to attach to their Christmas cards and gifts. "Well-known American artists" designed all the seals, Gluck explained. The stamps featured illustrations such as Santa holding his sleigh, a child scrawling a letter, and a tuxedoed gentleman examining an envelope under the line "The Club Man Enlists with the Santa Claus Association."

"Do you know the Santa Claus Association?" asked an ad in *St. Nicholas Magazine*. "It takes the appeals of very poor children which Uncle Sam's Post Office finds in the mail every year—and has them cared for. Isn't that fine? Do you want to help this good work? If you will send 50 cents to us, we will send as a receipt *ten* Poster Stamps." As with the requests the previous year for postage funds, Gluck couched these direct appeals for money as a way to offset administrative costs. The seals proved a boon for the group's fund-raising, so much so that toward the end of the season, the Red Cross threatened the association with an injunction for using its seal-sale method. Gluck reluctantly agreed to scrap the program the next year.

One of the seals stood out for its higher level of detail and realism. It depicted a scene of Christmas morning. An African-American boy in a white nightshirt reaches out excitedly at a red toy wagon on the floor,

The association sold holiday seals, which donors could place on the gifts they sent to children. GLUCK SCRAPBOOKS.

alongside a shabby Christmas tree decorated with two ornaments sitting in front of the fireplace where a small stocking hung. The seal replicated a painting by artist Angus Peter MacDonall, titled *Golly*. A popular artist at the time, MacDonall created illustrations of happy families, stern soldiers, and other idealized images of America for magazines like *The Country Gentleman* and *Life*, as well as more fanciful scenes like a family of bears taking tea together or Generals Lee and Grant enjoying a drink in the woods. His work shared an aesthetic with the younger and soon-to-be more successful Norman Rockwell. But in December 1914, readers adored MacDonall, and an original work reportedly fetched $4,000 (about $92,000 today).

MacDonall, a sentimentalist with a style that jibed well with the association, not only gave the group permission to use the image for its Christmas seals, he also gave them the original painting to help attract visitors to the office. So excited about the gift, shortly after receiving the small two-by-one-foot work in the association's Fifth Avenue executive office, Gluck put the word out to reporters about the painter's generosity and promised to display it for all to see. That proved unwise.

On December 8, 1914, the day after these reports ran, as Gluck and a few volunteers returned to the executive office after work at the

Hotel Astor, he noticed immediately the painting was gone. Gluck hoped someone misplaced it or moved it to the Santa Claus Cave, as they had been planning to do the next day. But after he spoke with several officers and volunteers, no one could identify what had happened to the painting, though the office door had been left open for the last several hours. Only one explanation made sense: *Golly* had been stolen.

Embarrassed and upset, Gluck put out a notice to the papers:

PAINTING *taken from room 1205, 347 Fifth Avenue, famous and cannot be pawned without exposure resulting. If returned immediately, nothing said.*

Angus Peter MacDonall's painting *Golly*, used as the design for one of the association's seals and the original given as a gift to Gluck. GLUCK SCRAPBOOKS.

Like the kidnapped Jimmie Colwell whom Gluck had promised to help find, he declared the association would also recapture the stolen work of art. He directed the US Boy Scout to give a notice to every secondhand store in the city to advise the association if *Golly* turned up. MacDonall had included a dedication to the group on the back, so it would be easy to verify its provenance.

As they had in other instances, several newspapers mistakenly credited the group's rival, the Boy Scouts of America, with helping in the hunt for the painting. Scout commissioner Lorillard Spencer angrily wrote a notice in the Boy Scouts of America's weekly column in the *New-York Tribune* (scouting had grown so popular at this time that dedicated scout columns and full-page sections were regular features in a number of city papers). Under the headline "A Warning," Spencer explained that the article about the scouts helping with the painting's search was "entirely unauthorized, as no such orders have been issued to the scouts either individually or collectively." It was one more tension between two enemies as they built to an all-out war.

⁓

Despite their efforts, the US Boy Scout turned up no painting and gathered no leads on who had stolen it. After a few days, Gluck called off the search. The association needed the scouts to run the Santa letter investigations. The stolen gift soon faded into the background of the season's excitement. Five days before Christmas, a call came from Ralph Pulitzer—one of the wealthiest and most powerful men in New York City since inheriting control of the *New York World* three years earlier from his father, Joseph. He saw Gluck's comment about the need for postage stamps and thought he might have a solution. His son, eight-year-old Ralph Jr., wanted to help Santa Claus and, according to his father, had "offered up his Christmas savings to cover the postage for all the letters." The blank check from the generous child gave the group all the money it could possibly need heading into Christmas. But Gluck continued to call for postage funds.

The association cruised toward Christmas Eve. The Madison Square Park tree lit up at 5:30 in the evening for the third annual gathering, kicked off with a bugle announcement from the stand in the center of the park. The snow, which had begun to fall that afternoon, added the final detail to an ideal picture of Christmas in the city. A Native American from the Mohawk tribe, Gabriel Deer, sang for the crowds. The Boy Scouts of America's Lighting Industry Fife and Drum Corps performed. The US Boy Scout spent their Christmas Eve aiding the Santa Claus Association.

Cars offered to the association shot through the streets of New York dropping off last-minute deliveries, while other volunteers played Santa Claus on foot. Two volunteers, referred to only as "financially independent women" by the *Tribune*, participated in the deliveries of food and toys, and "said they had experienced more happiness than fatigue" by the end of the day. Eight teachers from Public School 170 on 111th Street and Lenox Avenue worked with the association to provide for 150 of their students.

Gluck encouraged the volunteers to sing a carol when visiting schools, churches, or other institutions, that had been published a few months earlier by writer Elsie Traut and then republished in several newspapers. She described its aim as to "win the favor of children and adults and be sung with fervor by the masses when they gather around the public Christmas tree, which is growing in number and popularity from year to year in our country." It read:

> Come, rally round the Christmas tree and praise the Lord on high.
> Let trumpets blare and carols sound, until they reach the sky.
> Come mingle in one mighty song, let all creeds melt in one.
> The love of Christ unite us all in one grand Christendom.

The carol first caught the interest of the association's Toronto branch, which distributed twenty-five thousand copies to the area. As with the previous year's celebration and songs, this touched on the themes of Christmas as a time to remove long-standing barriers and bring all people together for a public show of fellowship. Gluck dubbed the song the association's "National Christmas Tree Carol" and offered to supply copies to any schools and churches interested.

But a violent accident kept Gluck from singing the carol himself on Christmas Eve. He sat in the back of a taxi heading north on Broadway to his room at the Hoffman House. As the driver passed Madison Square Park, perhaps because he was hurrying to get Gluck home or was distracted by the glowing holiday lights, the car skidded on the newly fallen snow and pulled in front of the Twenty-Third Street crosstown streetcar. (The reason for the accident, according to the *Tribune*, was because Gluck "rode in a taxicab instead of the conventional sleigh drawn by eight prancing reindeer.") The streetcar struck the side of the taxi, throwing Gluck from his seat and sending the car spinning into the gutter. His head struck the side of the taxi, and he was knocked unconscious. Gluck spent Christmas Eve and Christmas Day—his birthday—recovering from his wounds in the German Hospital on the Upper East Side.

In the end, the *Tribune's* lighthearted response proved appropriate. Gluck recovered, and the association's Christmas Eve push exceeded even the group's own expectations. The 1914 season shined even brighter than the year before, with letters representing thirty-six thousand children.

———

But the real miracle happened more than 3,500 miles away. As Gluck recovered in the hospital, Christmas morning arrived clear, cold, and beautiful in the French village of Houplines, near the border of Belgium. Charles "Buffalo Bill" Stockwell, a commander of the Second Royal Welch Fusiliers—a tough Welshman and a quick draw on his revolver— heard shouting from the Germans for much of the morning. His own men had been in a slightly cheerier mood thanks to Christmas cards received from the king and queen along with an embossed brass box from Princess Mary's Fund (each contained cigarettes, tobacco, a pipe, Christmas card, and photograph of Mary, totaling 2,166,008 boxes in all).

But the odd mood and unusually beautiful winter day could not prepare him for what he spotted across No Man's Land. Three German soldiers hopped from their trench, opening themselves up to their enemy, and then turned back around as men below handed them a large object. The Germans rolled it across the field toward the Royal Welch when Stockwell finally realized it was a barrel. "Don't shoot," one German hollered out in English. "We don't want to fight today. We will send you some beer." Baffled at the men's behavior, who seemed unaware that the Welsh troops could kill them with ease, the commander climbed over the parapet and called, in what little German he knew, for the opposing captain.

"He introduced himself as Count Something-or-other, and seemed a very decent fellow. He could not talk a word of English," Stockwell later recalled. He told them, "My orders are to keep my men in the trenches and allow no armistice. Don't you think it is dangerous, all your men running about in the open like this?" While several of the Germans agreed and hopped back down into the trench, Stockwell and five German officers remained on the field.

"You had better take the beer; we have lots," the German captain told him. Stockwell called up two of his men and instructed them to bring the barrel to their side. Not wanting to accept a gift without offering one in return, he ordered his men to bring up some plum pudding, which they had in excess in their trench.

"He then called out 'Waiter,' and a German private whipped out six glasses and two bottles of beer," Stockwell described, "and with much bowing and saluting we solemnly drank it, amid cheers from both sides. We then all formally saluted and returned to our lines. Our men had sing-songs, ditto the enemy."

This was not an isolated incident. From Christmas Eve through Boxing Day, an estimated two-thirds of the British-held sector saw some version of this sort of fraternizing. Opposing soldiers shared cigarettes, rum, plum pudding, and souvenirs. They exchanged buttons and badges, and in at least one case, the prized *pickelhaube*—a German spiked helmet.

An officer of the Queen's Westminster Rifles wrote in a letter to the *New York Times* that his holiday in the trenches was "the funniest and most amusing Christmas I have ever spent." On the morning of December 31, readers of the same paper that dismissed the idea of soldiers putting down their weapons on Christmas Day read about the officer's description of doing just that. "I went over in the afternoon and was photographed in a group of English and Germans mixed," the officer wrote. "We exchanged souvenirs; I got a German ribbon and photo of the Crown Prince of Bavaria. The Germans opposite us were awfully decent fellows—Saxons, intelligent, respectable-looking men. I had quite a decent talk with three or four and have two names and addresses in my notebook." He described it as an experience that "would have made a good chapter in Dickens' *Christmas Carol*. It was, indeed, a tribute to the spirit of Christmas."

It was just the spirit of Christmas Gluck had hoped to foster with his call for an armistice. The publicity man could hardly claim credit for these soldiers putting down their arms, but he could, and did, claim credit as one of the first to suggest the idea—even before Pope Benedict himself. "Mr. Gluck . . . was the first man to enter a plea for a Christmas armistice— a suggestion that was favorably entertained by high British officials and called to the attention of His Majesty King George the Fifth," the association would later write.

Further reports rolled in across Europe and the United States over the first two weeks of the year. Many of the soldiers believed their interactions only occurred in their brigade, not even aware that similar acts of good faith had taken place in the next battalion and certainly not all across the Western Front. It seemed too great a story to be true, and soldiers would acknowledge they might even think it "a bit of a yarn" had they not been there in person. Yet it was true. The Christmas spirit removed the divisions not just between rich and poor but also between Allied and Central Powers and, at least for a day, sworn enemies could unite over holiday beer and plum pudding.

Even as Christmas 1914 moved further into memory, the Christmas spirit continued to permeate the Santa Claus Association's executive office. At the end of February, a man with heavy stubble and sloppy clothes showed up at the office. He carried a rectangular parcel wrapped in brown paper under his arm and asked the volunteer inside if she could deliver the package to John Gluck. She agreed.

When Gluck returned to the office later that afternoon, he tore open the wrapper and set his eyes on a late Christmas—or perhaps birthday— gift. It was *Golly*, the valuable MacDonall painting, still in perfect condition. More pleasing still was the note that accompanied it, handwritten in a scrawl little more refined than the children's letters that had filled the Santa Claus Cave two months before.

> *Here is the oil painting I stole from you last December. I was hungry and had no place to sleep when I took it. I did not know what it was or what it was for when I stole it. If I had known that it was used to cheer up the kiddies for Christmas I would never have stolen it.*
>
> *I tried to pawn it two times, but couldn't. The first pawnbroker I offered it to showed me the name of the association on it. This was the first time I found out who owned it. I tried to wash off the name, but couldn't do so. The second pawnbroker also refused to take it.*
>
> *I have kept it with me ever since. I have often thought of how happy I was after Santa had been to my house when I was a boy. My mind*

*bothered me so much that I could not sleep at times, and I decided to
send it back by a friend of mine. I would have carried it back myself,
but I was afraid of being recognized by some one in your office.*

The note was signed "The Meanest Thief," likely a reference to one of
the headlines in December: "Santa Claus robbed: Meanest Thief Wanted."
Gluck could hardly have devised himself a more charming resolution to
one of the few sad moments of the previous season.

Unless Gluck had devised it himself. The thief's letter read a bit too
neat, a perfect advertisement for the work of the Santa Claus Association
right when the public would be losing interest after the holidays. Such a
happy story could keep the group in the headlines. Indeed, Gluck rushed
to the newspapers to tell them of *Golly*'s return. At least one reporter published the note in its entirety. But while the thief's restoration of the loot
seems suspicious in retrospect, no questions were raised at the time, and
no clear evidence can be found to contradict Gluck's version of events.

Then again, the return of the painting was eclipsed by even more
stunning news from the association later the same month. After hearing
the heartbreaking story of Isabelle Colwell's baby, the Santa Claus Association's secretary, Fannie M. Baker, had been particularly touched. She
put out a request to the group's members as well as its Toronto branch
and a handful of like-minded regional groups with which she had been in
touch, urging them to be on the lookout for any letters or clues with the
name James Mosgrove Colwell, senior or junior. The connected society
ladies began to ask around while the US Boy Scout leaders reached out to
their own chapters throughout the country. Weeks had passed since Isabelle's original visit to the Santa Claus Cave, but the effort to track down
little Jimmie continued. Baker refused to give up.

Then a break came: One of the volunteers in the Toronto branch
knew of a pair going by those names. After some digging, they located
their forwarding address—Colwell had taken his son to Chicago. The
volunteers' efforts helped to eventually track down clues to his where-
abouts. Without tipping off James Sr. that they had found his location, the Santa Claus Association provided Isabelle with the funds she
needed to go to Chicago herself and ensure the safe return of her boy.

Caught by surprise, Colwell gave up his son, and both mother and child returned to New York at the beginning of February, now staying at the Park Avenue Hotel.

"I got there just in time," Isabelle Colwell explained on February 14, as her energetic child ran about the hotel lobby making friends with guests, happy to be home. "My husband had tickets for San Francisco and meant to leave for there last night." She gave special thanks to the work of the Boy Scouts and the Santa Claus Association, without whose help her child would still be missing.

Another heartwarming, too-good-to-be-true tale, this time involving not one but two organizations Gluck promoted. Skepticism would seem merited in this case as well, especially considering the few details provided on how exactly the association and the scouts tracked down baby Jimmie, succeeding where the police failed. But no police records disputing the account could be found, and Isabelle Colwell would certainly have no incentive to stick by the association's claims to the press if they were false. Perhaps, like the Christmas truce, some unbelievable stories were actually true.

To close out the group's second season, the association returned to the Hotel Astor to present its proprietors, William Muschenheim and his brother Frederick, with a gift of gratitude for providing the group with the Santa Claus Cave. Though the association hoped to unveil the gift shortly after Christmas, it proved a trickier present to prepare than expected.

They tapped Czech sculptor Joseph M. Kratina for the one-of-a-kind piece. He had studied under Auguste Rodin in France, and since moving to Brooklyn, had gained a reputation for creating striking busts of figures like Abraham Lincoln and Alexander Hamilton. Over his career, he would sculpt from life Theodore Roosevelt, Woodrow Wilson, and Charles Lindberg, among others, but Kratina set aside his profitable projects in March 1915 to ready a special gift for the Santa Claus Association. At the Hotel Astor, F. D. Waterman, the fountain-pen magnate, stood next to Gluck. He created limited-edition pens especially for the association's volunteers as a gesture of support and covered the cost for the sculpture. A camera crew filmed the gathered luminaries.

After reading his prepared remarks and vociferously thanking the Muschenheims, Gluck unveiled the gift: a four-foot-high bust of Santa Claus, mounted atop a block of marble, and crafted with impressive skill, from wisps of his beard to the puffball at the end of his cap. But it was not the fine method of the sculpting that made it truly special, Gluck explained with relish. It was the materials.

Look closer, he urged the Muschenheim brothers, *notice the fibers of paper*. Upon further inspection, the astonishing true nature of the bust was revealed. Kratina had sculpted it not from plaster or stone but from the pulp of thousands of Santa letters—five thousand childish appeals to which the association had responded. At the bottom the inscription read, "A fortune was sent to poor kiddies, for fuel, food and toys, and five thousand of them no longer say there is no Santa Claus."

Joseph Kratina's sculpture of 5,000 children's Santa letters. SANTA CLAUS ANNUAL.

CHAPTER 6

Cathedrals of Commerce

This is our harvest time. Make it pay.

—FRANK W. WOOLWORTH

Just as he had set out to do, Gluck made a name for himself as a charity innovator and advocate of inspiring causes. Years had passed since his name last appeared alongside something so mundane as a customs ruling or shipping notice. But Gluck's higher profile hurt his pocketbook. The freelance fund-raising and publicity work failed to earn him as much as he had brought in at the helm of John D. Gluck & Son, or his tastes may have just gotten more expensive. Whatever the reason, his hotel and restaurant tabs grew and those around him heard Gluck complain of being "hard up" for cash with increasing frequency.

He proved an aggressive, skilled fund-raiser for the US Boy Scout, which brought him a steady stream of income. But beyond the "honorary vice presidents" scheme, the group began to practice even more shady fund-raising ploys. Gluck took part in a campaign to solicit $6,000 from businessmen to buy turkeys for ten thousand needy scouts at a Thanksgiving dinner hosted by General McAlpin. But at the dinner, just two thousand places were set, and fewer than four hundred boys showed up.

Gluck could excuse such misrepresentation partly as a way to save face against the USBS's rival. Tensions with the Boy Scouts of America had deepened since Gluck came on board. BSA chief scout executive James E. West, a savvy administrator, solidified his control over his organization, centralizing and standardizing every aspect of the BSA: handbooks for scouts and scoutmasters, creation of merit badges, disciplinary rules, ranks, and rewards. But he viewed the USBS as a major distraction. Unlike other scouting groups, they refused to be absorbed into the BSA. Worse, they continued to create confusion among parents and donors who mistook them for the BSA.

West challenged McAlpin and USBS treasurer L. W. Amerman to create a joint fact-finding committee to study both groups. McAlpin agreed, but it fizzled as soon as his appointee got a look at the BSA offices, with some sixty employees actively working, compared to the USBS staff of three. McAlpin and his crew scrapped any cooperation with the BSA and declared open war on the group. This behavior upset a number of USBS leaders, concerned about the group's obsession with fundraising and its disorganization under McAlpin and Amerman. Eight directors quit in protest on February 5, 1915. It was just three days before a major fund-raising event the group had planned for the middle of Boy Scout Week, the BSA's major annual gathering.

This loss of organizers required Gluck to do more to help spread the word and raise money. He sent uniformed scouts into the streets to sell tickets to a show of music, military drills, and a "Plain Talk" to be narrated by well-known actor Burr McIntosh. All proceeds from the twenty thousand tickets being sold were to go to "the most valuable military movement of the age." While West went to pains to make it clear in the press that the BSA had no connection with this gathering, the USBS promised the event would "show up the Boy Scouts of America" (McAlpin had asked McIntosh to explicitly denounce the rival group during his speech).

On February 8, the Century Opera House was packed, and McAlpin sat in his theater box enjoying the performance of the bagpiping Scotch Kilties. Then came the main event: McIntosh took to the stage to deliver his speech on "The United States and Its Menaces." The general leaned forward, his eyes wide in anticipation as he waited to hear the actor stick it to the Boy Scouts of America. Instead, McIntosh struck a conciliatory note. "Why could there not be a spirit of friendly rivalry between the United States Boy Scout and the Boy Scouts of America?" he asked. "Why should not this group be known as the 'boys with the guns' and the

Boy Scouts of America as the 'boys without the guns'?" He spoke highly of the BSA's work, every kind word jabbing into McAlpin's side. Angered that the event did not embarrass the BSA as they hoped, the USBS leaders directed Gluck and the other solicitors to spread vile rumors about the group. They were told to point out that a major sponsor of the group was the YMCA and imply their rival barred Jewish and Catholic boys from membership (never mind that Mortimer Schiff, a Jewish philanthropist, was on the BSA's executive board). It was a grubby business, but Gluck needed the money. With each new deception, he grew more comfortable with using trickery when the truth failed to get results.

So it came as a relief that Matthew Micolino, president of the Washington Market Merchants' Association, reached out for his assistance on a very different project. The organization of seventy-five butchers, sausage makers, and poultrymen needed some good publicity. New Yorkers derided their market as a filthy wreck, while city officials sought to tear down their stalls and livelihoods and make them pay for it. Gluck put himself forward as the man to solve both problems. Micolino accepted.

Covering an entire city block of downtown Manhattan, the parallelogram bordered by Fulton, Vesey, Washington, and West Streets served for decades as perhaps the most important produce market in the city. It had operated in the same place since 1812, when its stands numbered a few dozen and a two-story watchtower stood at the center, guarding against English ships engaged in the War of 1812. The stalls expanded northward from the vast retail building to a row of wholesale stores, then westward as landfill extended the island itself, creating West Washington Market. By 1858, it stood as the largest market in the country.

Everyone shopped at Washington Market. The city's working-class families, more fashionable members, and even tourists made a point of dropping by. Famous visitors included Abraham Lincoln, Ulysses S. Grant, and King Edward VII. The shoppers and merchants formed a community of their own, with decades-old customs and aged passageways that made the market a city within a city. But by 1915, its age showed. The city, which owned the land and building, and rented the stalls to the merchants, decided to raze the dilapidated shopping district and replace it with a modern market. Gluck would sell the new landmark to the public.

The old Washington Market at Christmas: an illustration of Cornelius Vanderbilt visiting the market in the mid-1800s, distributed by Gluck to the newspapers. SANTA CLAUS ANNUAL.

In a happy coincidence for the founder of the Santa Claus Association, his new client had also served as a crucial site for the cultivation of American Christmas. For much of its early development, the most important feature of the holidays was not gifts, Santa, or decorations but an extravagant feast. This made the market, with its lines of butchers, bakers, and fruit peddlers, the heart of commercial activity from the earliest days of seasonal celebrations in New York.

"Finest corn-fed gobblers. Choicest thing in the market," the poultry dealer in his starched white apron recited as shoppers pushed through the gas-lit aisles searching for the best bird to adorn their Christmas table. "Here you are, finest Christmas turkeys, just waitin' to be et." At the height of the holidays, the north side of the market housed as many as one hundred stalls selling turkeys, hung by their legs and displayed on high tiers of hooks. "Christmas pervaded everything," a *Sun* reporter described after a visit to the market. "Peddlers on the corners offered Christmas lemons, oranges, raisins, and nuts; a little girl sold Christmas shoe ties at five cents the dozen; a youth, with an evident notion of the fitness of things, hawked Christmas toothpicks." Whenever reporters sought to capture the bustle and merriment of New York City Christmas, to the downtown market they went.

In 1851, Mark Carr, a logger in the foothills of the Catskill Mountains looking for a way to make some money on the abundant fir and spruce trees covering his land, hauled thirty-six trees down the Hudson River by steamboat. He paid the Washington Market proprietor a silver dollar for the use of the strip of sidewalk at the corner of Greenwich and Vesey Streets. The city dwellers quickly bought up the firs, thrilled with not having to go chop down the trees themselves. With no small effort, Carr had invented the Christmas-tree lot right there at Washington Market. The steady supply of trees, easily purchased, led the practice to proliferate. By 1880, merchants sold hundreds of thousands of trees each season, costing fifty cents to one dollar, with Washington Market still a major hub.

But it was another event that played the most significant role in establishing modern Christmas, and the namesake of Gluck's expanding association. It was on his way to Washington Market to retrieve a turkey on Christmas Eve, 1822, when the idea for a Christmas poem occurred to Clement Clarke Moore.

Bundled in his fur cap, boots, and heavy coat, pulled by his horses down the unpaved, snow-covered Ninth Avenue, the wealthy gentleman endeavored to purchase the ingredients for the family feast. As his servant Patrick drove the sleigh, Moore could relax and appreciate that everything on which his eyes settled belonged to him—with the notable exception of the avenue itself, which in 1815 had become public land. Inherited from his mother, Moore's estate, called Chelsea House, stretched from the Hudson River to Eighth Avenue, bounded by Nineteenth and Twenty-Fourth Streets to the south and north.

The story goes that as he rode, Moore settled on the idea of a gift for his family, a poem that would enchant their minds as much as the night's feast would please their bellies. Moore's audience would include his wife

Eliza, his mother Charity, and his six children ranging in ages from eight months to seven years. He may have also considered the numerous domestic servants and his five slaves who might overhear part or all of the recitation.

Conceiving a poem as a Christmas gift made sense for Moore. He had published a Hebrew lexicon, knew French and German, and would eventually rise to professor of Greek and Hebrew literature at the Protestant Episcopal Seminary. But when topics of romance and imagination seized him, Moore dashed off rhyming verses. Upon his marriage to Eliza, he compared her to Minerva, "With sparkling eye, with rosy cheek, / With tongue that loved full well to speak." When satirizing New York's burgeoning temperance movement, he wryly proclaimed, "Away with all your wine-fill'd casks! / To atoms shatter all your flasks!"

So, with the crisp winter wind blowing in his face as his coach traveled down Ninth Avenue, Moore began constructing couplets. He arrived at Washington Market and began touring the aisles, picking out the finest ingredients for the feast (though Patrick likely carried them) at the same time that he selected the most appealing holiday images and phrases he could think of. From Washington Irving's *A History of New-York*, he plucked the notion of St. Nicholas flying over rooftops and "laying his finger aside of his nose." He also gathered Irving's descriptions of Dutch burghers with pipes, twinkling eyes, and physiques like "a beer-barrel on skids," exclaiming "Dunder and Blixem!" (Dutch for "thunder and lightning"). For transportation, Moore selected a sleigh, that not only brought him to Washington Market but appeared in the picture book *The Children's Friend*, published the year before—the first to depict Santa riding a reindeer-drawn sleigh (the book's publisher, William Gilley, was a neighbor of Moore's). He no doubt considered Pintard's 1810 woodcut as well but, opting to make the poem pleasing rather than didactic, he set aside the birch switch so prominent in the original illustration of St. Nick. Into this stew he added his own special ingredients: the one reindeer in *Children's Friend* increased to a more fanciful eight; the children's parents made an appearance, waking up at first frightened, then approving of the "jolly old elf." "A portly, rubicund Dutchman living in the neighborhood" provided Moore with a model for St. Nick himself, as he would decades later explain.

His groceries selected, Moore returned to his sleigh and headed back to Chelsea. Turning off Ninth Avenue and into his snow-covered orchards of bare apple and walnut trees, he continued to hone the lines. As his wife prepared the evening's feast, Moore put the final touches on the poem, polishing them into rhythmic verses that even his youngest—eight-month-old Emily—could appreciate.

That night, as the merchants of Washington Market closed up shop, Moore gathered his family around the toasty fire of the vast mansion's living room, and began:

'T was the night before Christmas, when all through the house
    Not a creature was stirring, not even a mouse.

Moore's audience of eight presumably relished the poem—enough to tell friends and other family members about it. After hearing of the piece, one unnamed relative copied the verses and passed them to her friend in Troy, New York, 160 miles north of Moore's estate. This friend then passed them along to Orville L. Holley, editor of the *Troy Sentinel* newspaper, who happily published the work in its entirety the following Christmas under the title "An Account of a Visit from St. Nicholas." It soon spread from there.

Santa would appear in wildly different forms over the decades after "A Visit" first appeared, but none had the staying power of that poem's imagery—a "chubby and plump" Santa with rosy cheeks, cherry-red nose, and belly that "shook when he laughed, like a bowl full of jelly." Moore proved expert at distilling the disparate ideas of St. Nick that had popped up throughout the preceding decade and pulling them together into an irresistible, highly memorable form. The poem exhibited what his biographer, Samuel Patterson, calls "a meticulous sense for the fitting word, a feeling for the precise rhyme, a sensitive regard for smooth rhythm." Less charitable, perhaps, is Santa scholar Charles Jones's assessment that "Moore's imagination was derivative. . . . He was not depicting, but assembling." But the details he selected, and the way he assembled them during his trip to Washington Market, set down the basic character of Santa Claus from that point forward.

Exterior of the old Washington Market. SANTA CLAUS ANNUAL.

Like Macy's or the packed holiday markets at Bryant Park, Rockefeller Center, or Union Square today, Washington Market was once the commercial hub of Christmas activity in New York. But over the many decades of its operation, these alluring sights and sounds were accompanied by far more unpleasant ones. As New Yorkers settled further north on the island of Manhattan, newer, smaller shopping areas sprouted up, putting into obvious relief the "dirty and crowded Washington Market," as the *Sun* called it. Reporters competed with one another to devise nastier ways to describe the conditions. One story headlined "Ugly Spots in Gotham That Might be Removed" and spotlighted the "dirty old Washington Market," while another asserted that "[T]here are few large stables in this city which are not cleaner and do not smell less unsavory than Washington Market." By the turn of the century, instead of Gotham's Christmas spirit, the market symbolized all that was outdated and unattractive in the city.

This growing distaste threatened the livelihoods of the hundreds of merchants who had operated from the market for decades. Without a major turnaround, the whole thing would be razed and replaced by a more modern commercial area, leaving these sellers with no way to make a living. So the market men came upon an idea: They would raze the market themselves, rip out the "filthy disgrace," and replace it with a state-of-the-art space worthy of modern New York. The plan got the support of the city, and Gluck was tapped to help tell this tale of transformation.

Gluck headed downtown to watch builders demolish the old space (the merchants moved to temporary stalls nearby), putting in a new, larger floor area and expanding the aisles. He saw them install marble-covered counters, discarding the disorderly arrangement of rails, iceboxes, and merchant gear. The builders installed systems for hot and cold water, drainage, and concealed electric lighting (making each stand "like a miniature theatre" as he described to one paper), and replaced the wooden floor with one of cement and terrazzo that could be hosed down, not just swept. Perhaps most transformative was the new refrigeration scheme. Instead of refilling their boxes with ice each day, the merchants could rely on new refrigerators, cooling each day what would take the equivalent of fifty tons of ice.

Gluck kept the papers apprised of each development, describing for reporters the refreshing color scheme of white and olive green, the porcelain tile and white marble, nickel and aluminum. But he ran into challenges. Although the market men hired Gluck, decisions required approval by the slow-moving city. Tensions simmered between the public and private interests, and Gluck found himself in a position he remembered well from his customs-broking days: trying to help his clients reach their goals but having to wade through a moat of bureaucracy and political agendas to get there. After making every major decision as the head of the Santa Claus Association, Gluck found the involvement of the borough president, controller, and superintendent of public markets on every matter a major encumbrance. He could not even get the city to approve an opening date. Initially slated for July 1914, they pushed back the grand unveiling over and over in the face of arguments over the plans' specifics.

To make matters worse, a sensational crime on Thanksgiving week diverted press interest from gleaming new aisles of produce to tales of corruption and murder. Chicken dealer Barnet Baff, owner of several stores throughout the city and a West Washington Market stall, was visiting with a customer when he received a phone call at about 6 p.m. on November 24, 1914, asking that he return to his stall. An independent dealer, Baff had faced harsh criticism a few weeks earlier at a meeting of the poultry dealers' association for exposing price fixing by other sellers, helping send members of the city's Poultry Trust to jail. Men who Baff believed were hired by business rivals made threats on his life and assaulted his business associate. As he strolled over to his stand on the chilly evening of November 24, pushing through the crowded sidewalk toward Thirteenth Avenue, two men approached Baff, raised their guns, and fired. They hit the poultryman first in the left shoulder and then the chest, the second shot proving fatal. In full view of dozens of shoppers, the men escaped in a car as Baff bled out on the market's filthy wooden floor.

The murder landed on the papers' front pages, raising suspicions about the other poultry sellers and shining a spotlight on their suspect business practices. Gluck was frustrated by the distraction. It was hard enough trying to overcome the public's image of the market as a dirty place; now he had to allay worries that the merchants were criminals or that a shopping trip might get one killed. He reached out to his press contacts to offer reassurance that shoppers had nothing to worry about and remind everyone of the new market on the horizon, but this could hardly compete with the drama of the poultryman murder. In December, authorities arrested a pair of chicken inspectors and known Hudson Duster gang members, but failed to convict them. After promising "we'll have everything cleared up completely" just weeks after the murder, the district attorney remained empty-handed almost a year later as Gluck finally prepared for the market's grand reopening.

Fortunately, the lack of new developments in the Baff murder kept the case out of the paper as the Merchants' Association and city officials finally settled on an opening date of October 25, 1915, timed to ensure that the mobs of holiday shoppers spent their money at the revamped market. Gluck commissioned an elaborate souvenir program to be distributed over the six days of events and was in the midst of creating press announcements for the city's papers. He determined to show Micolino and his association his skill not just at generating excitement about the new space but elevating the building to something magical as well. At the beginning of October, the major work completed, the sellers began the move from their temporary stalls to the permanent new ones. The slow-going process required hundreds of sellers to transfer all their scales, butcher's blocks, and equipment. At the rate the men were going, the move would take right up until the official opening date.

So Gluck looked on in disbelieving anger when he opened the *New York Times* on October 4 to a surprising headline: "Washington Market Ready."

Without consulting the sellers, Superintendent of Public Markets Sidney Goodacre announced that the new market was open for business. Perhaps eager to allay any rumors that the launch would again be delayed, Goodacre underplayed the fact that most of the sellers had yet to move into their new, tiled stalls, and confidently declared the shiny new market ready for customers. "Old Washington Market to Reopen this Week in new $116,000 Suit of Tiles and Concrete," read the *New-York Tribune* the same day, giving most of the credit for the modernization to "the supervision of Controller [William] Prendergast, President [George] McAneny of the Board of Aldermen and Borough President [Marcus] Marks."

Curious customers rushed downtown as soon as they heard. Pushing to get inside, they found it virtually empty except for a few half-prepared stalls. These disappointed shoppers collided with the merchants rushing to move their wares to the new market in order to meet the sudden rush, leaving their temporary stalls unattended. The Merchants' Association members were furious to be caught flat-footed and feared the bad press could ruin months of preparations. They also wondered how their publicist let this misinformation get through to the papers. Gluck rushed down to Vesey Street to speak with reporters and save his job. "Does this look like opening today?" he shouted, waving at the chaos surrounding him. "We've planned great things for the week of October 25, when the opening is scheduled, and now this announcement mixes everything up."

Despite his savvy with speaking to members of the press, Gluck's temper raged when he felt his reputation impugned, particularly when meddling government officials were involved. He told the *Tribune*, in a tone the reporter described as a "growl," that blame for the debacle rested on the city officials and their base desire for publicity. "Controller Prendergast and Sidney H. Goodacre wanted to see their names in print. So they took this matter out of our hands. Ridiculous to say the opening is to be this week. Look at us!" The market's grand reopening hung in the balance.

———

After Gluck's outburst at the superintendent of public markets and controller, the newspapers ran corrections clarifying the opening date. The Washington Market mob thankfully receded and returned to its more typical flow. Gluck took pains to shift attention to the excitement of the grand opening. He mustered all the publicity skills he had acquired to hype the grandeur and reached out to his old friend Paul Henkel to cater an extravagant buffet lunch in the mayor's honor. Henkel's grandfather had reportedly served luncheon to city officials when the market first opened in 1812, making his selection an easy sell. Despite the bankruptcy first of Keens and then of Henkel's Chop House, by the time he was tapped for this catering opportunity, Henkel had returned to managing Keens under new, more fiscally responsible ownership.

To showcase Henkel's banquet, Gluck delivered samples to the New York newspapers a week before the launch. One particularly impressed reporter at the *Sun* suggested the food must have been delivered by "some special means of transportation—perhaps a reinforced motor truck." He allayed any readers' doubts about the magnificence of the offerings under the heading "Just listen to this."

Listen, listen, listen:

Venison Steak				
Bear Steak		*Possum*		
Giant Lobster		*Tenderloins*		
Geese	*Geese*	*Geese*	*Geese*	*Geese*
"	"	"	"	"
"	"	"	"	"
"	"	"	"	"

Or, in a word, Twenty Varieties of Geese.

Scotch Woodcock   English Black Cock
    English Pheasant
    French Red Legs Russian Partridge
Scotch Grouse
Baby Turkey, &c, &c, &c

. . . After diligent inquiry last night, it was learned in a general way that the et ceteras will consist wholly of plain, substantial, solid—and liquid—food.

The reporter concluded that the Merchants' Association "has everything framed up to raise the very deuce." Gluck no doubt beamed with pleasure at this description. To other reporters, he provided notices on the history of the market with prints of the crowded old stalls during a Christmas visit from Cornelius Vanderbilt, along with preview photographs of the immaculate aisles of the new space.

Despite the false start, distractions from the Baff murder, and hostility between merchants and government officials, opening day arrived as promised, on October 25, and proved indeed to be "the very deuce." Spectators arrived by the thousands, receiving the hundred-page souvenir program commissioned by Gluck. Few of those leafing through the booklet could have imagined the opening to have been anything but a cooperative, friendly affair—just as Gluck intended. The brochure even opened with a "verse penned to commemorate the foresight, courage and ability of all those who have joined with the members of the Washington Market Merchants' Association":

> High in the midst of this most happy land
> A well-built white pyramid does stand;
> By which spectators know the time o' the day
> From beams reflecting of the solar ray;
> Its basis with ascending steps is grac'd,
> Around whose cleanly purveyors plac'd,
> Vend their most wholesome food, by nature good,
> To cheer the spirits and enrich the blood.

The gleaming tile and marble stalls in the new Washington Market. GLUCK SCRAPBOOKS.

Gluck left the poem's author anonymous, perhaps since it was written not for Washington Market's opening at all, but for the 1738 opening of London's Covent Garden. Gluck (or whomever he tapped to write the program) had cribbed the lines from another commemorative program, titled "The Humours of Covent Garden."

A band led a procession of city officials seated in luxury automobiles and forty firemen in antiquated fire engines from city hall to the site of the market. Mayor John Purroy Mitchel delivered the grand opening address, followed by Board of Aldermen president McAneny, who described with pleasure how "this building was a disgrace to the city four years ago" but now "offered as a promise that this in time shall be the standard of all markets of the city." Even borough president Marks, away at an exposition in San Francisco, managed to drop in, via long-distance call.

Following the public pomp, the crowds enjoyed afternoon concerts of opera, singing, and dancing. The Bay Side Winne performed a fox-trot while Heck Henry offered up a pigeon walk, with McKenna's Band closing out the evening. Special guests included a Mrs. Hackett who had served stews at the market since the Civil War, and Theodore Loges, who had sold cheeses there for more than half a century. At almost ninety years old, Loges told the crowd his secret to longevity: Eat lots of cheese. But the impressive new facilities proved the biggest attraction of the event. As the festivities continued for six more days, thousands of New Yorkers would shop in this transformed Washington Market. Gluck looked on with satisfied pleasure.

The gleaming tiles reflected a new Gotham, one moving into the modern era and building a more inviting public space for citizens to meet and conduct their business in. It also represented a new high for Gluck's promotional work, strengthening his connections to some of the city's most powerful merchants and politicians, among them a man who would give Gluck and his Santa Claus Association the opportunity to cross paths with another landmark in the commercial transformation of Christmas.

—◆—

As the purchase of trees became customary, merchants sold things to put on them. General Electric commercially distributed the first electric Christmas lights in the 1890s and in 1903 the Ever-Ready Company introduced string lights it called *festoons*. They replaced the dangerous candles that had proliferated over the previous decades. But the sale of Christmas ornaments created its own industry and the man most essential to catalyzing their popularity may have been Frank Winfield Woolworth. In 1880, he opened "Woolworth's Great Five Cent Store" in Lancaster, Pennsylvania, which differentiated itself by making an unabashed play for the budget-conscious shopper. The store sold out its stock in a few weeks, and within months Woolworth opened a larger store in Scranton. He sought out holiday products, partnering with Philadelphia import firm Meyer & Shoenaman, which made him a deal on American-made, glass-ball ornaments. "Most of them would be smashed before there was even a chance to sell them," Woolworth said, but was eventually convinced and bought a few dozen. They sold out in less than two days.

Convinced of the money to be made on Christmas products, Woolworth sold gold German tinsel and hand-painted American ornaments. After a trip to Europe in 1890, he added handblown glass pieces created in Lauscha, Germany (the chief glass manufacturing city in the country, and now part of Russia) to his stock. They proved the most popular decorations yet. "Give your stores a holiday appearance!" he wrote in an 1892 letter to his now more than a dozen stores. "Hang up Christmas ornaments. Perhaps have a tree in the window. Make the store look different. This is our harvest time. Make it pay."

While wealthy families were some of the earliest adopters of extravagant holiday ornamentation, these decorations succeeded because of their affordability. Garlands, faux evergreens, nativity sets, and toy trains soon joined them on the nickel-and-dime tables. "For good or ill, the F. W. Woolworth Co. played a large part in commercializing Christmas, forever altering the seasonal shopping patterns of the working class," according to historian Karen Plunkett-Powell. Woolworth helped democratize the holiday. Gift giving began as a tradition among the elite, with gentlemen paying calls and exchanging cakes, meats, or oranges stuck with cloves as a token of good fortune in the new year. While the feasts sourced from Washington Market remained central to holiday celebration, they shared attention with toys, gifts, and goodies. "The great trouble is to know *what to choose*," said a reporter for the *New York Evening Post* in 1860, cataloging more than two dozen gift categories and the stores that carried them. By the final decades of the nineteenth century, those at every social level took up the practice of Christmas celebration, and merchants, Woolworth prominent among them, happily met their demands.

By 1910, Woolworth had more than one thousand stores across the country and imported a huge volume of the ornaments, gifts, and decorations. Reaching this new level of prosperity, the self-made man decided to do something spectacular. He would build a monument—the tallest building in the world. Woolworth bought up the block on Broadway between Barclay Street and Park Place, a few blocks from the Washington Market, and tapped famed architect Cass Gilbert to design the structure. Gilbert drew on the European-inspired beaux arts style popular among New York architects, adding in unusual neo-Gothic elements. Beyond its height, the structure would boast a pyramid cap on top, with an observation deck, cream-colored terra-cotta, and hand-chiseled gargoyle figures, including bats, owls, and pelicans.

By the time it was completed, the project came in at $13.5 million, which the merchant paid for in cash. It would all be worth it to Woolworth on April 24, 1913, with the opening of the building and his ultimate moment of triumph. "55-Story Building Opens on a Flash," the *Times* declared on April 25, 1913, describing the extravagant dinner where Gilbert was guest of honor. Celebrated clergyman S. Parkes Cadman dubbed the stunning new addition to the cityscape "the Cathedral of Commerce."

Gluck borrowed this tone of grandeur and extravagance when helping to put together the opening of his own "well-built white pyramid" two years after the Woolworth's unveiling. Though not one of the lucky nine hundred in attendance that night, Gluck had crossed paths, in his previous life at the helm of John D. Gluck & Son, with Hubert T. Parson, the treasurer of Woolworth's. He had provided tariff expertise to the company that had proven extremely valuable to Parson, one of Frank Woolworth's most valued advisors. The executive had been impressed with how Gluck's "knowledge of the details pertaining to tariff questions, both legal and practical, covers a broad field," and he was happy to do him a favor. The success of the Washington Market opening only enhanced Parson's esteem of the Santa Claus Man.

As pleased as he had been with the Santa Claus Cave, Gluck had greater ambitions for his association. He wanted it affiliated with the building that New Yorkers could not stop talking about, even two years after its opening. Riding the success of the Washington Market's transformation, he reached out to Parson and asked if he could cash in that favor. He sent clips of the association's last two years and explained that it would be fitting for Santa to have a place in the world's tallest building.

As it happened, despite the building's fame, it was difficult to fill so many offices. The Woolworth had space to spare. Gluck received permission to bring his association into the Woolworth Building. For its third season, the Santa Claus Association was moving to the structure that represented all that was exceptional, enterprising, and remarkable about Gotham and its self-made men.

CHAPTER 7

Child Wonderland

Mr. Gluck bids fair to become christened the Santa Claus of America.
　　　　　　　　　　　　　　　　　　—NEW YORK AMERICAN

Leaving the "Cave" of the Hotel Astor for the thirtieth floor of the tallest building in the world felt like a major promotion for Gluck and his association. "From here he can keep an eye on every child in the world surely while he hammers on little horses and fashions speaking dolls," one reporter imagined. "No newsboy on Park Row escapes him, and as for the children of commuters over in Jersey and the babies on the barges which tie up at the docks—well, to put it mildly, he knows their inmost thought."

To help the group feel at home in its grand new headquarters—and attract additional visitors—Gluck borrowed the Joseph Kratina sculpture of Santa Claus from the Astor and displayed it in the office, inviting New Yorkers to come look at the bust made of five thousand children's letters and to pick up a few fresh letters while there. Some forty new vice presidents—society ladies and leaders of groups as disparate as the Friday Afternoon Club, Bay Ridge Reading Club, and Women Probation Officers' Association—moved about the new headquarters. These women oversaw much of the sorting and answering of the letters while Gluck continued to grow his list of "honorary vice presidents," which now numbered more than one hundred, to include some of the most well-known names in the city. In addition to former New York governor Martin Glynn

Children were invited to personally deliver their letters to the association's Woolworth Building headquarters. This image comes from an unknown newspaper
saved in GLUCK'S SCRAPBOOKS.

and Saks & Company founder Isadore Saks, Controller William Prendergast was now listed among the officers. Gluck apparently buried the
hatchet with the man he had accused two months before of pompously
announcing the Washington Market open so he could "see [his] name in
print." Now Gluck was happy to put his name in print.

The group's volunteer leaders included seventy-five-year-old Sarah
Barry. The *Evening Mail*'s Zoe Beckley, still Gluck's chief cheerleader,
lauded the recruitment of the matron. "Who says a woman, or a man
either, has no place in the world's work after youth is over?" Beckley asked
about the "brisk, plump little women of the type that life's troubles and
disappointments enrich without embittering." Gluck assured Beckley
that he believed age an excellent indicator of experience. "I am for gray
hairs every time," he said.

Gluck set up this billboard for the association at the corner of Seventh Avenue and Fifty-Third Street. GLUCK SCRAPBOOKS.

Gluck took out ads in *St. Nicholas Magazine* and elsewhere promoting the group's dazzling new headquarters. "Call and see how we play Santa Claus to poor children of two nations," it urged. New this year, he secured a billboard at the corner of Seventh Avenue and Fifty-Third Street. Featuring an illustration of Santa and abutting a Budweiser beer sign, the

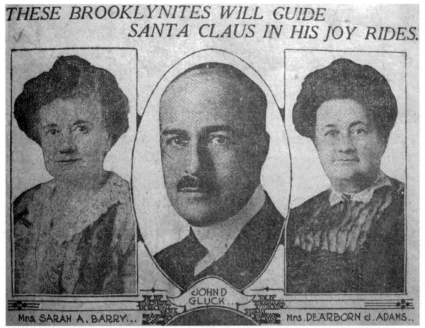

THESE BROOKLYNITES WILL GUIDE
SANTA CLAUS IN HIS JOY RIDES.

JOHN D
GLUCK..

Mrs SARAH A. BARRY..   Mrs DEARBORN d. ADAMS..

The Brooklyn chapter expanded the association's impact. Mrs. Dearborn J.
Adams (right) would soon be implicated, along with her daughter and Gluck, in
the dubious war charity American Convalescent Home Association. This comes
from the Brooklyn edition of the *New York World*. GLUCK SCRAPBOOKS.

billboard read: "Make some little kiddie's heart happy for Christmas: We
collect thousands of letters from the Post Office each year. Come get one
and play Santa Claus, filling request direct."

But the Santa Claus empire extended beyond the walls of the Woolworth. In addition to the executive office, Gluck opened a "field office"
in the Hotel McAlpin, thanks to his continuing fund-raising for the US
Boy Scout and its chief scout. On December 8, a Brooklyn office at the
Hotel Clarendon opened under the direction of Mrs. Dearborn Adams,
the fifty-two-year-old wife of a real-estate broker living on Sixth Avenue
in Brooklyn. The proprietor, A. G. Wegge, provided the space to the
group gratis.

Gluck claimed new branches in Cincinnati, Atlanta, Baltimore, Buffalo, and Boston. F. May Simpson, secretary of the Canadian branch,

reported on November 28, at the group's first 1915 session, that in its inaugural year the Toronto-based chapter had answered 2,783 letters. Margaret Lauriel Brown, the association's national secretary, toured the United States on its behalf. She sent Gluck a telegram through Western Union from Chattanooga, Tennessee: "Have had successful trip all cities ready for Santa Claus." The Santa Claus message spread.

Omaha introduced its own Santa Claus Association, partnering with the *Omaha Daily News* and a theater production to donate proceeds from the performance of a play called *Puss Puss* to the group. The Charleston, South Carolina, Santa Claus Association began publishing a list of "Santa Claus Assistants" and what each offered up to help the group: baseball gloves from Mrs. W. Way, toys from Louis Cohen, and a penny from Little Ann.

This careful accounting in Charleston pointed to the thinness of the financial reporting in New York City. Gluck announced at the start of the 1915 season that he had refined the system, cutting volunteers' work in half while reducing postage charges by a third. Yet the group's fund-raising efforts were more aggressive than ever. Although he asserted that the association had minimal overhead, directly connecting donors and recipients, in the same conversation Gluck would say, "We would like to have donations of printing, postage stamps, and money from those who are in a situation to give."

Specifically, the group needed funds for 50,000 two-cent stamps, he explained on December 10—the same amount requested in the group's first year. Nine days later, these needs doubled. "[W]hile no begging would be done in this year's campaign, 100,000 two-cent stamps were needed to carry it to a successful finish," Gluck told the *Tribune*, claiming the group was now $3,000 in debt.

Where was all the money going? The cost of the billboard, advertisements, and thousands of sheets of stationery must add up, but the New York newspapers did not report how much was donated or where it went. Instead, the reporters became more manipulative than Gluck himself in urging readers to donate. "What are you going to do to bring Christmas cheer to some little trusting bit of humanity who still has all faith in the good old saint?" the *Brooklyn Times* asked its readers.

Brooklyn's assistant postmaster Peter Cleary wanted to do his part. With his post office just across the street from the Hotel Clarendon, he made the daily trip to the group's new office himself in order to drop off the Santa letters. Cleary would have happily forfeited the cost of the missing postage, but that would break official Post Office Department law.

So he met with a handful of postal officials to devise a better idea to save the association money: They would pay the postage themselves. "Clerks to Pay Postage" and "P.O. Men Aid Santa" the Brooklyn papers trumpeted upon hearing the news. By Christmas Eve, the Brooklyn postmen had proved so generous they ended up with enough extra donations to purchase twenty-five dinners for needy local families.

Even with the Brooklyn postage covered, Gluck continued asking for more money. "Of course we do need some volunteer subscriptions to carry on the office end of the work," Gluck told a writer for the *Evening Sun*. "Stamps and money to buy more stamps are our chief needs just now. It isn't hard to find big-hearted persons who are glad to take over one or more of the kiddies' appeals, but we are rather put to it to defray the expenses of postage." A boy named Melvin Spencer took Gluck up on his

Working out of the Hotel Clarendon, the association's Brooklyn chapter enjoyed the enthusiastic support of Brooklyn postmaster Peter Cleary and his men. SANTA CLAUS ANNUAL.

offer, breezing into the Woolworth with three thousand stamps in hand, offering them up—only if he could lick and stick them himself.

On December 16, Gluck headed back uptown to the Hotel Astor. He was there to speak before the monthly gathering of the Theatre Assembly of New York, which held its meetings in the hotel's Grand Ballroom. He peeked out on an ocean of elegant women (estimates ranged from 1,200 to 3,000 attendees), each with her beribboned hat set primly on her lap. Latecomers stood in the back, hats remaining atop their heads. Gluck could spot a scattered man or child—but no open seats—among the flow of well-coiffed hair and delicate faces. Women filled the box seats to the sides and the gilded balcony at the back, with the ballroom's mirrored doors creating the impression that the group went on into the next room and the next. Gluck had quite an audience.

After the Theatre Assembly's president, Mrs. J. Christopher Marks, welcomed the hundreds of society ladies in attendance, she introduced her husband, who opened the program of performances with an organ recital of his own. The attendees then enjoyed a series of acts from stars of current Broadway shows: cellist Hans Kronold and fully costumed actors from the comedy *Hobson's Choice* and opera *Martha*. Marguerite Namara, a lyric soprano making her Broadway debut in the operetta *Alone at Last*, sang the swelling and heartbreaking ballad "Pretty Edelweiss." Though the twenty-seven-year-old remained an up-and-coming performer to the New York City crowd, composer Franz Lehár specifically wrote the role for her, which would launch her long and prolific career of musicals, films, and serious operas. As she sang, the attendees must have sensed that before them stood a star. Gluck waited patiently in the wings.

Among those taking in the show was twenty-one-year-old Symona Fermer Boniface. With striking brown eyes and dark hair, she fit in with the theatrical crowd. She personally knew a number of those in attendance, and had since she was a child. The daughter of George C. Boniface Sr., a playwright and actor since the early days of Broadway, she grew up in the world of theater. Eager to follow in her family's footsteps, both as a writer and actress, Boniface was nonetheless fiercely independent, having moved out of her family home to live in the center of the theater district before going off to Vassar College, where she was now finishing her final year.

In town for Christmas break, she diverted herself with all things theater. But watching the theatrics on stage, Boniface may have wondered why these actors were up there, instead of her. Outside of several college performances and scattered writings, she took few stabs at joining her father's profession. Her statement in the *Vassarian* yearbook captured the young woman's outlook as adulthood advanced: "Symona is going on the stage one of these days, but before she does she believes in getting a broad education." As she sat in the audience at the Hotel Astor, a man who would play an important role in this education strolled to center stage.

After a few enthusiastic words for the Actors Fund, Gluck described to the delighted crowd the workings of the Santa Claus Association. He explained that he was not there to ask the ladies in the audience for their money. There was something else they could do to greatly aid Santa Claus and for which they were particularly suited: Go to a show the next week. The success of the *Kick In* benefit the year before had led to several producers offering to donate the receipts from the earnings of a number of new shows this year. Over the next week leading up to Christmas, each respective performance would donate its earnings, selling tickets at the Hotel McAlpin's field office. If they wanted to really delight the kiddies, they could go to every one of the benefit shows:

- Monday night: *The Eternal Magdalene* at the Forty-Eighth Street Theater
- Tuesday night: *Under Fire* at the Hudson Theater
- Wednesday matinee and night: *Rolling Stones* at the Harris Theater
- Thursday night: *The Ware Case* at Maxine Elliott's Theater
- Friday night: *Hobson's Choice* at the Comedy Theater
- Saturday matinee (Christmas Day): *The Ware Case* at Maxine Elliott's Theater

Gluck explained that each show could mean thousands of dollars toward the effort to bring Santa to the city—as long as an audience

The vast membership of the Theatre Assembly of New York, gathered in the Hotel Astor's Grand Ballroom on December 16, 1915, where they enjoyed samplings of the latest Broadway productions as well as a speech from Gluck.
SANTA CLAUS ANNUAL.

showed up. To thank the performers, Gluck invited the principals of all five shows to share in a celebratory luncheon in the dome of the Woolworth Building. In addition to these donations, several managers of movie theaters offered the receipts of screenings to the group.

Gluck's Theatre Assembly presentation touched singer Marguerite Namara. Though *Alone at Last* could not offer up an entire benefit show, she passed the hat around to her fellow performers. The group together raised $13.25—not a vast sum, but it earned her credit as "a co-worker" of the Santa Claus Association in newspaper reports.

Also impressed with Gluck was Boniface, who approached the Santa Claus Man after his presentation to learn more about his work. She struck up a fast conversation with the impeccably dressed man two decades her senior and no doubt caught his interest immediately with her confidence, wit, and beauty. He invited her to come by the Woolworth to see the association in action. She accepted.

On the chilly morning of December 24, New York City postmaster Edward Morgan, the man whose permission launched the association in the first place, was busy as he always was this time of year. He worked at his desk in the General Post Office when a colleague alerted him that a visitor was here to see him. Waiting out on the vast front steps of the building, coat buttoned to the top and a fedora atop his head, was Gluck. He was joined by seventy-five of the association's volunteers, themselves wrapped in their fine coats and hats. Among them was Symona Boniface, in ankle-length fur coat pulled up just under her nose to keep out the cold. Gluck had insisted she join them on the outing.

Morgan expected their visit. Gluck had called the day before to ask if they could pick up the latest letters in person. At the head of the members, Gluck greeted Morgan and then asked Sarah Barry to explain the reason for their visit. With that, she unveiled the massive present they brought Morgan and his men: a twenty-five-pound plum pudding, a gift of gratitude for his continued support of the Santa Claus Association. Barry explained that the pudding had been made with a special English recipe, which had remained unchanged for six hundred years, from the country's Pemberton Hall. Morgan was delighted and promised to share it with the whole department—he certainly could not eat it himself.

As postmen dragged the ungainly gift inside, past the post office's Corinthian columns, several other mailmen exited, carrying the latest batch of Santa letters, neatly stacked and bound into manageable piles. Gluck urged the group to arrange themselves in a semicircle with the post office's grand pillars behind them. A photographer prepared to snap a few pictures in the same place where Gluck had stood with King Baggot the year before. The Santa Claus Man handed a few stacks to Sarah Barry, Mrs. Dearborn Adams, and the other main volunteers, and then gave a few stacks to Boniface, positioning her next to him at the head of the group and cocking his chin as the camera snapped.

That afternoon, Gluck announced that the organization had broken a new record. Santa had touched the lives of sixteen thousand families, and fifty thousand children throughout New York City—almost three times

The association's leaders, photographed after delivering to New York postmaster Edward Morgan a twenty-five-pound plum pudding and picking up the day's delivery of Santa mail. Symona Boniface and Gluck third and fourth from the right. SANTA CLAUS ANNUAL.

the number received just two years before. Gluck filled an entire scrapbook with the press clippings from 1915 alone, covering every aspect of the group's work and fund-raising from almost every area newspaper. But Gluck had one more announcement to make, one that would dwarf the twenty-five-pound pudding.

As the group's work wound down on Christmas Day and the piles of letters in the Woolworth office dwindled, suddenly the space began filling with reporters. Gluck stopped his volunteers and informed them he was going to make an announcement.

"Three years ago, in the rear of Paul Henkel's chop house, we started the Santa Claus movement," Gluck began. "This is now the largest organization of its kind in the world and thousands upon thousands of families have come to realize the true Christmas spirit. We will never know the ultimate good we did, as hundreds of families in this and other cities were benefited by being placed in direct contact with people who could do for them throughout the year—the opportunity for which was first presented by the unique, effective, and economic system of the Santa Claus Association." Then he dropped his big news: "The peculiar nature of our work calls for a building of our own."

Gluck had commissioned architects George and Edward Blum to create "the most unique building in America." The two men's firm had earned a reputation for innovative twists on the beaux arts style that had become familiar to New Yorkers, with materials like terra-cotta and tile, and their next project would be the Santa Claus Building. It would measure seventy-five feet wide on a plot one hundred feet wide, allowing for significant space and light. The exterior was to be made of white marble, treated in the classic manner, with long, simple lines. A massive arched portal, nearly twenty feet deep, would make up the front entrance, with a huge Christmas tree in the center, encircled by two sets of stairs. The façade would depict versions of Santa Claus from all the countries of the world, each created by an artist native to that country. Above them, the words "Santa Claus Association" would be engraved. A frieze about the base would depict dozens of children "in all their multitudinous moods." But the most spectacular aspect of this rather spectacular façade would be the massive stained glass window, which would serve as the tree's backdrop. Measuring thirty-five feet wide by fifty feet tall, it would depict Santa himself, dressed in traditional red and white as well as giving "the artist opportunity to portray the Christmas spirit in colors that will inspire."

A stable of prominent artists would collaborate on the project. Painter and illustrator Maxfield Parrish, known for his idealistic illustrations of children's books like the 1909 *Arabian Nights* and L. Frank Baum's 1897 *Mother Goose in Prose*, agreed to submit design ideas for the exterior, as had sculptor Gutzon Borglum, who would supervise decorations. The sculptor was at the time living in Stamford, Connecticut, having left New York City in frustration after resigning from the organizing committee of the New York Armory Show of 1913. A decade later he would begin the fourteen-year project of creating Mount Rushmore.

A celebrity even scouted the building's location. Douglas Robinson, perhaps the biggest realtor in the city, was tapped to find the site for the Santa Claus Building. He was an aggressive Scotsman who managed the Astors' landholdings and led the effort to secure the blocks of Manhattan on which the Pennsylvania Railroad had built Penn Station. Now he could use his substantial connections to secure the association a prominent place in Manhattan.

The ground floor would house the offices of the association as well as other willing charities. It would include an auditorium where children's plays would be performed year-round and lectures about education and childhood development would be given, along with a library of children's books. On the second floor would be the Lilliputian Bazaar—a huge market where new toys from around the world would be sold or given away. Toy makers from around the country would display their newest products. "This department," Gluck said of the toys, "is my hobby. I wish I had the time to play with them. . . . Personally I do not believe in ugly dolls and toy soldiers and numerous articles such as throw the child into a negative state of mind and depict destruction. I believe in things that spell construction."

There would be a large-scale service kitchen and salon, allowing for the feeding of as many as one thousand people at a time, as well as a high-end restaurant and rooftop garden. It would be charity focused, but also extravagant. "The proposed Santa Claus Building will be a national monument," he declared—a real-life Santa's workshop, as well as a place of international celebration of the "Christmas spirit." Even more than the Woolworth Building, the Santa Claus Building would blend spiritual ideals and consumerism into a true "Cathedral of Commerce." But to be sure there was no confusion of what nation was bringing the gifts of Santa to the world's neediest, Gluck concluded, "The building will be a manifestation of America."

The media rapidly spread the word about the proposed building, with a bevy of names to describe the palace: "child wonderland," "Santa Claus's new home," "all-year palace," and "a building that should be to the main factory of S. Claus and Co. as the New York Sub-Treasury is to the National Treasury in Washington." Many printed a large drawing of the proposed building. Across the country, papers lauded that Santa Claus was being "Recognized at Last!" "While the structure will be constructed for utilitarian purposes, it is intended to exemplify the spirit of Christmas," the Hartford, Kentucky, *Herald* reported. "All effort like this should command commendation, and for the one simple reason, if for no other, that it tends to enrich the lives of children," added a paper in Portland, Oregon.

Moviegoers across the country learned of the building as well. On December 30, among such news stories as the collapse of a $25,000 bridge in Spokane, Washington, and the examination of the liner *Minnesota*, which was suspected of being damaged in a war plot, the new Hearst-Selig News Pictorial clips included a cheerier announcement. "The only building in honor of Santa Claus in the world will be erected by the International Santa Claus Association," it proclaimed, running illustrations of the building for thousands of viewers to see across the country.

Every detail seemed to have been carefully considered and provided to the press—except how it would be paid for. Just a week earlier, the Santa Claus Association sought funds to relieve its $3,000 debt. Now Gluck announced this new project that was expected to cost about $300,000 to complete with only the sketchiest plans for bankrolling it. "The idea is one which should lend itself to the hearty cooperation of the public," Gluck explained. "We will probably begin a campaign to ask the mothers of America to contribute to its construction." The organization emphasized its economic value, as a place to bolster the toy industry, but it would also be the most tangible tribute to the Christmas spirit.

"Where the money will come from is the simplest problem in the world," concluded the *Sun*. "Everybody in the world—that is nearly everybody in the world—owes something to the old gentleman with the snowy beard and the capaciously filled red suit; and it is self-evident that the nearly everybody who can possibly afford it will be delighted to give something to the erection of a building in the gentleman's honor, especially when the chiefest and mainest aim of the building is to make his system so perfect that not only nearly everybody but absolutely everybody will be a partaker of his undoubted blessings." This boosterism for the Santa Claus Building made sense coming from the *Sun*. This was the same paper, after all, that eighteen years before had responded to an eight-year-old girl who feared that Santa might not be real with the definitive reply: "Yes, Virginia, there is a Santa Claus."

One reporter predicted that such a national Santa Claus monument would conclusively relocate Santa's headquarters to America. "What a fascinating wonder spot that New York temple to the children's patron saint would become as it was made known to children from the center to the remote confines of the country," he wrote. "It is as if we proposed to Americanize this world potentate among children; as if we were to acquire as our very own his court and retinue and his more direct and intimate consideration."

Gluck may have drawn inspiration from the beaux arts style of the Hotel Astor, or the stunning new post office on Eighth Avenue, or the glistening new Washington Market. Whatever gave him the idea, like Woolworth, Hearst, and other accomplished men of this period, Gluck became convinced that a man captured the world's imagination using brick, mortar, and marble. These detailed, spectacular plans in many ways eclipsed the Santa Claus Association itself.

A decade earlier, the suggestion that New York City could house a monument to Santa Claus would have been laughable. But likely so would the idea that the man who invented the five-and-dime store would erect the tallest building in the world—that it would be not just a tribute to its namesake, but a cathedral to commerce itself. It would have been difficult to imagine that New York City would usher the resources, talent, and will to create a monument to service and dedication in the form of the largest post office in the country, or transform the city's reservoir into a shrine to knowledge in the form of a grand public library, or a "monument to movement" whose astrological mural 120 feet above ground elevated arrival and departure from the city into something magnificent.

But in 1915, all these were a reality, all of them not only spectacular but of such practical use that they had transformed the daily lives of the city's population in ways both large and small. At a time when miracles actually happened, a Santa Claus Building providing needed assistance to the city's young and poor, while celebrating and protecting the spirit of Christmas itself, would not seem that outrageous. At such a thrilling time in New York City, it did not seem ridiculous to trust the Santa Claus Man, but rather, ridiculous to doubt him.

Sketch of the proposed Santa Claus Building. GLUCK SCRAPBOOKS.

PART II

CHAPTER 8

Doors to Deception

Dear Santa Claus—Do you live far? Would you please come up my house Christmas day? I, Rose, ten years of age, wants a doll; John, seven, wants a engine; Alice, about five, wants a doll; Beatrice, just more than three, wants a set of dishes, and Andrew, not two yet, wants a Teddy bear.

—BEGGAR

Dear Santa Claus—I heard about your great kindness to poor children and I hope you will be good to us. I have a little cripple sister and a baby sister and brother. My little cripple sister is only five, and my papa has been out of work all summer. I hope you will answer soon and won't forget us. Your little girl friend,

—MANIPULATOR

Dear Santy—I wants a nice small train, not a expensive one—one that's just strong and will last long time. This is all I want, and we can't afford nothing this winter. Yours truly,

—FRAUD

Christmas 1915, the day Gluck announced the Santa Claus Building, was one of the most tremendous days of his life. Rushing around the Woolworth office, he answered reporters' questions and frantically sent press announcements to newspapers far and wide. He helped wind down operations for the year, and he and Symona Boniface likely enjoyed dinner together in celebration of his birthday. They had struck a fast connection—his larger-than-life personality and confidence and her wit and beauty pulled the two together. Boniface's connection to the theater world was especially magnetizing to a man so enamored with Broadway and the culture surrounding it. Within a few months, the two would wed. It would be Gluck's second marriage since his short nuptials with Katherine Wheeler a decade earlier. But uncharacteristically for a pair of showboats, no public announcement would be made of the marriage.

Amidst the Christmas Day hubbub, Gluck made time for his daily routine of reviewing the day's papers. Despite the dozens of fawning stories about the group's work and the avalanche of coverage depicting the Santa Claus Building, one piece caught his attention and irritation. In an editorial titled "Opens Wide Doors to Deception," the *New York Times'* editors questioned the approach taken by the Santa Claus Association and the ease with which someone could abuse it for private gain. The *Times* was not raising questions about Gluck or his increasingly dubious fund-raising practices; they worried about deceitful children.

The association, they wrote, "has been widely advertised, and the inevitable result has been the inspiration of not a few children quite without belief in the myth of the gift-bearer to exploit the obvious possibilities of the situation." Most of these kids probably don't even believe in Santa, they fretted, and Gluck's work more likely provided "a lesson in mendicancy mingled with deception for the young plotters, and a worse lesson they could hardly learn."

It marked a reversal for the paper that had a few years before been one of the most vocal proponents of releasing the letters to the public. They had once assumed the best intentions, pleading with the post office to see that the "trusting children," who "never doubt[ed] that their missives received the proper attention from Santa Claus" not have their innocent letters sent to the Dead Letter Office. What had changed?

The likeliest explanation began with a winter stroll *Times* publisher Adolph S. Ochs took on Christmas Day 1911. The story went that, while walking off his turkey dinner, Ochs crossed paths with an unkempt man on the sidewalk who explained his tough circumstances and asked the newspaperman for a few dollars. Struck by the holiday mood and the man's sad tale, Ochs obliged. The rush of pleasure Ochs felt inspired him to use the *Times'* platform to launch a worthy charity of his own—one that would shift the focus from general city troubles to individual narratives of need.

The next year, the paper trumpeted that it was launching a campaign to help the Hundred Neediest Cases in New York. Unlike the Santa Claus Association, however, reporters would work with the city's leading relief organizations (the same "old-line charitable agencies" Gluck dismissed as wasteful and inefficient) to determine the individuals or families most deserving of readers' generosity. The very first case involved a father locked in a state asylum and an overwhelmed mother trying to care for seven children—two of them tubercular and the rest underfed—on $5 a week. The second case was a nearly blind widow, desperately holding on to her job as a brush maker to support two children at home. The paper dedicated pages to the individual stories.

The *Times* put a premium on conducting thorough investigations, partnering with select organizations known for taking an incredulous, investigative approach to figuring out who deserved charity: the Association for Improving the Condition of the Poor, the State Charities Aid Association, and the Brooklyn Bureau of Charities, among them. These groups had the ear of the *Times'* editors when it came to the subject of assisting the city poor. And most vocal among the five groups guiding the *Times'* Neediest Cases campaign was the Charity Organization Society. The group had established itself as a vociferous enemy of inefficiency, charity fraud, and, strangely enough, Santa Claus letters.

—◦—

The Charity Organization Society (COS) had been launched as a response to the urban poverty created by the Industrial Revolution—disease, starvation, and more violent dangers resulting from cities' growing populations. Following the model of the London Charity Organization Society, the US version started in Buffalo, New York, during the "Long Depression" of the 1870s and expanded to major cities throughout the country.

Reflecting the industrial era in which it began, the COS made "efficiency" central to its alleviation of poverty. It maintained that charities should adopt a scientific approach to their efforts, and anyone requesting assistance should be investigated, registered, and supervised (much of these efforts were conducted by trusted volunteers, making door-to-door visits to those applying for charitable relief, a model Gluck imitated with the US Boy Scout). The COS aimed to be more than just a charity group; it was a hub connecting credible agencies and churches in each city with one another, identifying worthy recipients, and avoiding any duplication of effort. The "friendly visitors" were intended not just to aid but also to elevate the lower classes, providing them with positive influences and the "inculcation of habits of providence and self-dependence," as its constitution stated.

One of the most outspoken branches was that in New York City, which viewed assisting unworthy recipients as a danger worse than poverty itself. It created a Committee on Mendicancy, which apprehended street beggars and investigated "Begging-Letter Writers"—the unemployed who sent letters to former employers asking for support. As emotional and ineffective charity blossomed during the holidays, the group pressured Gotham newspapers to discontinue their annual distribution of Christmas dinners, instead pushing them to run it through an approved charity group or abandon the practice entirely.

Those looking to make Christmas donations could instead visit the COS office or simply mail in their donation and be informed of exactly where the funds went. When a Miss Pollock living in Gramercy Park dropped in, the district secretary told her about Mrs. Dee—a single mother trying to raise six kids and keep her oldest daughter in school while on a cleaning-woman's salary of $20 a month. Pollock cut a check for $10 and was later informed, "They had a very pleasant Christmas. The children had a tree which had been donated to us with all its trimmings. They had a good dinner and Joseph had substantial gifts in the shape of an overcoat, shoes and rubbers." The secretary added that she hoped Pollock's interest in the poor would not end with the Christmas season. These donations were not wrapped in elaborate paper and ribbons or delivered under the auspices of Santa Claus. They were tied in simple bundles with the family name plainly written on the parcel. COS members meticulously tracked the donations, keeping the focus on relieving essential needs, not on some vague notion of pleasing the emotions or spreading the Christmas spirit.

So in 1907, when Postmaster General George von Lengerke Meyer lifted the federal ban on Santa letters and the newspapers filled with unverified, woeful tales of children in need, the COS grew alarmed. Although the press and public applauded the letters' release and the outpouring of generosity throughout the holiday season, the effort to answer these letters possessed all the hallmarks of the emotion-driven largesse the COS disdained.

New York COS superintendent W. Frank Persons had heard his fair share of pitiful tales from New York's poor, and the reprinted letters appearing in the New York newspapers struck him as suspicious. While the *Times* and other New York papers criticized the "red-tape-bound officialdom" of the Post Office Department, Persons culled reports on letters to Santa from around the country and found "a commingling of sensationalism, bathos, and lack of humor," as one COS executive summed it up. "Children were represented as being in alarming numbers fatherless, and, paradoxical as it may seem, fathers, in alarming numbers, were assumed to be indifferent to and incapable of taking any part in providing of Christmas cheer for their children. A carnival of gloom was the impression we got from reading some of the newspaper statements." The coverage assumed the best intentions of the letter writers and cast them as the epitome of innocence. The COS superintendent knew better.

Persons and his investigators contacted the leaders of the groups who answered the letters. Little consistency, oversight, or even logic could be found. A representative for the Chicago Bureau admitted that its method "was superficial, and doubtless resulted in the rejection of some letters from extremely poor families and the inclusion in the charity list of some letters from families in comfortable circumstances." Persons felt the whole approach to be elaborate and inefficient. Why ask that requests for help be submitted under this cover when existing systems—city relief programs, established philanthropy societies, or the COS itself—allowed for needs to be met, no silly invocation of a mythical saint required?

Persons needed a counterweight to the media's naïve promotion of these letter-writers' appeals, to show these sentimental stories were exaggerations and were pulling funds from people actually in need. He needed proof the kids were lying. Persons charged his organization's Investigative Bureau to look into the letter writers, using the inspection methods the COS had refined over the previous quarter-century. This began with gathering a sample of the letters themselves. He looked no further than the morning news—with no Santa Claus Association to answer the letters in 1907, New York's newspapers served as intermediaries between Santa's mail and the public, printing children's charming missives in their pages, along with home addresses.

"Dear Santa," read a letter from Lizzie Cleary in the *New York World*. "Would you please give me something for Christmas, as we are very poor and have no papa? My mamma works downtown in offices and sometimes she takes in washing and does the best she can. You see, Santa, it is very hard for me also, for I get up very early and have to send my sister and brothers to school. I don't care for much so long as my mamma and sister and brothers has a happy Christmas."

Persons sent an investigator to Cleary's home to see how difficult life really was for the girl. The visitor was invited in by Lizzie's mother. She looked about the home, spotting a doll and "no evidence of want" and reported back that assistance from the public was hardly needed.

A woman wrote to Santa Claus of her friend, Mrs. Murtha, living at West Sixtieth Street, asking: "Will you help her to get work in behalf of herself and young boy? She wants cleaning, washing or any work. She is absolutely penniless."

Upon investigation, the COS representative "felt confident that woman had a man lodging with her and she finally admitted that there was one there. . . . Mrs. Murtha made a very unfavorable impression on visitor."

Looking into the Ross family, whose daughter had written to Santa Claus claiming the family was out of work, the investigator "Learned that family consisted of woman and daughter, both of whom went out for day's work."

In one case after another, the investigator found a letter writer who exaggerated his or her need or who was already receiving assistance from the COS or one of its charity partners. It was plain to the group's leaders that the popularity of answering Santa Claus letters was a case of sentimentality over substance, and the campaign was draining precious resources—donations, volunteers, and press attention—from more vital relief work. On October 26, 1908, after several drafts, Persons sent a letter to Postmaster General Meyer asking he reconsider the "unwholesome publicity" that gathered around the release of the Santa letters:

> *Many of these letters delivered by the postal authorities to private individuals and even to newspapers were widely published without concealment of names and addresses of the writers. There was, as should have been expected, a very great increase in the amount of such mail, immediately following the first publications of these letters. Thousands of them were written obviously for the sole purpose of attracting attention and securing charitable assistance. This degradation of the Christmas spirit was further accomplished by the ostentatious, public distribution of presents by newspapers and other agencies in answer to these requests.*

He added that there were "many obvious instances of parents teaching the children to beg for relief" and that "a very considerable evil will result" if the letters continued to be released as they had been. Similar letters were sent by many of the society's chapters. The postmaster general received them with great interest. They confirmed concerns he himself felt about the release of the letters and gave him the cover he sought to rescind their release in 1908.

"Complaints having been received from many charitable organizations of abuses of the privilege extended in Order No. 934, dated December 13, 1907, permitting delivery to such organizations of letters addressed to 'Santa Claus,' the privilege will not be renewed at this time," Meyer wrote in an order to his department. It was back to the Dead

Letter Office they went, and the Charity Organization Society claimed a strategic and moral victory.

———

The arguments made by the COS in 1908 were still true in 1911 when talk about releasing Santa letters resurfaced. But Postmaster General Frank Hitchcock, who succeeded Meyer in the position, had a different attitude toward the letters. When the question came up during his tenure, he decreed that in order "that many poor children may be blessed with a happy Christmas," he would release the letters "and thereby assist in prolonging their youthful belief in Santa Claus."

Alarm bells rang out in the COS headquarters. Fortunately, they knew just what to do—draft a letter to the postmaster general and explain, as they had so successfully before, why freeing these letters was a bad idea. "Grave harm resulted from the public use of these letters by private individuals, charitable agencies, and by newspapers in 1907," COS executive Francis McLean wrote in a December 11, 1911, letter. The New York chapter's W. F. Persons sent a copy to New York City postmaster Edward Morgan, noting that it was cosigned "by the heads of the six most representative and prominent charitable organizations in this city." If the postmaster general moved fast enough, there would be time to reverse his position and halt the release of the letters this season.

But the 1908 strategy did not work in 1911. Hitchcock was a very different postmaster general than Meyer. He had a far sharper sense of how to manage the media and what made a great story: just a few weeks earlier he and Morgan had appeared on the front pages of newspapers across the country as they oversaw the first, dramatic, airmail delivery. At the time, Hitchcock was also laying the groundwork for the new parcel post, which was sure to excite the public.

The media itself had transformed in just a few short years, with an explosion of newspaper and magazine titles boasting record-breaking circulations. Readers liked the tales of Christmas charity, and it was easier than ever for these outlets to cast the Post Office Department as Ebenezer Scrooge for obstructing Santa's work. Hitchcock was not interested in getting into a debate over the nuances of effective relief work; he just wanted the Post Office Department to be on the right side of Santa.

"With many thousands of poor children, the letter to Santa Claus is only an appeal for what their parents are unable to give," James Britt, the third assistant postmaster general, responded to the COS, speaking for his boss. "To send these appeals to the Dead Letter Office, to be opened and returned to expectant children merely as an empty message, seemed to be a cold and heartless thing, and the Postmaster-General was unwilling to do it." He concluded that "the Order will, therefore, remain unchanged."

The shift in the postmaster general's attitude between 1908 and 1911 reflected a larger shift, as Christmas became a more public, spectacular holiday during the first years of the twentieth century. "Santa Claus is a part of the family idea of Christmas, and from time immemorable children have written him their wishes and their parents have fulfilled those wishes as they were able," a member of the COS wrote, urging that the letters remain in the home. Another executive added that giving these missives to the public "did seem to threaten a method of treating the Santa Claus legend that would work its destruction." Although this position had won the day in 1908, within a few years the postal officials and the country as a whole had changed its opinion. At a time when holiday displays were more extravagant than ever and civic Christmas gatherings proliferated, most now felt that Santa was not restricted to the home. He belonged to the city.

In the face of these forces and the sentimental arguments from the Post Office Department itself, the COS was outmatched. McLean wrote back to Britt, accepting Hitchcock's decision, and adding in a wounded tone one clarification: "The point of our letter was not to avoid the work or trouble which would be occasioned by receiving and dealing with the so-called Santa Claus letters but rather to protect the homes of the innocent writers of these letters from unnecessary visitation and molestation." But the fight was over. The domestic Christmas spirit the group sought to protect had already escaped or, in the eyes of the COS, been destroyed.

From that point forward, the Charity Organization Society was sidelined from the debate. They lobbied newspapers, public authorities, and private philanthropies but could not compete with the sentimental tales of Christmas spirit the papers published each season. The COS's relationship with the *Times* and its Hundred Neediest Cases provided a valuable opportunity to push back against the use of Santa letters as a meaningful charity strategy.

But these opportunities were rare. When Gluck launched the Santa Claus Association in 1913, the COS wrote that in light of the fact that "one man has recently started an organization to act as Santa Claus to these children," there were "Four Things to Remember." These included that "Nine times out of ten the really needy poor do not bring their wants to the attention of the public" and "the city child becomes sophisticated at so early an age that he soon ceases to believe in Santa Claus." No major paper carried the release, and the COS instead published it in the trade journal *Bulletin of the Merchants' Association*.

The same year, the Post Office Department made the release of Santa letters permanent, with the postmaster general's assistant commenting in a letter to his boss that the practice "has been found to be a very happy method of disposing of that class of undeliverable matter." That would be the final word on Santa letters—until fifteen years later, when the actions of Gluck and his Santa Claus Association forced the Post Office Department to change its position.

❦

Despite having won the public debate, Gluck moved quickly to rebut any criticism of answering Santa letters. Upon reading the *Times'* accusation that his association "opens wide the doors to deception," Gluck grabbed up a red pen and underlined the sentence that his group offered "a lesson in mendicancy mingled with deception." "To this conclusion I take entire exception and for my part assume that the writer of the article must be imperfectly acquainted with our work," he wrote in a pointed response published the next day. After explaining how the system of matching individual New Yorkers to each child's appeal helped to smoke out any cases of dishonesty, Gluck concluded that "This is a material age, but don't you think it is a good thing to try and preserve as long as possible the children's faith in the unknown, in their belief that once a year some one whom they never see will answer their prayers?

Santa Claus may be a myth to us of mature age; to children he is a living reality."

When Santa was involved, reporters and readers took virtually all Gluck's claims at face value. "The association keeps a sharp lookout for fake letters," the *Brooklyn Daily Eagle* reported as the group ramped up for its 1916 season. "According to the results of the investigations made this year, about 2 percent of the appeals so far were found to be the letters of professional beggars." This was about the same negligible amount of phony letters the group cited in previous years.

While Gluck explained that this was a sign of the trustworthiness of the letter writers, it was a strikingly small number when compared to the Charity Organization Society's findings a few years earlier that virtually all the New York City requestors had exaggerated their needs in some way. It was also a fraction of the 34 percent of letters that had been rejected by the Baltimore Federated Charities, the 69 percent of letters rejected by the Chicago Bureau of Charities, and the 85 percent rejected by the Cleveland Associated Charities when they attempted similar operations to the Santa Claus Association. When it came to trusting childish innocence, it was clear Gluck's group was the outlier.

The association did agree with at least one of the COS's arguments: The release of Santa's mail had led to more kids writing to him with each passing year. About twenty-five thousand letters were received and responded to in 1916—more than double that of the group's first year. Despite the Santa Claus Association's claims of its investigations and accounting, it ran a far less thorough operation than that of the COS and saw significant turnover in volunteers and leaders each year, making it hard to run a truly effective charity—and it did little to ensure its other chapters were being run any better. But as always, the press cared about the heart-wrenching letters, not accuracy.

Although COS criticisms remained focused on the letter writers, no questions were raised about the motives of the Santa Claus Association itself. Despite Gluck's frequent claims that the group was a different type of charity, one that did not collect funds but simply facilitated the connection between donor and recipient, plenty of money was coming in to the group. Requests had begun for postage stamps, then to help pay for gifts that the association's "gift-buying committee" handled, then to cover vague "administrative costs." Though the association operated again from the Woolworth Building for its 1916 season, Gluck directed a number of its volunteers to help solicit funds for its $300,000 Santa Claus Building. Though the major announcement the year before had generated a burst of donations, the association made few reports on the progress made toward this grand goal.

To help raise awareness of the group and raise funds for the building, in 1916 the association began to publish the *Santa Claus Annual*, a souvenir book celebrating the group's work, its supporters, and the magic of Santa himself. For twenty-five cents, anyone could buy a copy of the decorative volume. The cover featured a full-page photo of the Joseph Kratina sculpture of Santa Claus, made from the pulp of five thousand letters. It included dozens of portraits of the group's officers and honorary vice presidents—elegantly attired ladies and suited men, many of who no doubt bought themselves a copy, or several. The list of honorary vice presidents only grew, now including representatives of societies such as the Betterment League of New York and Rainy Day Club (an organization advocating that women wear short skirts and high boots on drizzly days).

It also included photos of the group's varied activities, with some questionable claims. The picture of the delivery of Postmaster Morgan's twenty-five-pound plum pudding claimed "there were a thousand visitors with this committee," despite the fact that newspapers reported only seventy-five in attendance.

The *Annual* included a story called "How Mary Katharine Became a Member of The Santa Claus Association," in which "the Moonman" whisks away a young girl losing faith in Santa Claus and gives her a guided tour of the group's operations. He shows her poor children with their noses pushed against the toy-store window and a cold tenement room where a child writes to Santa asking for coal. Then he takes Mary Katharine to the Woolworth office where she sees the volunteers in action, before joining one of the US Boy Scouts on his investigative rounds, as he brings cheer to a fatherless family. "Mr. Moonman," she says on her return home, thrilled by what she saw, "I never knew before what happiness Christmas can bring."

But Gluck's attention was being drawn elsewhere, assisting with publicity campaigns and serving as a "consultant" to other groups in their charity and fund-raising efforts. Prominent among these was his continuing work with the United States Boy Scout. In the six years since the USBS and the Boy Scouts of America had been founded, the concept of scouting had spread fast, especially in large cities, as a positive way for poor newspaper boys and tenement dwellers to spend their free time and develop their character.

But as the United States entered the Great War, US Boy Scout patriotic efforts would help put it, and Gluck, into the national spotlight. It would soon be revealed that Gluck was mailing out his own fraudulent Christmas wishes, and that the Charity Organization Society should be less concerned about the deceptions of the children sending letters to Santa Claus than the man who was answering them.

CHAPTER 9

Naughty List

This, then, broke upon me as the poetic age of our city . . . and open, like the early and obscure early days of ancient Rome, to all the embellishments of heroic fiction.
—WASHINGTON IRVING, *A HISTORY OF NEW-YORK*

Now here is a worthy cause, Gluck likely thought to himself as he set his smoldering Camel on the ashtray and uncapped his fountain pen, jotting "five dollars" onto the check in front of him. He then printed the name of the recipient: the Sun Tobacco Fund, which sent cigarettes to American soldiers overseas. Gluck wore a dark suit, his left wrist bulged with an expensive watch, a sizable ring on his hand glinted in the afternoon light. So far, the war had been good to him. Now he was sharing a little of the wealth.

Gluck sat at the desk in the new studio apartment he shared with Symona, at 28 East Twenty-Eighth Street, catching up on the business of a number of clients and campaigns. It was late September 1917, and he had just set up his home office to his liking. Two phones sat on the desk among the piles of papers. On the wall above, he placed framed newspaper clippings, a few certificates of commendation, a photo of his wife, and one of his father. In the center of these framed pieces he placed a startling trophy: the stuffed head of a wolf, set above the revolver he had used to kill it during a hunting trip—a recent hobby he had taken up, since his purchase of a new car had made it easier for him and Symona to get out of the city. Gluck liked to say that while he was an outdoor sportsman, his

Gluck in his "studio" at 28 East Twenty-Eighth Street, surrounded by clippings, commendations, and a stuffed wolf head. GLUCK SCRAPBOOKS.

favorite indoor sport was to keep the wolf from the door of those in need. After purchasing a new camera, he had also taken up a different kind of shooting, offering to photograph his friends and brothers in his office, or as he became accustomed to calling it, his "studio," stamping the photos with his name and home address.

Gluck capped the pen after signing his name and set it back in its holder, tucking the check into an envelope and retrieving his cigarette. His donation might have been modest, but the *Sun* would give it a special mention the next day, noting that the man "who makes the dreams of poor kids

Gluck enjoying the New York City winter. He noted on the back of this photo that an assistant took the picture. COURTESY OF FRANCES GLUCK.

come true" had spared a few dollars to give the soldiers some smokes. The paper's campaign might have sounded humble, but it had grown into a massive effort. At the time Gluck made his donation, the *Sun* had raised enough to send twenty-six million cigarettes to those fighting, and sought triple that "as the time for the soldiers' baptism of fire draws near."

This was hardly the only wartime charity to see a huge influx of donations. Since the United States had entered the war in April, hundreds of charities, funds, and associations had materialized, asking for money and supplies to send to the men overseas (before many even boarded ships). Parades, benefit shows, and galas were held in soldiers' honor. The National Red Cross Week from June 18 to 25 introduced the "week" idea of publicity campaigns and brought in $114 million to the organization. The YMCA raised $30 million in its September 1917 national drive. The group teamed up with the Knights of Columbus, Salvation Army, and four other major charities to form the United War Fund Committee, together raising in its United Fund Drive $203,179,038—the largest sum ever raised through public philanthropy in the history of mankind. It was "the nation's first great outpouring of charity dollars," according to historian Scott Cutlip, with much of the money coming from "the contributions of middle-class America giving on a hitherto undreamed-of scale."

Organizations popped up to cover every aspect of war work, troops needs, and patriotic missions: Committee for Men Blinded in Battle, Dollar Christmas Fund for Homeless Belgians, American Committee for Training in Suitable Trades the Maimed Soldiers of France, and of course, the Sun Tobacco Fund.

The association's Committee for Needy Children of German American Descent, introduced after the United States entered the First World War. SANTA CLAUS ANNUAL.

Gluck made donations to his pet causes, but he had much more coming in from his own operations. At his desk, he had devised ways to tap into the nation's apparently inexhaustible patriotism by making the Santa Claus Association speak for a nation at war. He had just promoted the group at the War Relief Bazaar at the main floor of the Brighton Beach Hotel. Only a few of the organizations that had originally signed up for the event were there—many had pulled out when rumors swirled that the bazaar was fraudulent, with the gate receipts going only to the organizers. The concerns were significant enough that President Wilson, scheduled to launch the event with the push of a button in Washington, DC, withdrew his participation. But for Gluck, an opportunity was an opportunity.

Now he was working out details of his newest plan: a "Red Card System" that asked whether letter writers were the children of soldiers or sailors who had been shipped overseas. Those who answered yes would be given special priority from the group's donors. While he was at it, Gluck decided to give the association an extra name to fit the times: War Santa

Association volunteers at work mapping out where gifts would be delivered.
SANTA CLAUS ANNUAL.

Claus. He did not limit the group's patriotic work to American-born New Yorkers. He emphasized the accepting nature of Santa Claus at a time of bitter division in the world (and earned the association a few more headlines) by creating a chapter to respond specifically to Germans and Austrians living in New York City. "We found children of alien enemy parents badly in need and also children of German and Austrian American descent facing a sad Christmas," he explained in the 1917 *Santa Claus Annual*. "Knowing the liberality of New York people and the fact that Santa could only be a true Santa when he took all children, of all races, who believed in him, [the] Santa Claus Association created a Committee for Needy Children of German American Descent." The group of sixteen volunteers promised to give special attention to the German and Austrian children whose parents might have lost their jobs or faced other discrimination through the recently passed Espionage Act.

But while he laid out ambitious plans for the association's 1917 season, including a move to the Hotel McAlpin, Gluck's attention was

Gluck used his connection to the US Boy Scout organization to rub shoulders with military men, such as Major Halstead Doray, pictured to the left of Gluck at the training camp in Plattsburgh, New York. COURTESY OF FRANCES GLUCK.

taken up mostly with a more urgent concern: a public military drill for the United States Boy Scout. He needed the November 10 event to raise funds and publicity for the group's lucrative Liberty Bond drive. But he also hoped it could serve as a rebuttal to criticisms he had been facing since the summer: that the USBS was illegitimate and that Gluck himself was using it for his own profit.

Julius Kruttschnitt, chairman and director of the Southern Pacific Company, had been surprised when a friend contacted him toward the end of July 1917 to say, with a bit of pride in his voice, that he just donated to the United States Boy Scout Camp Pershing Committee. The friend received a letter from the group explaining they had begun a boys' camp in Massapequa, Long Island, and were seeking donations. On the lengthy list of "Honorary Commissioners" running along the side of the letter, the prominent names included Adolph Ochs, W. K. Vanderbilt, and

Julius Kruttschnitt. Seeing that his friend supported this scouting group, the man had happily cut a check. Known for his easy, dignified style (he had been a teacher at Baltimore's McDonogh School for Boys and then an engineer, prior to jumping into the railroad business), Kruttschnitt uncharacteristically lost his cool.

The railroad man was livid. A man from the USBS had contacted him just the week earlier, asking if he would be interested in accepting an appointment to something called the "Executive Committee of the National Advisory Council" for the USBS. Kruttschnitt had declined, but now his name was being used as an honorary officer. As a man whose tenure at Southern Pacific had been marked by a high degree of transparency in the company's dealings and accident reports, the duplicity especially piqued him.

He fired off a letter to L. W. Amerman, whose signature appeared at the bottom of the mailer. "As this use of my name is without authority, and indeed ignores my refusal to allow you to use it, I must request that it be deleted at once, and that you inform me when this shall have been done," he fumed.

Word got out to the *New York Times* about the misappropriation, and a reporter contacted other names on the list. S. Stanwood Menken, president of the National Security League, was angered to learn of his inclusion, and wrote to the USBS on July 27 that "My name is being used on your note paper to my great embarrassment and without any authority on my part." He asked them to immediately remove it.

American military attaché Lieutenant-Colonel S. L. H. Slocum refused his assignment to vice president of the group. "Have never authorized United States Boy Scout to use my name in seeking appointments by telephone or using it in any other way since my resignation from that organization four years ago," he wrote to the *Times* reporter investigating the campaign. Judge E. H. Gary, chairman of the United States Steel Corporation, contacted the USBS to ask for details of their finances. The group responded back with a request for a personal interview, which he refused and asked that his name no longer be used. One by one, the rest of the listed men pleaded ignorance or anger at having been included—shoe manufacturer John H. Hanan, dye works mogul Albert Blum, jeweler

Pierre Cartier, and former senator Chauncey Depew. None of them had agreed to be included on the list.

The *Times* tried to get answers about why the group had so brazenly misused these names. The paper's reporter reached out to Amerman, as his name was on the mailer, but got no response. He tried several more times before finally receiving a call back—not from the group's treasurer, but from the man who had orchestrated the entire "Camp Pershing" campaign: John Duval Gluck.

At the start of the war, recognizing the prime opportunity it presented for an organization promoting a patriotic and character-building message, Amerman had expanded his fund-raising team and elevated Gluck to "commissioner at large" of the group. The offer was attractive: as commissioner, Gluck straddled the line between fund-raiser and officer, making money through both roles. He continued to receive a 40 percent commission on all his fund-raising, while pulling in an additional salary to oversee the group's team of canvassers and running its publicity operations. With the explosive interest in scouting of all types, a sizable income was all but guaranteed. He did not enjoy the gig just for the money, though. Under his pseudo-military position, Gluck visited actual military training camps and used the scouts' military drills as an opportunity to rub shoulders with men of influence in martial affairs.

But by accepting the position, Gluck graduated from being merely a hired gun to someone entwined and responsible for the group's operations. He moved from following directions to devising his own sly ways to earn the scouts money. His own malleable morals and desperation to bring in enough money to continue in the lifestyle he and his new wife had come to enjoy combined with the permissive culture of the USBS leadership to dislodge something dark inside the Santa Claus Man.

Amerman and his USBS fund-raisers taught Gluck how to use "honorary vice presidents," but since rising to commissioner at large, Gluck devised some additional innovations. Tapping the Santa Claus Association's lengthy list of contacts, he parlayed them into publicity for the USBS. His began using the names of prominent people unless they explicitly told the group not to, "taking for granted that silence gave consent," as Gluck explained to the *Times* reporter. In other words, Gluck could add any businessman, leader, or politician—all the way up to the president of the United States himself—to the fund-raising requests for the US Boy Scout, simply by mailing them a letter. As for those who explicitly declined, such as Julius Kruttschnitt, that was just a case of miscommunication between the members of the fund-raising team, and he had corrected it as quickly as possible.

The USBS would later entirely blame Gluck for this sneaky strategy. "Gluck used several names of men as Committeemen without their sanction," the organization's lawyer would admit as it sought to distance itself from the practice, claiming that once the leaders learned of the misuse of names, it destroyed all printed material carrying them. But while this exposure was an embarrassment the USBS wanted to move past, it made no move to demote or fire Gluck, probably because he brought in lots of money and most of the other leaders were involved in their own unscrupulous money-raising schemes.

General Edwin McAlpin, who saw the boys' mock battles as a way to prepare them for real battle, was one of the last members of the USBS leadership who saw it as anything more than a fund-raising scheme. And he had died suddenly of a cerebral hemorrhage the same April week President Wilson declared war on Germany—a sad irony for a man who felt the country was never strongest than when it was in the midst of war.

Under Gluck, the fund-raisers drew commissions of at least 35 to 40 percent of the total they raised. How much the group brought in and what expenses they covered remained opaque. The USBS would claim to have collected $42,000 in 1917 and spent $9,000 on expenses, but provided no support for these claims or documentation of where the money went. One of Gluck's fund-raisers would later admit that the organization "was using a handful of loyal, earnest lads, located mostly in and around greater New York, to obtain large contributions." These boys would pay for their own uniforms, board, and lodging for camp.

It seemed the only explanation could be that the fund-raisers were pocketing almost all the money themselves. Making this more likely were the questionable morals of the fund-raisers. While the Santa Claus Association was made up largely of society ladies, the team Gluck worked with at the USBS was composed of hired solicitors with few qualifications beyond their ability to raise money. At least one, J. E. Smith, was an ex-convict (he had served a term for bigamy in Indiana), and the others were far from the cheery charitable volunteers who filled the Santa Claus headquarters each year.

But even the money Gluck and Amerman pulled in was apparently not enough. After agreeing to provide solicitor Francis W. Winch with a 35 percent commission, Amerman soon after demanded the commission be split with him. Collector Edwin Southard brought in $10,000 for the organization, but when it appeared he was keeping most for himself, Gluck accused him of having "double-crossed" him and fired the canvasser. A torrent of money rushed into the USBS, and Gluck and Amerman could not get enough of it.

This growing malfeasance was not lost on BSA chief scout executive James E. West. He continued to grow his own organization and sought ways to put a stop to the increasingly corrupt USBS. The BSA had won a major victory the previous summer when Congress granted the group a federal charter, protecting its name, insignia, and terminology from imitators. The arrival of the war and unprecedented amount of fund-raising by the USBS forced West to use the charter to try to put an end to the USBS. On July 31, 1917, the National Council of the Boy Scouts of America launched a New York Supreme Court lawsuit to restrain the USBS from using the words "Boy Scout" or any version of the phrase in its name.

It was likely no coincidence that this was the same week that the Kruttschnitt scandal broke in the *Times*—West made a practice of calling up the names of officials who appeared on USBS letterhead to see which organization they thought they were supporting. West was as skilled with using the press to his advantage as Gluck, and the embarrassing story offered a nice burst of negative publicity against the USBS as the case got underway.

Gluck scoffed at the lawsuit and assured the press there was no merit to it. It would take another year and a half before the Supreme Court would decide who was right. West was confident in his case, but he did not anticipate how hard, and dirty, Gluck would be willing to fight.

The US Boy Scout was not the only organization using the emotional power of the war to fill its coffers for questionable purposes. With thousands of war relief organizations and millions of dollars flowing in with no oversight, opportunities for inefficiency, overlap, and exploitation were rife.

As with the sentimental power of Santa letters, the inspirational message of aiding soldiers and the country as a whole blinded the American public and authorities to the widespread ineffectiveness—or worse infractions—of these efforts. And just as with the Santa Claus letters, one of the only, and most vocal, critics of the undisciplined outpouring of wartime generosity was the Charity Organization Society of New York.

"At first little was thought of it," wrote Barry C. Smith, secretary of finance for the New York COS's Bureau of Advice and Information, in the *Times* the same week the paper reported on the Kruttschnitt kerfuffle. "Needs in Europe must be met—they required huge sums of money, and the money must be obtained—so the work went on. The motives and standing of the people connected with many of them could not be questioned, and so no organized attempt at supervision has been undertaken."

Smith complained that because the war was such an all-consuming concern, New Yorkers and city officials took almost no steps to verify the legitimacy of groups asking for money. "Philanthropic work is to a large extent so unregulated that it offers a fertile field for the exploitation of the public by individuals who, with great ease and facility, get funds to meet the expenses of their 'organization.'" Was it really necessary to have more than one group charged with aiding Italian orphans or distributing free milk to Belgian babies?

He explained that since no other organizations had stepped forward, his Bureau of Advice and Information would begin investigating and publishing lists of reputable charities. The bureau was figuring things out as it went—like the war relief groups themselves, the charity watchdog scrambled to meet explosive demand in the first months of the war. Smith's July 29 column marked the first of what would become regular features in the paper distinguishing reputable charities and frauds.

But with so many groups to vet and few tools to take on wrongdoers, Smith urged state legislators to pass comprehensive restrictions on war relief, requiring that groups incorporate and face periodic investigations by the State Board of Charities. Smith did not name the United States Boy Scout or the Santa Claus Association in his criticisms. It probably should have relieved Gluck not to have any extra attention drawn to his dubious civic schemes. Instead, it baited him.

"I believe that Mr. Smith's plan would have been good about 1860, but not today," Gluck challenged, in a letter published by the *Times* a few days after Smith's. He urged that instead of auditing small charity groups, the smart approach would be a "complete wiping of the slate and a fresh, new, up-to-date plan which will conform to the conditions of the era in which we live." This would consist of a "charity service league," divided according to districts devised not by the State Board of Charities but

S.C.A. Staff Artist

CHARITY MANDARIN ENTERING HOME OF POOR CHRISTMAS MORNING:
This is an outrage, putting the people in direct touch with the poor. My private society should handle the public's money. I will cause secret reports to be sent out condemning the idea.

Gluck began presenting himself as a charity expert, criticizing those who questioned the Santa Claus Association as self-interested or backward in their understanding of philanthropy. This cartoon, appearing in the SANTA CLAUS ANNUAL, captures a typical denunciation.

rather the Police Department and Board of Health ("the real guardians of the poor" as Gluck called them). While oversight was valuable, Gluck cautioned that "it must not be at the cost of entirely eliminating the warm, personal, human interest which alone makes possible real charity."

This, in addition to his call to the *Times* about the USBS's shady fund-raising, showed that Gluck was not concerned about keeping a low profile, even as criticism of unregulated charities grew. He was not satisfied with merely rejecting criticism of his work; he truly believed himself a charity expert. As Gluck saw it, he simply understood philanthropy better than the COS and his other critics.

"Our records are absolutely correct, but as yet no others have apparently made any effort along the lines of accuracy in their reports on the matter," he would later state. Gluck asserted that the association's records "are interesting and demonstrate what may be accomplished in a short space of time."

———

But editorials were just one of the weapons in Gluck's arsenal. On November 10, he launched the grand public event he had been planning for weeks to draw attention to the USBS's Liberty Bond sales drive and prove to New York City that the US Boy Scout was a powerful patriotic force. He and the other leaders mustered every scout they could in Washington Square Park and began a patriotic march up Fifth Avenue. It was a clear, beautiful fall day with a slight breeze providing relief to the scouts in their heavy khaki uniforms. Hundreds of uniformed boys moved in procession, a rifle set on each scout's left shoulder, as a handful of musicians helped them keep time with drum, fife, and trumpet. Lieutenant General L. W. Amerman (he had recently given himself a promotion from colonel) dressed in the elaborate uniform of a USBS officer for the event, but Gluck preferred civilian clothes—his usual three-piece suit. Nonetheless, the seven-block march at the head of the mock military cavalcade gave Gluck a thrill.

As he and the scouts reached Union Square, Gluck saw their destination: the USS *Recruit*, a wooden mockup of a battleship that the US Navy had built in the center of the park. As its name implied, the "land man-o'-war" served as a recruitment tool, operating as a fully equipped, commissioned warship where a staff of bluejacket guards arose every morning at 6 a.m., scrubbed the decks, washed their clothes, and stood guard, answering questions from passersby. Like the scouts, these soldiers were performing for onlookers eager for an up-close replica of the action happening overseas. Civilians could come aboard to see how a military ship operated and, if so inclined, sign up for the US Navy or Marine Corps (the *Recruit* would eventually draft about twenty-five thousand men).

Atop the ship's afterdeck, the USBS honored the winner of the group's Liberty Bond contest. The honoree was not a Boy Scout. She was not even a boy, but twelve-year-old Pauline Henkel, the daughter of Gluck's longtime friend and manager of Keens Chophouse, Paul Henkel. Amerman pinned the medal to the cheery girl's fur-lined coat, where it fought for attention with her colorful boutonniere and a decorated, wide-brimmed hat sitting atop her head of flaxen curls.

When asked how she managed to sell $25,000 worth of subscriptions—far more sales than any scout made—she cheerily explained it was in part through enlisting her friends at Public School 67, but also through personal solicitation among "business men on Broadway." No doubt her father, who by now had fully reclaimed his position at the center of New York City's bustling business and theater community, had something to do with his daughter's impressive numbers.

Toward the end of the ceremony, Commander Charles Adams, who ran the navy's recruiting in New York, addressed the scouts. "You must be worthy successors, and be ready to follow when the country calls," he told the gathered boys. Just how many he spoke to seemed to increase with every report. Although the original story reported one thousand in attendance, another quoted it at three thousand. In an article that ran a week later, the number of US Boy Scout members had grown to five thousand.

Although these numbers were dubious, young Pauline was unquestionably a fund-raising force. Thanks to her dad's connections and the fame she earned from the USBS drive, the girl would become well known for her record-breaking bond campaigns, far exceeding this first haul with $1.25 million in bond sales by her fourth effort. In total, she sold nearly $4 million of bonds over the course of the war.

It was not clear how many of the deceptive fund-raising strategies Gluck used in the USBS were also applied to the Santa Claus Association. The leaders of the association were a much more trustworthy lot than Amerman and his band of solicitors. But Gluck's next major leadership move left many of these respectable individuals baffled.

Gluck and Symona Boniface's relationship grew more tempestuous. The spirited personalities that drew them to each other in the first place led to blustery arguments as the months passed. She earned a reputation among his brothers as a prima donna—competing with her husband to be the life of any party. His grandstanding and exaggerated stories began to lose their earlier charm. But there was still plenty of warmth between the two. Gluck doted on her, buying clothes, gifts, and baubles for his young wife, providing her with far finer a lifestyle than might be expected from a man on a publicist's earnings. He racked up debts throughout the city, but the spending did not slow. She called him "My Santa Claus."

It had been his work with the Santa Claus Association and his connections to the city's acting elite that initially attracted Boniface to Gluck. So perhaps it was for this reason that he gave her an early Christmas gift in December 1917: the presidency of the Santa Claus Association.

It was a startling choice considering her lack of experience in anything but college coursework and socializing with theater crowds. When he launched the organization in 1913, Gluck stressed that his business acumen and investigative background made him uniquely suited to play Santa Claus. By contrast, the new twenty-two-year-old president had just two leadership qualifications Gluck could cite: at Vassar she had been a member of the Student Aid Society and president of something called the Flags for All Society.

It gave Boniface the opportunity to rub shoulders with the producers and actors with which the association organized benefit shows. But rather than the move of a man trying to please his wife, a more likely explanation is that Gluck wanted to distance himself from the association as scrutiny of the USBS grew. He continued to serve on the treasury committee managing the group's finances, and the organization's correspondences

Symona Boniface, suddenly elevated to association president, at work at the group's executive headquarters. SANTA CLAUS ANNUAL.

continued to feature his signature style. Gluck had stepped down only in name and still exerted his influence on the group. Putting Boniface in charge ensured he could continue to profit from the group without attracting as much attention to himself.

On the rainy Saturday that officially kicked off the 1917 season, Boniface stepped into her new position. Wearing a high-waisted skirt and satin blouse, her hair done up in a stylish chignon, she took a seat at her new desk in the association's executive headquarters, telling volunteers of the plan she had discussed with Gluck: to divide the city into one hundred districts, and match letters from those in need with others who lived near them. While most of the junior volunteers went along with the change unaware of any impropriety, the switch deeply irritated several more veteran leaders. Not only were they concerned about the idea of a twenty-two-year-old woman taking charge of the organization, but they were dismayed at the nepotism and the apparent unseriousness of the association it revealed. Several members quit in protest.

But one of these angered volunteers believed there was deeper corruption in the association office. She had seen more than just a lack of rigor in Gluck's methods and wrote to the US Secret Service outlining her suspicions and some grave accusations against the leader. The tip would come back to haunt the Santa Claus Man.

— ◆ —

Mounting complaints from the Charity Organization Society and others about the egregious swindling taking place in the name of charity began to stack high on the desk of newly reelected New York City district attorney Edward Swann. One of Swann's first acts during his new term was to assign Assistant District Attorney Edwin Kilroe to take action against the glut of patriotic charities sprouting up. Kilroe was not just to investigate the more questionable schemes but to also build a broad case for the sort of state, and perhaps federal, regulation of war charities outlined by Barry Smith in his July 29 *Times* column. On November 16, Kilroe began his investigation. He would focus on little else over the next year.

As the 1917 Christmas season quietly wrapped, with minimal press coverage for the Santa Claus Association compared to two years earlier, one of the complaints Kilroe investigated came from S. B. Habicht, of the importing firm Habicht, Braun & Co. It was another of Gluck's scout scams. Habicht received a letter from the "Seventh Regiment of the United States Boy Scout," explaining they were a patriotic group seeking funds to support the organization's character-building efforts. Habicht paid twenty-five dollars, thinking he was supporting the Boy Scouts of America, but after speaking with several people knowledgeable of the group, realized he had been deceived. He wrote to Swann about his concerns, and the prosecutor took action.

Swann called Bernard H. Fry, "major" of the "United States Boy Scout Seventh Regiment," who had sent the letter to Habicht. He demanded that Fry, along with treasurer Ralph H. Korn and commissioner at large Gluck, come to his office and explain their fund-raising scheme. The men declined.

"They said they didn't like to be obliged to be out in the heavy rain," Swann explained. "I consented, but ordered them to come down [the next day], whether it was raining or not." The following day, the men, along with Arthur L. Van Veen (the USBS's "director"), marched to the DA's office.

Swann asked Korn how many members the Seventh Regiment claimed. "One hundred fifty boys, but most of them are inactive as far as the military activities of the organization," he admitted. Swann asked how much the group had collected. "$1,200—for fifes and bugles, and one hundred rifles," Korn replied. "We teach poor boys military training and we supply them equipment that they cannot afford to buy."

Korn initially claimed that Gluck received a salary of $500 from the group. But when Gluck was cross-examined, he admitted to having also pocketed $823 of the $1,277 he had personally collected for the Seventh Regiment for "services rendered"—a 64 percent commission.

The further Kilroe and Swann dug into the USBS, the clearer the group's corruption became. The officer scouts grossly inflated the number of its members, and as far as Kilroe could tell, the only people benefiting from the funds were Amerman, Gluck, and their band of unscrupulous solicitors. The assistant DA concluded that "These flagrant examples of the abuse of public confidence and the misdirection of patriotic impulses call for official scrutiny and control."

But wasn't Kilroe just the sort of official to provide such scrutiny and control? His options were limited. While section 934 of the New York Criminal Code allowed Kilroe to prosecute individuals for fraudulently obtaining property for charitable purposes—sending them to jail for up to three years—still only the most outrageous cases could be pursued. Sufficient evidence was hard to acquire (Kilroe would for two years pursue another charity huckster whom he called an "out and out crook" but fail to gather strong enough evidence to indict). Another barrier to prosecuting frauds was that a group could formally call itself a "charity" by doing just a slight amount of actual philanthropic work. The fact that pennies of the dollars raised went to actual patriotic work could be enough to ensure the organization's survival.

Many of the institutions Kilroe pursued, the USBS included, kept no records, or very limited ones, which made it hard to prove any laws had been broken. "In failing to make or keep such records no law was violated and no punishment could be meted out," Kilroe complained. When they had trouble making a clear legal case, Swann and Kilroe used what they referred to as "pitiless publicity" in order to educate the public about how its money was being wasted—a weapon with which they struck this branch of the scouts.

As clearly dishonest as Gluck and the other USBS officers appeared, the most Swann and Kilroe were able to extract from the scammers was that they agree to drop "Seventh Regiment" from their title. They had used the term to play on sympathies for the Seventh Regiment of the New York Militia, the oldest military organization in the state. The men reluctantly agreed to drop that part of the name and left the DA's office.

It was a miniscule victory in a herculean effort to expose and reform the city's vast apparatus of wartime charity fraudsters. Kilroe added his interrogation of Gluck and the Seventh Regiment to the 1,500 witnesses he interviewed, 4,463 queries processed, and almost 3,500 pages of typed statements gathered. In all, Kilroe and Swann discontinued some 384 corrupt charities and indicted twenty-six of the most egregious hucksters, with five convictions.

But there was so much more work to be done. Kilroe and Swann knew the only lasting success would come from building a larger case against the war charities and for legislation to allow better control and prosecution of these groups. Assembling all his findings and condensing them into specific recommendations, Kilroe got the endorsement of New York senator Henry Ashurst, and presented US Senate Bill No. 4972. If passed, the bill would put the regulation and supervision of patriotic societies under the purview of the federal government—the Department of Justice, Department of the Interior, or Treasury Department—supplemented by state and municipal laws.

The recommendations read much like those outlined by Barry Smith in the *New York Times* when he first called for wartime charity reform— the suggestions Gluck dismissed as more fitting for 1860 than the twentieth century. Indeed, Kilroe credited Smith by name—and no other charity experts—as a man who "generously gave counsel and attention to the work." But Smith himself did not provide an endorsement, nor did anyone from the Charity Organization Society. Despite consulting with Kilroe, the organization kept its distance from the bill. In the time it took for the assistant DA to get the legislation drafted, Smith decided that such an approach would be too easily abused and would "automatically [force] nearly every war charity good, bad, or indifferent, to discontinue its activities, through the mere impossibility of compliance."

Smith was not the only one with reservations about the final bill. After a thorough presentation before Congress, the ambitions of Kilroe and Swann's recommendations proved too great. Smith's concerns, added to the drained sense of urgency since the bill did not go to a vote until after the war had already ended, left the bill dead on the Senate floor. The city and country resisted reform of charities during this patriotic period. As with the debate over Santa letters, a logical case against war relief fraudsters could not compete with the outpouring of emotions and generosity the country was too eager to provide. Kilroe's marathon investigation collapsed just feet from the finish line. If Gluck's ambitions were to be checked, it would not be through reforming patriotic charities.

Perhaps it would be through his involvement in more serious crimes.

In the midst of building his case for the congressional bill, Kilroe received a visit from a sharply dressed man from the Bureau of Investigation. He was there to find out what Kilroe knew about John Duval Gluck. But to the assistant DA's surprise, the agent was not much interested in the man's fraudulent fund-raising. He was visiting Kilroe because he had reasons to believe Gluck was a German spy.

CHAPTER 10

German Intrigue

We want these German habits—these birth-day and Christmas festi-
vals—this genial family-life.
 —CHARLES LORING BRACE, *HOME-LIFE IN GERMANY*

"I have just a few reasons to believe that the Mr. John Duval Gluck referred to in [the] paper as Founder of this Santa Claus Association, may be a German spy," began the anonymous letter sent to the US Secret Service.

The writer explained, "I happen to be one of the women whose names are given as one of the 'Honorary Vice Presidents'" of the association. But she had become suspicious of Gluck during her time volunteering. The letter came just weeks after Boniface was elevated to president of the group, and the writer was likely one of those disgruntled volunteers who left the association in the face of Gluck's apparent abandonment of any sort of rigor or prudence in operating the group. But she had deeper concerns about the Santa Claus Man.

First, there was Gluck's German heritage. Though "outwardly he professes a great dislike of the Germans," she felt the fact he was only two generations removed from the enemy country meant Gluck must feel an ingrained support for his fatherland. That he had created a committee specifically to assist New York's German-speaking population also struck her as suspect.

In addition, "ever since the outbreak of the war in 1914 he has traveled extensively between the U.S. and Canada," and mentioned visiting further abroad. His reasons for taking the trips would vary with whom he spoke—sometimes it was for a publicity client, other times for customs-broking advice, or to help promote the Santa Claus Association. There must be darker reasons for his travels, the letter writer suggested.

More curiously, Gluck would speak openly about his membership in the US Secret Service, claiming he dedicated his free time to rounding up German spies himself. "How extraordinary it really would be if a man was in the employ of the U.S. Secret Service that he would tell it to a casual acquaintance," she wrote. The honorary vice president was correct about that. The Secret Service, which received her letter, quickly verified Gluck was no member. So why would he claim he was?

"I have no doubt you receive many such letters as this—and I hope this won't add to your burdens any, which I know must be very great," she concluded. "I hope against hope that this may be a wrong clue I am giving you but the whole thing looks very formidable to me, however, and I believe this Santa Claus Association is just a blind."

The Secret Service did indeed receive many such letters. Since the United States had entered the war, letters to the Secret Service were almost as numerous as those to Santa Claus, with thousands of tips and warnings pouring in, then assigned and reviewed by department staff. Distrust of Germans ran rampant throughout the country and came straight from the top. President Woodrow Wilson accused the enemy of having "filled our unsuspecting communities with vicious spies and conspirators" who "sought to corrupt the opinion of our people." Incidents such as the explosion of Black Tom Island in New Jersey—a mile-long pier opposite the Statue of Liberty blown up by German saboteurs in July 1916—showed the very real threat of Germans conducting nefarious activities within the United States. These concerns led to the passage of the 1917 Espionage Act, which gave law enforcement officials and prosecutors wide latitude to crack down not just on suspected spies but also on socialists, antiwar agitators, and anyone viewed as insufficiently patriotic.

But it was not just official branches of the US government looking into any threat of "German intrigue," as it came to be known, but quasi-government groups, such as the American Protective League (APL). This organization would conduct vigilante campaigns against those supposedly assisting the enemy. Its membership rolls expanded as the war continued, with more than 3,300 members in New York City alone (although neither Gluck nor any of his brothers joined the APL, his cousin Ferdinand was a member). The Justice Department and Bureau of Investigation needed the APL, as the government lacked the resources to conduct such extensive intelligence gathering themselves. When the bureau began its investigation of Gluck, New York's APL chapter was one of its first stops.

Gluck's connection to the shady practices of the US Boy Scout and the possibility that he was impersonating a member of the Secret Service raised sufficient concern within the bureau. J. W. Kemp was assigned the task of looking into him and his German connections, which is what brought the investigator to Edwin Kilroe's office in the summer of 1918.

Kilroe told him what he knew of the Santa Claus Man. He had not heard about his impersonating the Secret Service, but the man had been running the Seventh Regiment USBS, which feigned a connection to both the Boy Scouts of America and the military in a play to bilk confused donors. Then there was the American Convalescent Home Association. During his exhaustive study of the city's war charities, Kilroe had uncovered that Gluck was helping run this group, the brainchild of Helen Florence Adams, a cabaret dancer and daughter of Santa Claus Association Brooklyn chapter president Mrs. Dearborn J. Adams. The young Miss Adams set out to collect half a million dollars to establish a home in France for recuperating American officers. The Convalescent Home Association sought to purchase a chateau where military men would be entertained by "handsome, young, unmarried American girls." Gluck and others took up collections in restaurants and hotels while the girls entertained guests. Not surprisingly, this idea did not go over well with military wives, one of whom wrote, "It seems to me that while in France there must be some officers' wives of the other allied armies capable of entertaining American officers without these unattached women hunting the job." The State Board of Charities had rejected its application for incorporation in February 1918.

A colleague of Kemp's at the Bureau of Investigation looked into both the younger and elder Adamses. The twenty-eight-year-old daughter was "a very affected talker" according to the report and claimed to have spoken with Secretary of War Newton Baker and others, all of whom approved her work. The agent concluded that "There is no question but that the Am. Convalescent Home, etc. was run for the benefit of the Adams family." Gluck enjoyed some of those benefits as well.

Anything else you can tell me about Gluck's German connections? Kemp asked Kilroe. There was one odd fact the assistant DA had uncovered: The USBS actually targeted German firms, or those with a German name, when running its fund-raising. Those who declined to donate to the scouts would receive a follow-up call in which their patriotism would be questioned and they would be threatened with exposure. The only way to prove they were truly loyal, the USBS fund-raisers would imply, was to subscribe to the group. It seemed a strange scheme for someone who was assisting the Germans.

"He's out for the money," Kilroe told Kemp. The agent duly noted in his case file that "[Kilroe] believes him to be willing to take part in anything where there is a chance to make money." But there seemed something deeper than simple greed at play, Kemp considered. If Gluck were a spy, it would explain some of his recent behavior: elevating Symona Boniface to the top of the association, maybe to keep his own German name from the spotlight. Even his duplicitous fund-raising work with the United States Boy Scout could make sense as a move to undermine the Boy Scouts of America's patriotic efforts while lining his own pockets. Gluck so easily shifted from customs broker to publicist to charity expert, perhaps his loyalty was just as fluid.

Leaving the DA's office, Kemp knew he had a few more stops to make if he were going to understand this man's motives.

⁓

Kemp first went to his office and surveyed the newspaper coverage of Gluck over the previous decade. Beginning with his customs broking and freelancing with the American Merchant Marine Commission, the volume of coverage increased exponentially as Gluck launched the association and ramped up his fund-raising for the USBS:

Dec. 6, 1913–New York World–<u>P. M. Burlson</u> [sic] *instructed that letters be turned over to Santa Claus Assn. in Paul Henkel's Chop House.*

Jan. 18, 1914 – New York Times–"Played Santa Claus," article by <u>Edward Marshall</u>, giving praise for Gluck's idea of Santa Claus etc.

Jan. 29, 1914–New York World–"'Santa' not a Bankrupt." Paul Henkel was forced into bankruptcy. Gluck complained of article.

There was the arrest at the Mardi Gras festival, the calls for postage funds, the announcement of the Santa Claus Building with virtually no updates after the initial flurry of press interest. He read up on Gluck's involvement with the USBS and their current Supreme Court battle with the BSA, which continued to crawl along due to the USBS's obstructions and delays. Then, in the midst of his search, Kemp found the source of Gluck's Secret Service claims. A 1916 article in the *Evening Telegram* described a "Citizenry Secret Service" that Gluck had founded then folded. "It costs nothing to enroll and every member will be provided with a numbered identification card, bearing his photograph," Gluck told a reporter at the time. "A duplicate copy will be forwarded to the Secretary of State at Washington." The card included the organization's address— Suite 2238 of the Woolworth Building, the Santa Claus Association's executive office that year.

The secretary of state of course would have known nothing about the Citizenry Secret Service even if Gluck forwarded duplicate copies of the cards to him, which he almost certainly did not. Shortly after the article ran, government officials moved to quash the group for the confusion it would create with the US Secret Service. Gluck obliged by renaming his group the Citizenry Information Bureau. But Kemp would learn in the course of his investigation that the name change had not stopped Gluck from frequently telling others in casual conversation, whether an association volunteer or his landlord, that he was "a member of the Secret Service."

Kemp headed uptown, to Seventy-Second Street and Central Park West. Overlooking Central Park, directly across the street from the Dakota Hotel, rose the Hotel Majestic. Kemp was there to speak with Copeland Townsend, the managing director of the property who also managed the Imperial Hotel, where Gluck spent a lot of time. Townsend was a manager who made it his business to take part in the hotel's activities (he never missed any of the Imperial's tea dances on its famous roof garden) and got to know his guests.

After several months of observing Gluck, Townsend did not like what he saw. "He always appeared to be hard up for money," the hotelier told Kemp. Gluck had been in debt to the Imperial's restaurant and always had one reason or another for neglecting to pay up. He was a "shrewd person who lived by his wits," and he struck Townsend as devious.

Adding to the manager's distrust of Gluck, he had recently seen the man pay visits to a young woman named Virginia Rhodes, who had been staying at the Majestic. Never mind that Gluck was married, Ms. Rhodes had been vacated from her room when another guest made a complaint that the woman was conducting a blackmailing scheme through the mail. The ex-wife of Chicago engineer George Dixon, she had apparently been extorting money by cable from a man in South America. Townsend suspected Gluck had something to do with the ploy, perhaps helping her compose the letters, but the guest making the complaint provided few details and only circumstantial evidence to connect the Santa Claus Man to the scheme.

Kemp noted these revelations in his case file but pressed Townsend about whether Gluck seemed like he might be a spy. *I don't trust him*, was all Townsend would say for sure. The hotel manager had passed the blackmailing information to C. P. Hoagland, a Navy Intelligence officer with an interest in international mail fraud. Kemp headed to his office all the way back downtown, at 15 Wall Street, to discuss the suspected spy. Hoagland had paid a visit and personally searched Gluck's apartment—at 28 East Twenty-Eighth Street—for any hard evidence of his involvement in the blackmail. He saw Gluck's framed newspaper clippings and stuffed wolf head. Ruffling through his desk he found Santa Claus Association circulars sent out to German Americans, appealing for funds for "alien babies." This outreach to Germans specifically seemed like the sort of cover that a spy might use to help fund the enemy, Kemp considered.

The investigator tracked down a handful of other individuals who had done business with Gluck and come away feeling cheated. Whitehead & Hoag, a Newark, New Jersey, based company that patented the pin-back button, a staple of political and fund-raising campaigns throughout the country, was owed $108 by the Santa Claus Association. The firm's bill was months overdue, leading Whitehead & Hoag to sue. The Ralph R. Polk publishing house, which produced the *Trow's Directory* listing tens of thousands of New Yorkers and their addresses, had also sued Gluck for default on a bill. Sharing the assessment of the others to whom Kemp had spoken, the representative from the company told the agent that they "regard him as a crook."

But most telling was a letter Gluck himself had written—to President Wilson's private secretary, Joseph Tumultry, earlier that year. It not only explained the purpose behind Gluck's campaign to help "alien babies" but also revealed the man's most questionable motives.

———

Kemp plumbed the depths of Gluck's deceptions, trying to discern if they went so far as treason. He certainly seemed like the sort of fellow who might sell out his country if there were money to be made in it. But as the agent worked to determine if Gluck's strange schemes might include aiding the enemy, he had to keep in check prejudices against Germans coming from all directions.

As wartime set in, New Yorkers sought ways to de-Germanize almost every aspect of the city and its culture—a tricky demand considering the large German population. The Metropolitan Opera House banned German performances, with the single exception of staging Friedrich von Flotow's German-language work *Martha*—as long as it was sung in Italian. Schools cancelled German-language courses. (The City College of New York took the more moderate step of just reducing the number of credits given to German classes.) The German Hospital and Dispensary, which had treated Gluck after his car accident on Christmas Eve 1914, became Lenox Hill Hospital.

Some of the most vociferous protests against Germans came in response to the enemy tainting the American celebration of Christmas. When a ship carrying five thousand tons of German-made toys (purchased before the war but kept in Rotterdam for over a year) landed on US soil, a phalanx of society ladies threatened to rush the ship and throw the toys overboard. "Let us do as my ancestors did so long ago with the tea in the Boston harbor," said New York State Assembly candidate Mary Lilly to a ballroom full of concerned citizens at the Hotel Astor. Kemp had to consider that perhaps the volunteer who tipped off the bureau was as excitable as these crusaders.

When it became impossible for F. W. Woolworth to continue buying the handmade glass Christmas ornaments from Lauscha, Germany, he partnered with an American manufacturer to create ones as similar to the originals as possible and ceased to advertise their German heritage. By 1918, the *Times* reported that "American manufacturers are rapidly approaching the efficiency commonly attributed to German manufacturers of these goods." New York City was at pains—commercially, culturally, and historically—to strip any whiff of German-ness from Christmas.

What a difference a few decades made. During the second half of the nineteenth century, New York City embraced German culture in no place more so than in its celebration of Christmas. In 1853, social reformer Charles Loring Brace published *Home-Life in Germany*, in which he recounted the gift-laden trees, decorated homes, and joyful children he saw while touring North and Central Germany, and he urged Americans to "recognize that there is a religion in Christmas feasts." Upon observing the growing popularity of German-style Christmas trees and fairs catching on in 1859, writer Julius Froeres wondered whether it was the mission of Germany to "go out into the world and teach the nations how to amuse themselves." The spread of Christmas was a welcome German invasion throughout the Western world.

In fact, it was a German immigrant who gave the United States the definitive image of Santa Claus. Thomas Nast, who had moved with his family from Landau, Germany, to the Lower East Side when he was six years old, found huge success as an illustrator of political cartoons for *Harper's Weekly*. But Nast's Christmas illustrations of Santa Claus, the first of which appeared in 1863, proved particularly popular and became an annual tradition. In each new appearance, he refined Santa's image. The character grew from the elfin figure dictated by Clement Clarke Moore's poem into a full-grown man. His girth expanded and his cheeks appeared rosier. Nast filled Santa's workshop with the lively clutter that resembled his own crowded home, which he stuffed with trinkets and souvenirs (porcelainware, snuffboxes, clocks, and exotic "beheading knives") year-round, and elaborate processions of paper dolls and presents during Christmas. He popularized the idea of elves helping with the building and delivery of toys. Through the high-circulation *Harper's* as well as books and cards bearing his illustrations, Nast's version of Santa Claus, influenced by his German roots and New York City home, spread and solidified the character throughout America.

But by 1918, with the United States deep into the Great War, Germans' role in the invention of Christmas in America was a distasteful thought. A man of German descent playing Santa Claus for New York City was cause for suspicion. In many ways, these suspicions proved justified—just not for the reasons Kemp expected.

—⁓—

"I desire to enlist my services with the United States Government, my Government, without pay, if need be," Gluck wrote to President Wilson's secretary, who since the start of the war had been fully engaged as the Oval Office gatekeeper. Gluck described his particular skills in "matters of grave importance and along lines that a very few citizens are trained." Specifically, the effort to "control aliens living in this country—aliens at large."

Gluck said he wanted to meet in person with someone of authority who would give his plan a fair listen. He already met with William J. Flynn, chief of the Secret Service—a burly, hard-charging "anarchist chaser," as he would be known. The two had met for two hours in Gluck's office at the McAlpin Hotel, but the Santa Claus Man had left with the sense that the detective failed to fully appreciate what he had to offer. "I was impressed by the chief's utter lack of knowledge of certain conditions," Gluck wrote. "Mr. Flynn was not capable of grasping the full extent of my plan." As this may have been the same meeting when the Secret Service ordered Gluck to discontinue his Citizenry Secret Service, it's likely Flynn was not in an especially receptive mood.

So Gluck wrote that he wanted to bring his idea to the president himself. His pitch was simple:

*If trouble breaks out it will come from the poor. A man who has had no
breakfast, no lunch, no dinner and doesn't know where his supper is coming from, all on account of the war—is a dangerous alien to permit to
roam at large. All the more so when he sees plenty of work for citizens—
but no work for him, the alien. Nowthen [sic], when he sees his children
want for food and clothes—then he is all the more dangerous—He does
not know himself any moment when the hell in him will manifest itself.*

Gluck asserted that the poor were not simple downtrodden innocents
as the Santa Claus Association had for years presented them. They were
time bombs, ready to detonate as soon as conditions worsened. He suggested to Tumulty that the United States create a surveillance system that
would "keep tabs" on the poor, and poor Germans in particular, without
their knowledge—and that he should oversee the whole thing. Gluck's
qualifications for running this project were his connection to the poor, the
German community, and the information he had gathered on both while
serving at the helm of the Santa Claus Association.

While Gluck's claims were grandiose, he was asking the right man.
Tumulty was acutely concerned about the dangers posed by German
supporters living in the United States. The secretary urged prepared-
ness against Germany long before that became a popular position, and
Tumulty would later describe his concerns about "a sinister purpose on
the part of the German sympathizers in this country" in his memoir of
his time under President Wilson.

To sell his qualifications, Gluck included press clippings describing the association's work, a photo of his newly introduced Committee
of German Americans, and stories from New York's German-language
newspapers describing the association. These pieces were "in themselves
proof that I have been helping poor Germans and Austrians. I know
them. They trust me and my associates"—and for that reason, he was the
man to spy on them. The letter was signed "John D. Gluck, Esq." Despite
the fact that he had never gone to law school, Gluck would begin making
a habit of adding the designation after his name.

Tumulty forwarded Gluck's letter to the Bureau of Investigation, where it was sent up the chain of command and answered by

"Chief"—Alexander B. Bielaski, the bureau's chief since 1912. He let Gluck know that "the statements made by you concerning a plan for controlling alien enemies have been noted," and recommended that Gluck reach out to the bureau's New York City representative, William Offley, in the Park Row Building. Gluck scrapped the plan almost immediately after receiving Bielaski's response, claiming he had gotten a more financially remunerative opportunity for his ideas. But the bureau held the letter in its files, for Kemp to discover in the midst of his investigation.

To the agent, the letter captured in one document Gluck's desire for public esteem and willingness to bend his morals ever further, happily selling out the poor Germans he claimed to aid. Dodging bills; raising money on one apparently false claim after another—helping children, helping patriotic boys, helping the country, helping Germans; spying on and threatening those same Germans in order to make more money; blackmail. Kemp was astonished by how many schemes the man was juggling and how brazenly he ran them. Gluck's shady dealings had attracted the suspicions not just of the Bureau of Investigation but also of the Office of Navy Intelligence, the New York district attorney, the American Protective League, and countless individuals who had crossed his path. But thanks to his obfuscations and the obstacles in gathering concrete evidence of his wrongdoings, each case against him seemed to dissipate into vapor before it could yield results.

He's a crook all right, Kemp concluded, but there was little he could do about it.

"At this time it seems that there is little or no dependable reason for suspecting Gluck or the U.S. Boy Scout of German intrigue," the agent wrote. "[B]ut it seems to be the consensus of opinion that Gluck is a schemer and a faker who engages in everything in which there is an opportunity to make money by fair or foul methods."

CHAPTER 11

Poor Boy Gets Nothing

So many tears, so many fears,
For older folk, this Christmas Day!
But there's that Scout with a smile on his lips
And here's to the Scout, I say!
So much to do, such heavy tasks
For one and all, this Christmas Day!
But along comes a Scout with a blithe "I'll help"
And here's to the Scout, I say!
—Anonymous, "A Toast" in *Boys' Life*

It was tough for inspectors and reformers to pierce the fog of patriotism and sentimentalism that seized the public during the Great War. But with half a dozen investigations into Gluck's work, it was not a governmental or law-enforcement group that would finally set him off and put in motion a chain of events to halt the Santa Claus Association. It was the Boy Scouts of America.

If there was one man who would have been unsurprised by the criminality in J. W. Kemp's report on Gluck, it was James E. West. In a few short years, the chief scout executive of the BSA had built his organization into a formidable institution, with almost a quarter-million members. The responsible, honest lads in uniform served as a welcome counterbalance to the troublemaking newsboys and bootblacks who until then had been the more typical models for adolescent urban males, and the entry into war had only increased support for the BSA's character-building mission.

But as effectively as West had solidified his own personal power and positioned the BSA as the authority on building good boys, the nagging irritation of the rival USBS remained. After almost ten years of directing inquiries and public-information campaigns against the US Boy Scout, West knew more about the group's solicitors and corrupt inner workings than perhaps even the USBS's own leaders.

Having finally taken the rival group to the New York Supreme Court, the BSA was in the midst of a months-long court battle with the USBS. The USBS had dragged its feet every step of the way, delaying the proceedings and refusing to provide documentation when requested. But on March 25, 1918, as West's years of campaigning against the rival neared a final showdown, he received a copy of a letter sent by Gluck that left even the tough-as-nails scout leader dumbstruck.

"I, John Duval Gluck," began the letter, which had been sent to the Justice Department and then forwarded to West, "respectfully petition your honorable Committee to investigate the methods of financing of the Boy Scouts of America." On thirteen single-spaced pages he laid out twenty charges against the BSA, and West in particular, claiming he pocketed public funds, used the post office for fraudulent campaigns, and published "expensive and useless statistics all of which tend to build a huge money-getting machine of which the poor boy gets nothing." Among the accusations:

> *[T]here has been a palpable misuse, by the said James E. West, of public funds, intended for the Boy Scouts of America. That said James E. West is aware of the acts of PROFESSIONAL MONEY SOLICITORS WHO CHARGE SEVENTY FIVE PER CENT COMMISSION for their services, the proceeds of which <u>never reach the boy</u> and very little the organization.*

> *Your petitioner further alleges on information and belief that both the American public and the American boy, are completely misled by the methods employed in obtaining and disbursing money as directed by Mr. James E. West. Your petitioner further alleges on information and belief that of the $1,357,000.00 canvassed and collected by James E.*

West for the fiscal year ending December 31st, 1917 not one cent for so much as a shoe lace was expended for the poor boy.

And on he went. West would not have been surprised to find out about a new moneymaking scheme from the USBS. But to receive a long list of accusations against the BSA that perfectly characterized Gluck's own organization was shocking. The conviction of Gluck's statements may have been the most startling part, as if by writing lies onto a letterhead, he could turn fiction into fact. He seemed to believe his own obvious inventions.

The BSA was already battling the USBS in the Supreme Court. But this piece of make-believe compelled West to confront his rival head on.

James West had seen for himself how strong civic organizations and personal development could help young men escape a bad lot in life. Losing both his parents by the time he was six years old, West suffered a childhood illness that left him with one leg shorter than the other. While he shied away from physical activities, West dedicated himself to reading and crafts, succeeding in public school and serving as an officer at his Washington City Orphanage, helping to improve the experience of the other children.

Determined to help pull up unfortunate boys like himself, West worked his way through law school and went into private practice in 1906, campaigning in Washington, DC, for playgrounds, the establishment of a juvenile court, and homes for orphaned children. He was inspired by Sir Robert Baden-Powell's original vision for scouting but was hardly the charismatic leader of his British counterpart. After taking over in January 1911, West began to reshape the BSA in the image of the bureaucratic social agencies he worked with and admired. At times the approach could be harsh (West publicly drove out Chief Scout Ernest Thompson Seton, who held a more sentimental view of boys' development), but it worked. Gluck followed all of these developments with interest: clipping, saving, and jotting notes on articles about the BSA's progress. It may have been that Gluck admired West's acuity. Or just as likely, he wanted to borrow ideas for his own ongoing USBS campaigns.

When they weren't lambasting the BSA, the USBS deceived donors into thinking they were the same group. Under Gluck's direction, checks written explicitly to the "Boy Scouts of America" were endorsed and cashed by the USBS. The group secured an office at 200 Fifth Avenue, from which it sent out solicitations—the same building the BSA had occupied for years. In a fund-raising drive to raise $1 million for the USBS, mailers stated that the group had two hundred thousand members and was trying to increase the number to one million. It was no coincidence that this was the same number of members the BSA legitimately aimed to recruit at the same time.

All of these shenanigans had finally led the National Council of the Boy Scouts of America to launch the New York Supreme Court lawsuit the previous summer. West tapped the law firm Hughes, Rounds, Schurman, and Dwight as counsel. The first name in the firm's title was that of Charles Evan Hughes, former governor of New York and, just two months before the BSA filed its lawsuit, the associate justice of the US Supreme Court. L. W. Amerman tapped the more modest and affordable Blauvelt & Warren to represent his side. The prosecution quickly secured the deposition of scouting's patron saint, Sir Robert Baden-Powell. He firmly expressed his support for the BSA.

After the USBS's delaying tactics ran their course, Gluck took a new tack, acting as if the years-long antagonism between the groups was just a misunderstanding. He submitted an editorial to the *Times*, explaining that he recently attended a conference at the BSA headquarters and came away impressed by West's leadership, whose work he claimed to have followed for years. "May I suggest that it is a pity that the Boy Scouts of America and the United States Boy Scout should be in controversy, legal or otherwise, in the public eye at this of all times?" Gluck asked in his most thickly mollifying tone. "Surely this is not helping the boys or their cause, which, as I understand it, is what we all have at heart. I warn the officers of both institutions that the result can only be injury to both parent organizations." He could not help but add that it was the BSA that had something to worry about, as there had been "a tremendous movement" to the militaristic USBS since the declaration of war. Gluck and the USBS followed this up on January 19, 1918, offering to settle with the BSA for $8,000.

On February 15, James West offered his response to Gluck's gestures of goodwill: he filed an affidavit to the Supreme Court charging that the USBS was "in substance the personal property of L. W. Amerman, dealer in jewelry and a public accountant." West accused Gluck and his crew of solicitors of dividing among themselves at least $30,000 collected as part of their "Million Dollar" fund-raising campaign. They challenged Amerman, Gluck, and the rest to provide an inventory and account of the property and liabilities of the organization. Gluck punted.

"I had nothing to do with raising the funds and Mr. West knows that I hadn't," he countered. "I didn't touch a penny of the money." He threatened to start libel proceedings.

Four days later, apparently forgetting he had just claimed to have had no connection to the USBS fund-raising, Gluck came forward with a new suggestion: that the USBS become part of the BSA. "There is only one solution," Gluck declared. "The United States Boy Scout must yield, providing they are permitted to do so with honor to the boys. I blame the officials of the Boy Scouts of America entirely for the delay. I could have brought about an agreement long ago if [not for] certain officials of the Boy Scouts of America." The public pressure and legal costs were taking a toll on Gluck and his fellow leaders of the USBS. They needed an exit before they ended up humiliated and broke. Gluck concluded that "If there has been any misuse of funds on the part of any one in our organization—suit or no suit—that person will be punished. I don't think any one is guilty." West ignored Gluck's olive branch, pointing out that the case was already before the court to decide.

At this point, a more coolheaded publicity man, or more skilled con artist, would have recognized he had exhausted his options. He would have acknowledged that odds were not in his favor and the chances of winning against the far stronger BSA and its powerhouse legal team were slim. But Gluck was angered that West rejected his gesture and hoped to mete out some damage on the BSA's reputation.

"James E. West issues numerous tables, publishes fancy but useless charts together with elaborate reports and pictures, which in the bulk, looks formidable," he wrote in his thirteen-page diatribe against West and the BSA. "They throw no light, however on what becomes of thousands of dollars." Gluck listed the "compulsory equipment" which "the little fellow faces when he joins" in order to go to camp, on hikes, and participate in parades: a mess kit for $1.25, poncho for $2.50, and canteen for $2.25. All told, he claimed it cost $20.50 per boy. This contrasted with the USBS, "which equips a poor boy free."

West, hardly believing Gluck could be so brazen, suppressed his better judgment to refrain from commenting on the accusations and shot back that this was simple retaliation. "This is a sort of last stand of the rapidly dwindling forces of the United States boy scout, for whose officials troubles are multiplying," West wrote. "I only hope the attorney general will find that he has jurisdiction in the matter." He added that "the sooner this matter is thrashed out in the courts, the better it will be for the great boy movement in the United States under the organization of the Boy Scouts of America."

Attorney General Thomas Watt Gregory did indeed send a letter admonishing Gluck for attempting to use the Department of Justice to settle a grudge. "The statements contained in these news items were not based upon anything derived from the Department of Justice, either directly or indirectly," Gregory said. "It is evident that there was a plan to injure the Boy Scouts of America and to use the Department of Justice as a vehicle to accomplish this end." Along with his letter, Gregory included all the materials Gluck had sent to the Justice Department, and noted that because the accusations were so empty and erroneous, he did not even want to keep the complaint on file.

"Any person can mail a complaint to the Department of Justice, no matter how irrelevant its subject matter may be," he wrote. "I now see that this procedure may be used as a means to injure innocent persons. I herewith return to you your 'complaint and petition' with the distinct statement that it contains no allegation, much less proof, of any wrongdoing on the part of the officials of the Boy Scouts of America, and that it should never have been submitted to the Department of Justice." Charles Evan Hughes promptly made the letter public, and it appeared in newspapers throughout the country. He rounded it off with a condemnation of the USBS: "It is not only unfortunate but unpatriotic for the little group of promoters, of which Gluck is a leader, to thus prey on the Boy Scouts."

The legal and public-relations pressure finally broke the USBS. The group settled to allow it to avoid additional legal expenses and negative publicity. In March 1919, the court handed down its decision, ordering that the USBS could not use any version of "Scout" or "Scouting" in its name, effectively ending the group, which had already sustained too much public embarrassment to continue.

"It is with great satisfaction that I am able to definitely inform the National Council, and through the National Council the whole constituency, that the suit of the Boy Scouts of America against the United States Boy Scout has concluded," James West gloated in his organization's annual report for 1919. West could not hide his pleasure at having finally undone the United States Boy Scout. By vanquishing his final Boy Scout rival, the once-crippled orphan boy solidified his ownership over the very concept of scouting and the proper way to instill ideals into America's young men. Under his leadership, the Boy Scouts of America would grow into a vast operation, with millions of members and no serious competitors.

———

The Boy Scouts of America claimed victory as the cloud of war lifted from the United States and the wider world. The Allied forces defeated Germany, and the signing of the Treaty of Versailles left the enemy country virtually powerless. The United States turned inward. Americans lost their appetites for international engagement. When Woodrow Wilson's progressive successor, James Cox, ran on the platform of instituting the League of Nations to strengthen the international community, he was soundly beaten by the more isolationist Warren G. Harding. Americans wanted to close the door on the violence and complications of the wider world.

It could afford to. Since taking over manufacturing of products it had previously sourced from Germany and Europe, the United States now sold many of the same products back to international buyers. "Some of the most popular toys with French shoppers this season are of American origin," the *Herald Tribune* noted. By 1926, the United States would be producing more toys and playthings than any other country in the world. The country found that after emulating France, Germany, England, and the Netherlands in its celebration of Christmas, now it was dictating the style, traditions, and supplies the world used in its own celebrations.

This time of postwar optimism and rise of America's position in the world, and increasing commercialization of Christmas, should have been an ideal moment for the Santa Claus Association to spread its message. But Gluck was too distracted, drained, and humiliated by the Boy Scout debacle to manage anything beyond the most basic operation of the group. His reputation as a publicist and charity expert had taken a beating and his customs work had long been dried up. He took a job as managing editor for a local New Jersey newspaper, the *West Hudson Record*, spending more of his time across the river, away from the excitement of Manhattan that had so electrified him.

As Gluck's professional life contracted, his wife's was on the ascent. Theater audiences were suddenly seeing a lot more of Symona Boniface. She joined the Shea-Kinsella Players at the Warburton Theatre in Yonkers, New York, in the play *Hindle Wakes*, staged at the start of 1919. Later that year she performed in the comedy *A Young Man's Fancy*, on Broadway, at the Playhouse Theatre. Like her father, she was interested in writing as well as performing, and found time to study playwriting at Columbia University. But her first true feel of the spotlight came as an understudy for *Bluebeard's Eighth Wife*. The actress in the title role fell ill and with less than twenty-four hours to prepare, Boniface took over. One critic called the performance "praiseworthy. In fact her performance was even better than that of the woman for whom she was substituting."

Soon after this bravura turn, Boniface repeated the trick. When actress Mary Newcomb was unable to make it to Broadway's Eltinge Theater (later named the "Empire Theater") to perform the lead role of *The Woman on the Jury*, Boniface was called in to save the day. Arriving at the theater at 7:46 p.m., she got her lines, the outline of the plot, and fifteen minutes to rehearse before the curtains rose at 8:30 p.m. "Naturally she was uncertain about her lines but not uncertain enough to mar the performance," critic Wood Soanes said. "Her stock training served her in good stead."

It may have been that Boniface's rising star and Gluck's implosion proved too much for the marriage. Or that Gluck's antics, which once charmed the young actress, now wore her down and embarrassed her. Whatever the reason, the two divorced.

As it happens, Boniface would eventually enjoy her greatest fame while suffering the clownish capers of a very different type of perpetrator: the Three Stooges. After a string of successful stage performances throughout the 1920s, Boniface and her mother relocated to Los Angeles where she found regular film work. Beginning in 1935, she appeared in more than a dozen of the Stooges' short films, delighting audiences as the matronly foil to Larry, Curly, and Moe. Playing dowagers with names like Mrs. Van Bustle, Mrs. Gotrocks, and Mrs. Smythe Smythe, her upper-class pretentions would be capsized as the Stooges wrecked her elegant home, disrupted her stuck-up social gatherings, or threw pies in her dismayed face (though Boniface also holds the distinction of being the first person to *throw* a cream pie in any Stooges film).

It was probably not the legacy Boniface longed for all those years before, as an aspiring actress sitting in the audience at the Hotel Astor, listening to Gluck describe the work of the Santa Claus Association, but it earned her long-lasting fans. Though her grave in North Hollywood's Pierce Brothers Valhalla Memorial Park sat unmarked for decades, in 2005 the Three Stooges Fan Club raised funds through its members to commission a marker recognizing her and her work. Visitors to Symona Boniface's grave will now see her youthful face, wearing just a hint of a sly smile, engraved above the epitaph "Forever on the Screen, Forever in Our Hearts."

Following Gluck's divorce from the actress and defeat at the hands of the BSA, the Santa Claus Association was no longer in Gluck's heart. The distraught and humiliated Gluck decided to leave the group behind. In the fall of 1919, ahead of the Christmas season, he asked the Salvation Army to take over the work. More than even the Santa Claus Association itself, the Salvation Army had become synonymous with Santa Claus since the 1890s, as their volunteers had begun appearing on city streets dressed as St. Nick, accompanied by bell and kettle. It made a certain sense for them to take over the work of answering Santa letters.

Publicly Gluck stated he was giving up the association because it had become too successful: They received so many requests, they were simply unable to handle them all. "The immediate success of the Santa Claus Association is not the question. That is already assured," Gluck said in his pitch to the Salvation Army. "We believe we are voicing the sentiments of Colonel Peart, Colonel Parker and other members of the Salvation Army Board when we state that if the Santa Claus Association is not taken over by them it will not be because the SCA movement is not a worthy one. . . . So, as we see it, the real question at issue is, can they take us over and do justice to both movements."

The organization's leaders responded with speed. On November 7, a representative for the Salvation Army declined the opportunity, saying that transferring the responsibility "could not do justice to your organization . . . or give the required study and attention necessary to its continued success."

It was hard to imagine Gluck or the association had much of a future.

PART III

CHAPTER 12

"Santa Claus as a Business Man and Advertiser"

The disillusions that come from contact with the larger activities of a man's life cannot dispel the sentiments that cling to Christmas-tide.
—POSTMASTER GENERAL ALBERT S. BURLESON

Doug and Mary had a train to catch. Hollywood's original celebrity power couple, the second- and third-highest-paid actors in the world, were, as usual, in a rush on the chilly Friday morning of November 24, 1922. Escorted from an artist's studio where they had spent the first part of the day having their portraits done, Douglas Fairbanks and Mary Pickford sat in the backseat of their car as it barreled toward the Ritz-Carlton at Madison Avenue and Forty-Sixth Street. Their train was scheduled to leave from Grand Central Station in less than half an hour, transporting the actors back home to their eighteen-acre Beverly Hills estate, known to the press as "Pickfair." The stars had just cancelled a planned trip to Mexico since there was too much work to be done back in California.

Despite the hurry, the two looked elegant as always. Fairbanks wore a carefully pressed suit and tie complete with pocket square, all as tidy as his pencil mustache; Pickford's hat, set on her head of dark golden curls, complemented her long, dark dress and jacket. Her pale skin contrasted with the rouged cheeks popular in the day.

Fairbanks had just wrapped the road show of his new film, *Robin Hood*. A little more than a month earlier, it had been the first film to premiere in Hollywood, opening up the brand-new Grauman's Egyptian Theater. It was reportedly also the first to cost more than $1 million to make, with the largest set ever constructed in Hollywood—the castle dining room alone measured as large as the Grand Central atrium. A month after its premiere, it looked like the gamble was paying off. It opened to stellar reviews and the crowds were rapturous. Refusing to rest on his laurels, Fairbanks was eager to return to the United Artists (UA) studios to work on his follow-up, *The Thief of Baghdad*, which he hoped to be even grander than *Robin Hood*.

Pickford had been enjoying a resurgence herself since producing and starring in 1921's *Little Lord Fauntleroy* and 1922's *Tess of the Storm Country*. She was "the most universally beloved person in the world to-day," as one fawning reporter described. But with all their power and influence, as they were raising the country's conception of entertainment to levels never before imagined, the two could not stretch time itself. Exiting their car to cheers and flashing cameras, pushing past the excited crowds on the sidewalks, the two made their way into the Ritz-Carlton. It looked unlikely Doug and Mary would have time for the final item on their packed itinerary. The duo had earlier agreed to assist one of the few people in the world who was arguably more famous than they: Santa Claus.

Standing in the lobby, smiling and welcoming the most famous couple in the world as if they were old friends, was John Duval Gluck Jr. Closer in height to Mary than Doug, the forty-two-year-old Gluck now waxed his mustache into tight curls at the ends and slicked his ring of hair down using pomade. He had spent extra time readying himself that morning and wore his best suit. For some reason, he also held a blue Western Union cap in his hand.

When she wasn't starring in, producing, and writing dozens of films, Pickford made a part-time job of assisting St. Nick. The year before, she had visited the 250 tenants of a county poor farm, learning what each wanted prior to her visit, and delivering to every one of them a pair of bedroom slippers and a stocking full of candy and goodies, as well as their special requests—comb, corset, and newspaper subscription among them.

The same year, papers described her as a "Partner of Santa Claus" when she patented a new doll in her likeness. Pickford would later be the celebrity to turn on the lights of Hollywood's Santa Claus Lane Christmas parade and would for years continue to promote various Santa-related charities for impoverished children.

So it was no doubt Pickford who had agreed to lend her and her husband's wattage to this curious group that answered letters to Santa Claus. Heading to the elevator, with just fifteen minutes to go until they had to be at the train station, Fairbanks, or at least some of their assistants, may have expressed skepticism about whether they had time for this stunt. Whatever the arguments, Pickford won out, and it was decided they would do as they had agreed—after all, Santa had made arrangements to come to them. As the stars and their retinue made their way to the Ritz-Carlton's corner suite, Gluck explained that the electricians he hired had just completed the addition to their room. Everything was ready for Doug and Mary's performance.

The grand suite they entered was the stars' home away from home, known to reporters as "Pickfair East" since it was always here they stayed when in New York City, whether to open a new picture or supervise their UA business. The space was full of photographers and reporters—a constant presence. On any given day, this was a place of frantic activity: Doug giving an interview while Mary read a script, assistants asking for wardrobe decisions while maids packed or unpacked luggage, the phone ringing and ringing.

Many of the same entertainment reporters had been at the hotel a few weeks earlier for the press junket for *Robin Hood*, when Fairbanks went up to the hotel's roof with bow and arrow in hand to pose for photographs. Though he was warned not to shoot, the swashbuckling jokester could not pass up a great photo op and let an arrow fly across Madison Avenue, figuring it would bounce innocently off the windows across the street. The twenty-six-inch projectile instead soared through an open store window and lodged its steel tip into the chest of fur dealer Abraham Seligman. Thankfully for everyone, the man's thick coat and vest blunted the point's impact and he was only superficially wounded. Fairbanks settled with him for $5,000 and a personal apology at Seligman's hospital bedside—learning his lesson that some fairy tales should remain in the imagination.

The stars took notice of the addition in the corner of their suite that Gluck had installed and paid for: a brand-new telegraph machine. Set on three wooden legs that came to just below Fairbanks's chest, the machine looked like nothing very complex—a basic telegraph system on which messages could be transmitted by tapping letters on a tiny keyboard.

But its reach was vast. This particular one had been installed in order to connect to twenty-five cities across the United States and Canada, sending out a simple message: the Santa Claus Association was open for business. Not wanting to keep the stars any longer, Gluck handed Mary a slip of paper on which he had written the one-line message she was to send out announcing the start of the Santa Claus season. To Doug he handed the blue cap, with small brim and Western Union's familiar logo of a winged globe. Fairbanks smiled his thousand-watt grin, his thin mustache rising as his eyes lit up, and he popped it on his head. As Gluck moved to the side, photographers stepped in and Pickford read out the words while her husband pressed the telegraph buttons. The cameras snapped. Ever the professionals, Doug and Mary wrapped everything up quickly and made their train without a minute to spare.

Douglas Fairbanks and Mary Pickford helped the association launch its 1922 season, sending a telegraph out to twenty-five cities from their suite in the Ritz-Carlton. SANTA CLAUS ANNUAL.

Just three years earlier, Gluck had lost his marriage, his steady income from the USBS, and his reputation thanks to his public drubbing by James West

The New York Times
Times Square

December 2, 1925.

Santa Claus Association,
Knickerbocker Building,
New York City.

Dear Sir:

    As requested, we are sending you the enclosed letter for your attention. We shall continue to send all such letters that come to us during the 1925 campaign of our Hundred Neediest.

               Very truly yours,

               THE NEW YORK TIMES,

Despite Gluck's exposure for his involvement with the USBS and other schemes, Santa letters kept coming to the association, not only from the post office but from other charities and newspapers such as the *New York Times*.
SANTA CLAUS ANNUAL.

and the BSA. He had given up on the Santa Claus Association. But since that time, Gluck had somehow pulled his organization out of its spiral and returned the group to higher-than-ever levels of esteem and fund-raising power. How could this be? Several factors, and a hefty bit of luck and good timing, had given the Santa Claus Man a second life.

After Gluck's painful downfall, he kept a low profile. He moved to a bachelor apartment and commuted to the *West Hudson Record*, finding some respite in the dull rhythm of work editing the local news of a New Jersey neighborhood. He made few, if any, attempts to promote the Santa Claus Association and scaled back his publicity work. But while Gluck distanced himself from the association and the Salvation Army refused to take it over, the Santa letters kept rolling into the post office. An occasional individual—"a pianist of international reputation" or "prominent Wall street man"—would step forward for a letter or two, but the rest had to go somewhere, so they went to the Santa Claus Association, which in 1920 was Gluck's home address.

It wasn't just the post office that continued to forward Santa's mail there. The American Red Cross, St. Joseph's Settlement, St. Francis' School Association for the Aid for Crippled Children, and the Children's Aid Society, among others, forwarded those Santa letters mailed to them or written by youngsters in their charge. Kids kept writing to Santa. Whether Gluck actively promoted it or not, the association's work continued to pile up.

Gluck did not rescue the association on his own. Key to reenergizing the group was Samuel Brill. Senior member of the men's clothing and furnishing company Brill Brothers, he had built, along with his three younger brothers, a small retail empire in the city. As he got on in years, the clothier began to dedicate himself to philanthropic work. Brill had responded to children's letters the first few years of the association's operation, and he noticed as soon as Gluck pulled back from the group and no Santa letter came his way. "[W]henever you are ready be sure and let me hear from you, and if there is any little personal service that I can do, I will try to do it," he wrote to the association. "You have a splendid work before you and you deserve all encouragement." Gluck decided to take him up on his offer. As Gluck withdrew as the public face of the organization, Brill happily filled the leadership vacuum, taking on the position of president and actively promoting the association. During the first years of the 1920s, Brill replaced Gluck as Santa's chief spokesman.

Like Mary Pickford, Brill prided himself as being young at heart. Upon assuming leadership of the association, he penned a letter to the *New York Times*:

The illusions of childhood are its most precious heritage, yet many children of the poor go to bed Christmas Eve with hearts full of hope and cheer only to awaken Christmas morning to the same empty, barren spectacle of their drab existence. They wrote their letters to Santa Claus, but their prayers were not answered. . . . The association needs, not money, but more good people to help in the work—men and women who feel the obligation of their own happy childhood and have a bit of Santa Claus in their hearts, who will read the letters and play the role of Santa Claus as the condition of the writers and their own conscience dictate.

His enthusiasm for the group made for a strong advertisement of its work. Brill's comments proved so effective that the association submitted the identical letter to the *Times* the following year, which it again published. Brill deepened his involvement with the association for business reasons as well as philanthropic ones. His business relied on the holiday gift giving that had increased exponentially over the more than three decades since he had founded Brill Brothers.

But despite the growing extravagance of the Christmas season, the clothier worried about a call for a "buyers' strike" due to rising prices and extreme deflation at the start of the decade, which threatened to reduce the amount of money spent during the holidays. Combined with moralistic efforts by groups like the Society for the Prevention of Useless Giving, still up and running since its founding in 1912, Brill saw an affront to Christmas itself. As head of the Santa Claus Association, he publicly lambasted such refusals to buy holiday gifts as creating a "Black Christmas."

Brill's worries would pass. While the United States slogged through months of recession until July 1921, it would arrive on the other side in the midst of extraordinary economic growth and individual wealth, seen most opulently in its holiday shopping. By Christmas the same year, the *Times* reported that the "rush of buying, according to the shopkeepers, was unprecedented." Such unrestrained holiday shopping, with merchants eager to meet demand, would only grow more extravagant in the coming years.

With Brill's passion helping to revive the Santa Claus Association, Gluck's own interest was slowly rekindled. With Brill's assistance, Gluck reapproached Vincent Astor. After the basement of his Hotel Astor had served as the association's headquarters in 1914, the businessman and philanthropist decided to offer the group a space in another of his famed Gotham properties: the Knickerbocker Building. Named after Washington Irving's fictional historian, the structure, at Broadway and Forty-Second Street, had been converted from a hotel to office buildings in 1920. The Knickerbocker would remain the group's headquarters for the next seven years, with Astor forfeiting the $1,500 monthly rent each December.

The "Santa Claus Cave" of the association's second year was now the "Santa Claus Clearing House," with a central office of more than two thousand square feet and an adjacent private office for the executives. Delicately, Gluck returned to his work with the Santa Claus Association. He found volunteers still interested in assisting. He set up areas to process the letters, with a sturdy wooden table in the center where the postman deposited the day's delivery. Miniature Christmas trees covered in tinsel brought holiday spirit to the room, along with full-sized trees erected

The association's main room in the Knickerbocker Building, where it would be headquartered for most of the 1920s. SANTA CLAUS ANNUAL.

throughout the office and crepe-paper streamers hung across the ceiling. Even the room's support column was made to resemble a chimney, with a wrap of redbrick corrugated paper.

Gluck kept his name out of the press. Though he orchestrated events in the Ritz-Carlton suite the day Doug and Mary launched the 1922 season, none of the newspapers mentioned him. Though still listed at the top of its masthead as "Founder," no longer was Gluck presented in the group's *Annual* as the unique genius who had devised the association's system. "Guided by a happy thought, it has been our work to see that these missives to Santa Claus did not die," read the annual address to association members, opting for the collective pronoun rather than the first-person singular that had been his standard. "So we came to take from the Post Office these strangely directed letters and to meet the requests they held in the name of the rosy old Saint of Yule." This essay and many others in the *Annuals* during the 1920s were unsigned or given a generic byline such as "Cub Reporter." To glance at them, one gets the impression they were written by a dedicated team of association volunteers or officers. In fact, virtually all came from Gluck's own pen, but he chose not to disclose this in the official publication.

As it turned out, there were plenty of others—in addition to the most famous couple on the planet—happy to help spread the Santa Claus Association's message. Actress Margarita Fisher and actor William Faversham took photos with St. Nick. The group tapped the famous war hero Mike "Fighting Irishman" Donaldson, recipient of the Congressional Medal of Honor for rescuing six of his comrades from German attack, to help keep belief in Santa alive.

"Yes, I believe in Santa Claus just as much as I did before I received the blow the day I was told that he didn't really exist," New York City postmaster Thomas G. Patten, who served in the position for four years before Edward Morgan returned to the role, explained from behind his desk in the grand General Post Office as another busy Christmas season began. "I don't believe in his physical being as I did then, but I am none the less convinced that he is alive. The older I get, the younger I grow in my beliefs." He made no mention of Gluck. When the *New-York Tribune* wrote its annual Santa Claus Association story, the reader would have no

The image of the generous businessman became central to the association as Gluck mounted a comeback in the 1920s, with the help of prominent retailer Samuel Brill, who stepped up to serve as the group's president.
SANTA CLAUS ANNUAL.

notion of who founded the group, who continued to oversee almost every part of its operation, and who collected the money donors sent in.

Placing Samuel Brill at the top of the masthead made plain the importance of retail and business savvy in how the organization was run. Business leaders were not just wealthy or prominent donors (though they were often that too—the *Herald Tribune* would note that Brill "had assisted [the association] financially"), they represented an American ideal that reached a peak in the 1920s. Gluck described businessmen as "the best charity experts" and the system he promoted followed the efficient, innovative thinking of the business leaders of the era. In an unsigned letter in the 1922 *Annual*, Gluck wrote that "The Santa Claus Association desires to introduce the poor to the Prince of Princes—the American business man."

In this period, the businessman was seen not just as worthy of respect but of worship. In 1925, advertising executive Bruce Barton, who first gained attention by running the wartime publicity for the record-breaking United Fund Drive, published *The Man Nobody Knows*, in which he recast Jesus Christ as the original businessman. Christ was a "forceful executive" in Barton's telling, and "picked up twelve men from the bottom ranks of business and forged them into an organization that conquered the world." If Christ were alive in the 1920s, he would not be giving street sermons but "be a national advertiser" in newspapers and magazines. From 1925 until 1927, *The Man Nobody Knows* was the best-selling nonfiction book in the country.

But Jesus was not the only idealized figure remodeled into a 1920s businessman. The same year Doug and Mary launched the association's holiday drive, Roy Dickinson wrote for the advertising trade publication *Printers' Ink* an article titled "Santa Claus as a Business Man and Advertiser."

> [C]onsider the change in Santa's problem. From the simple problem of long ago, he has had to change his distribution methods to fit the giant apartments which may shelter hundreds of families under one roof, with a very small chimney thrown in to make his task harder. It is no wonder, then, that about ten years ago, like other great manufacturers, he had to change his methods . . . with his newspaper advertising to search out the concealed love of kids in the hearts of crusty old bachelors, the big mailing list, the modern lithographed labels, and the Christmas morning visit to a little tenement home, the new joy that comes with it.

Dickinson had visited the association's headquarters and reported that Santa Claus had become a modern man of business. "Despite the charitable character of its work, the Santa Claus Association is business-like in all its dealings," another reporter covering the group in 1922 wrote. A poem in the *Annual* even updated Santa's workshop to the times. Instead of the cluttered room depicted by Thomas Nast, where Santa and his elves manufactured toys, it spoke of "a great big office in this strange land, where the letters to Santa Claus go." And, as Dickinson's headline implied, the association also took out advertisements. Gluck bought space in the *Sun* under the headline "Don't let them say 'There ain't no Santa Claus,'" noting again that they were seeking "*not money*, [but] men and women with a bit of Santa Claus in their hearts" to aid the organization.

The Santa Claus of Clement Clarke Moore's poem—a jovial "pedler" with a sack of goods on his back—had appealed to store owners of nineteenth-century New York City looking to attract buyers. As the mercantile class gave way to the managerial class, it made sense that giving Santa a more business-friendly image, working from an office, might help ingratiate him to the city's growing population of corporate workers—and potential donors. The 1920s saw the final version of Santa Claus—thick black belt, bright red suit—solidified through the covers of *Saturday Evening Post* by J. C. Leyendecker and Norman Rockwell, but just as importantly through his ubiquity in advertisements. Though Coca-Cola is erroneously credited with casting the final version of Santa (it did not start using him in ads until 1931), according to historian Karal Ann Marling, "It is fair to conclude that advertising codified the appearance of the modern American Santa Claus." These advertisements—and the American-made toys and products they promoted—spread beyond the country's borders, making the distinctly American, and New Yorker, version of Santa a global character.

America's political establishment encouraged this veneration of the businessman. Following the sudden death of President Warren G. Harding in 1923, Calvin Coolidge rose to the executive position and embraced the philosophy that "the chief business of the American people is business." He encouraged a laissez-faire ideology that scorned regulation that could impede profits. This was particularly the case with charity and

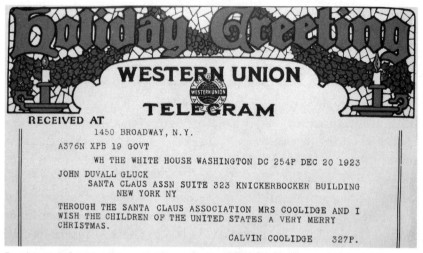

WESTERN UNION

TELEGRAM

RECEIVED AT

1450 BROADWAY, N.Y.

A376N XPB 19 GOVT

WH THE WHITE HOUSE WASHINGTON DC 254P DEC 20 1923

JOHN DUVALL GLUCK

SANTA CLAUS ASSN SUITE 323 KNICKERBOCKER BUILDING
NEW YORK NY

THROUGH THE SANTA CLAUS ASSOCIATION MRS COOLIDGE AND I
WISH THE CHILDREN OF THE UNITED STATES A VERY MERRY
CHRISTMAS.

CALVIN COOLIDGE   327P.

President Calvin Coolidge, working with Secretary of Commerce Herbert Hoover, encouraged greater privatization of charity work throughout the country and endorsed the work of groups such as the Santa Claus Association. SANTA CLAUS ANNUAL.

relief efforts. Spearheaded by Secretary of Commerce Herbert Hoover, Coolidge encouraged "associationalism" that tapped private welfare federations, corporate service departments, and philanthropic foundations to fill in as a national welfare program. Rejecting the federal safety nets typical of Europe and fueled by the postwar sense of individualism and faith in the wisdom of the businessman, Hoover, with Coolidge's encouragement, put responsibility for caring for the poor on private groups and local communities, rather than working to provide federal funding or oversight. He left charity regulation in private hands as well, and the sort of national reform Kilroe and Swann proposed in 1919 faded further from view.

Coolidge's boosterism of private charities extended to the Santa Claus Association. When the new president sought to wish the country's children a merry Christmas, he tapped Gluck's group to do the honors. "Through the Santa Claus Association Mrs. Coolidge and I wish the children of the United States a Very Merry Christmas," the president telegraphed to the Knickerbocker Building from the White House on December 20, 1923.

Gluck had been exposed just a few years before as a fund-raising fraud, investigated for everything from blackmail to espionage, and forced to discontinue his United States Boy Scout group. But as he returned, first tentatively, then more aggressively, to the work of the Santa Claus Association, he found the city and country more willing than ever to give St. Nicholas a hand. He found himself in the midst of a period of optimism and expanding economic growth, which brought Americans better fortunes than they had ever experienced. Millionaires were sprouting up faster than ever, many with more money than they knew what to do with. The massive fund-raising of the war years had revealed the wells of charity funds available to organizations able to make a compelling plea. The arrival of radio gave solicitors an even more powerful medium than print through which to get their message out (indeed, Gluck launched a Santa Claus Radio Department from which Santa Claus spoke "to the kiddies direct from the North Pole"). Newspaperman-turned-publicist Cornelius M. Smith would later recall of this period that "almost anyone of good appearance with a flair for selling, organizing, and publicizing could conduct successful campaigns to raise moderate sums for popular causes." Fund-raiser John Price Jones summed up the decade of 1919–1929 as "the golden age of fund-raising."

Parallel to the network of gift buyers and letter writers, Gluck ramped back up his complex operation of fund-raising, for which almost no one but him was accountable. He quietly introduced a subscription list that individuals could send to friends and encourage them to sign up. A letter among Gluck's papers, from A. M. Eichman of the J. C. Rabiner & Company brokerage firm, explained that "the following paragraph heads a subscription list which I am today starting on its errand of good sportsmanship throughout our organization," followed by a notice aimed at the businessman set:

BE A SANTA CLAUS!

You crusty old bachelors with no kiddies of your own; or you happy fathers whose youngsters lead tenderly sheltered lives; you who are so

*far away from your boyhood that you never look back, just stop a min-
ute and think.*

*Don't you remember how your heart thrilled with pride and gratitude
over that big bonehandled jack-knife given you by that Prince of Good
Fellows, Uncle John? And what about that wooden sled, those club
skates, and that bag of agates from some other Uncles? Those were the
days of real sport, and the days of Real Sports, too.*

*Just remember—there are a lot of youngsters just now that haven't any
generous Uncle Johns. Remember this, and then dig down deep, and
make yourself a member for life in the Good Sports Club.*

A. M. added at the end, "Incidentally, Charlie, I have investigated the
Santa Claus Association through various local newspapers, and through
other channels, and I find that it is a 100% philanthropy, with practically
no overhead to charge off." The note reads like something Gluck himself would have written but is apparently genuine (though A. M.'s judgment in his associates is questionable—within months of the letter, J. C.
Rabiner & Company would file for bankruptcy).

In addition to the funds coming from donors to the association's "gift-
buying committee," hundreds of retailers, manufacturers, dry goods sellers,
banks, and trust companies—Lord & Taylor, F.A.O. Schwartz, Drake's
Cakes, and even Ex-Lax—bought ads in the *Santa Claus Annual*. "A large
part of the funds obtained through the projection of advertisements was
applied toward *immediate aid cases and executive expenses*," Gluck wrote
in the yearbook, but offered no data to demonstrate specifically how the
money was spent. Also unaccounted for were the donations raised for the
Santa Claus Building, a project for which the group continued to solicit
funds in its *Annuals* and when speaking to the press, despite having made
no progress on the building itself.

Another source of funds came from the association's benefit events.
Gluck showed that the group was back and better than ever with a grand
New Year's Eve party on December 31, 1923. A society organization known
as the Once a Year Club cohosted an elaborate gathering for the group

NEW YEAR'S LAND
ATOP the WALDORF
December 31st 1923

Parties grew more elaborate throughout the Jazz Age, and the association hosted its own New Year's Land party, full of celebrities and entertainers, atop the Waldorf-Astoria to welcome in 1924. SANTA CLAUS ANNUAL.

atop the Waldorf-Astoria, with the door's receipts going to the Santa Claus Association. Called New Year's Land, it started at 11 p.m. and continued well into the next morning, as guests grabbed breakfast at the hotel's famous restaurant, Oscar's.

Attendees included English actress Violet Englefield, wearing jewels so extravagant that she had been escorted to the party in an armored car. Dancers Constance Evans and Albertina Rasch entertained the gathered crowd. Jazz musicians "set hearts athrobbing and feet atapping," as the *Santa Claus Annual* would later describe. Fannie Brice and Lionel Atwill presided over the Reception Committee. In a blast of noise, confetti and party favors rained from the ceiling, mixing with the cacophony from the live band. The roof garden's bright flowers provided a colorful backdrop to the huge Christmas trees decorated in gold and white. Spanish matador Chickerito wandered about in full costume, facing off with "the famous Hippodrome dancing Bull." As it was a fake creature, Gluck could rest easy that he was in no violation of animal-rights laws.

The most famous man in attendance was championship heavyweight boxer Jack Dempsey. Three months earlier he had fought Argentinian Luis Firpo for his fifth title in as many years and won in just under four minutes—what the *Times* had dubbed "the most exciting minutes of the sporting year." Before a crowd of ninety thousand, Firpo hit the canvas seven times before coming at Dempsey with a powerful blow that knocked him headlong through the ropes. It looked like the great champ

The most famous man at New Year's Land: heavyweight boxing champ Jack Dempsey, gamely facing off with "the famous Hippodrome dancing Bull."
SANTA CLAUS ANNUAL.

had finally been bested. But Dempsey recovered and knocked out Firpo at the start of the second round, thrilling the crowd and earning him the half-million-dollar purse. This New Year's Eve, his only rival was the dancing bull, whom he pretended to tussle with in pictures of the event.

Not only did Dempsey help sell papers, but the champion's promoter, Tex Rickard, was also not shy about paying reporters for glowing coverage of his biggest client. He would pay as much as $25,000 per fight directly to sportswriters—what he considered an advertising expense. Rickard and boxing manager Jack Kearns both dropped into Gluck's New Year's Land wearing tuxedos but gamely donning novelty hats for the photographer.

Each attendee paid to get in the door and many made additional donations, but just how much was raised, the Santa Claus Association never disclosed. While it may have earned Gluck money, New Year's Land was also a rich vindication for the Santa Claus Man. Not only did it make it appear that the association was back on top, but it was a flashy response to a different fund-raiser that had taken place a couple of weeks earlier—a fund-raiser he was supposed to have been running.

Dempsey's promoter, Tex Rickard (right), a celebrity in his own right, chatting with boxing manager Jack Kearns.
SANTA CLAUS ANNUAL.

Gluck had been engaged by the Samaritan Hospital Building Campaign Committee to help raise money for the creation of a new hospital. It was his first publicity gig in a while, earning him a lucrative $250 a week in addition to his *West Hudson Record* salary, and he no doubt wanted to make a big impression on the client. The project would transform the seven buildings of the Samaritan Hospital into a six-story exemplar of modern medical technology, with two hundred beds and two operating rooms, a large roof, promenades, and sun parlors. It was a big contract, and Gluck felt some of the old magic and confidence from his heyday of publicity work return.

Plans immediately got underway for a spectacular benefit event at the Thirteenth Regiment Armory, running the entire first week of December 1923. Gluck spoke with the Ladies Auxiliary of the Samaritan Hospital in February, letting them know they would have to get involved in the fund-raiser. The "Streets of Paris" was to be the theme of the winter festival, with some $13,000 worth of gifts raffled off to attendees. Prizes included trips to California, Bermuda, and Florida, as well as a gold fountain pen and cash. The winners would be announced in the *Brooklyn Daily Eagle* after the event. Five hundred hospital employees were charged with selling one million tickets, and during a meeting of the hospital's young nurses, Gluck hired a photographer to capture the discussion.

Looking for a way to add some class to the drive, he sent out the image of the young women to newspapers at the end of August, along with some attention-grabbing copy under the headline "Society Girls Aid Samaritan Hospital Drive."

> Brooklyn's younger set has taken an interest in the drive for the Samaritan Hospital, which is soon to be erected at Fourth Avenue and Seventh Street. Representatives of Brooklyn's best families visited the headquarters of the committee in charge of the drive at 625 Fulton Street and were formed into teams to canvass the borough. . . . It is expected that one of the first affairs to be arranged by the young women, in conjunction with their canvassing, will be a "social tea" to which leading members of the theatrical profession are to be invited. As the plans for this tea are as yet in the initial stages, no date has been fixed.

No date was fixed, because none of it was true. Gluck had recast the working nurses as society girls and invented the "tea" to give the fundraiser a whiff of social prestige. Rather than being pleased with Gluck's bending of the truth in the name of generating publicity, the campaign's director, Henry M. Rynehart, was furious. "The fact of the matter is, these girls, while they are just as good as any society girls ever born, are merely employees who, for the most part, are working here at $15 a week, and this sort of thing is ridiculous," he said. With disgust he spat out his estimate of Gluck: "Publicity men, perhaps, may not be supposed to tell 'the truth, the whole truth and nothing but the truth' all the time, but there should be a limit to the extent they may go in taking liberties with the truth." Clifton Bogardus, the general chairman of the committee, immediately fired Gluck and sent a notice to the papers: "This is to inform you that Mr. John D. Gluck is no longer connected with the Samaritan Hospital in any capacity." Gluck's preference for fantasy over reality, placing average New Yorkers several rungs above their station on the social ladder, had again run him into trouble.

It was fortunate for the leaders of the campaign that they cut ties with Gluck when they did. The headlines about the fund-raiser and its impropriety caught the eye of an organization called the Brooklyn and Queens Charity Investigating Bureau. The watchdog group (like the Charity Organization Society, it was a private group unaffiliated with a government body) had recently sprouted up. Its managers, Thomas and William Norton, took special interest in solicitors like Gluck who pocketed a huge share of the donations they generated.

"I have seen a contract entered into between John D. Gluck and officials of the Samaritan campaign committee which provides a salary of $250 a week for Gluck as director," said Thomas Norton. "I have been informed that certain of the professional solicitors working for the fund receive $50 of each $250 they collect, which approximates 20 percent. This leaves 80 percent out of which the salary of Gluck had to be paid until his dismissal recently and all of the other expenses incidental to the campaign had to come." Norton asked that the matter be taken to the public welfare commissioner, who oversaw city charities and hospitals.

The Nortons knew that reaching out to this official would get results. The notoriously tough commissioner Bird Sim Coler had been in his position since 1918 and had earned a reputation as a pitiless critic of waste in the city's relief work. He was one of the only officials to make real progress in cracking down on the city's fraudulent philanthropies and was not a man to overlook charity chicanery.

This reputation no doubt inspired trepidation in Bogardus and Rynehart as they headed downtown to present their books to Coler at the Manhattan Municipal Building. They met with the thin, sad-eyed Coler in his office on the morning of September 17. The fifty-six-year-old commissioner wore a salt-and-pepper mustache and bow tie as he coldly reviewed their report on the campaign's donations, salaries, and expenses. "We welcome any examination," Bogardus declared. But after spending time examining the details of the Samaritan Hospital's accounts, Coler determined that with the dismissal of Gluck and a thorough accounting of its books, the organization's fund-raising campaign appeared clean. The hospital's fund-raisers exhaled in relief as Coler announced, "I am convinced that those directing the drive are earnestly striving to give

Brooklyn an institution which would fill an urgent need," he said. "Should I be requested I would gladly attend meetings and lend my voice in aid of what I consider a worthy movement." It was a rare endorsement from a city official who most often used his position to criticize and close dubious fund-raisers.

Gluck responded with a small item, defying both Rynehart and the Norton brothers to prove any of their accusations, adding that he was "the best and most economical promoter in the business." The *Eagle* editors opted not to run it. It was a reminder to Gluck that he should keep a low profile, that it was in his interest to stay behind the scenes, and that his skills at playing the press to his personal advantage were not as strong as they had been a decade earlier. They were reminders he would ignore.

It was also Gluck's introduction to the man who would finally prove his undoing: the eagle-eyed public welfare commissioner Bird Coler.

CHAPTER 13

Order Out of Chaos

When out on the lawn there arose such a clatter,
I sprang from my bed to see what was the matter.
—CLEMENT CLARKE MOORE, "A VISIT FROM ST. NICHOLAS"

For Bird Coler, Christmas seemed to get crazier every year. The public welfare commissioner sought some sort of control over city charity to see that the influx of donations went to worthy places and to tamp down on those taking advantage of New Yorkers' generosity. He knew the holidays were a bustling time—but not usually this busy. For Christmas week 1923, the stern official had not slowed down since investigating the Samaritan Hospital's "Streets of Paris" drive. Every day brought new calls about fraudulent charities to his cramped office downtown in the Manhattan Municipal Building. Coler, with a strict Catholic view of right and wrong, unfailingly responded to each tip.

On Monday he apprised District Attorney Joab Banton, Edward Swann's successor, of five questionable relief campaigns claiming to help the needy—the National Disabled Soldiers' League, the Beth Israel Aid Society, and Needy Children's Free School among them—and saw that they were investigated. Tuesday he requested investigations of two more charities. Coler simultaneously halted a large-scale ball at the Hotel McAlpin, planned for a group called the Emergency Ambulance Drivers, which claimed to aid the city's emergency hospitals but did nothing of the kind. He initiated an investigation into Guardians of the Poor and

Needy—whose president pulled in a salary of $2,080 of the $3,000 they raised for the year—and saw that it was closed. By Thursday, he had shut down drawings taking place at a holiday mahjong benefit for the Catholic, Jewish, and Protestant Big Sisters organizations. Since the summer, Coler had been targeting these sorts of benefit block parties for offering games of chance, accusing them of having "degenerated into commercial enterprises, where petty gambling is indulged in and morals of young girls are endangered."

Throughout the week, he collected stacks of cards from a number of legitimate relief groups, including the Charity Organization Society. On each card was written the name of a person who requested a donated basket filled with the fixings for a Christmas dinner. This was a popular holiday program, but one that had gotten out of hand when half the city's welfare groups launched their own basket campaigns. Coler and his team went through the stacks of requests, personally weeding out any duplicates, keeping them all on file as part of the Christmas Basket Central Registration he had just created. It was the type of thorough process to which the Santa Claus Association had once aspired.

The same week, Coler had learned that his and his wife's own names were being falsely used as "endorsers" on solicitations. "The overzealousness of professional solicitors . . . will result in disorganizing the reputable charitable organizations of our city," Coler fumed. He offered a one-hundred-dollar reward to anyone who could give him information leading to the arrest of those misusing his name.

To Coler, the holiday season was not a time for sentimentality but for wariness. He looked out from his tenth-floor office window and saw a Wild West in need of a sheriff: street solicitors harassing passersby, fund-raising mailers piling up on businessmen's desks, the constant cacophony of benefit shows and block parties supporting who knew what. It was up to him to clean up New York charity. The targets of some of his harshest criticism were the kindhearted but gullible society folks who enabled these charity cheats.

"If you women are on the level, I shall be glad to have you cooperate," Coler told a roomful of startled members of the Woman's Municipal League at the Hotel McAlpin. They had invited the commissioner to speak about how they could donate time to city relief efforts and expected the usual cheery commendations for their benevolence and generosity. Instead they got a dressing-down. "It is very easy for professional charity adventurers and adventuresses to make a statement to you ladies and you will swallow it," Coler chided, assuring the women that he and his department were "going to take care of the poor and the children, but not the people who can afford to pay." After finishing his diatribe, the women got a chance to ask questions. None made a peep.

But in the blitz of Christmas 1923, it was clear that curbing charity fraud in New York City was too much work for one man, no matter how dedicated he might be.

Public welfare commissioner had never been Coler's dream job. He had wanted to be governor. The public servant began his political career as the first comptroller of Greater New York City, following the consolidation of the five boroughs in 1898. Chief accountant of the vast new city, he had done his job well. "He brought order out of chaos, and established the finances of the new and greater city upon a firm and acceptable basis," State Senator David B. Hill wrote of Coler when he ended his term. "If he made some enemies they were largely the enemies of decent government and honest politics, whose hostility was to his credit."

He was certainly not afraid of making enemies. Coler was a Democrat eager to keep his distance from the Tammany machine. His investigation of spending on drinking water uncovered leaders from both parties giving preferential contracts to a private company that overcharged the city. He pushed his own party to support reform and eventually worked alongside Governor Teddy Roosevelt to quash the deal. Coler's meticulousness and antagonism to moneyed interests gave him a burst of support. When Roosevelt was called up to serve as William McKinley's vice president, Coler hoped to ride his popularity as an independent-minded leader to the top position in the state. But despite his exceeding expectations in New York City, his opponent more than made up the margin with upstate Republican strongholds. Coler lost the governorship by just 8,500 votes.

After he took the consolation prize as Brooklyn borough president, his career stalled. He opened up a brokerage firm; wrote books on public education, religion, and the dangers of socialism; and started a magazine on public policy. Then, in 1918, political opportunity once again came knocking. On the first of the year, New York City mayor John Hylan tapped Coler to turn his punctilious eye to the city's welfare programs, as commissioner of public charities, soon renamed the commissioner of public welfare. The responsibilities were substantial: Fifteen hospitals, shelters, and institutions to care for destitute children, elderly, mentally or physically disabled, and those otherwise unable to afford home or health care, with Kings County Hospital, Sea View Hospital, and the five welfare institutions on Blackwell's Island among them. Some fifteen thousand impoverished New Yorkers were now his responsibility to manage. He was one of eight board members overseeing the operation of Bellevue and its four allied hospitals, and coordinated with dozens of private and state-affiliated organizations. This also meant he was the city's main charity cop, with both the power of publicity and the purse at his disposal.

Coler had been interested in charity reform since the earliest days of his career. But he was at heart an accountant and generally unimpressed by the heartbreaking stories of charitable need made by many of the city's relief societies. Coler would recall later his first brush with public charity: the daily visit to the comptroller office of an old whiskered man by the name of Mr. Lyons who ran the New York Free Ice Water Society. He stopped into Coler's office asking for $750 he was owed by the city for the service he provided. When Coler asked Lyons how much of that went into his own pocket, he was angered to hear that the man took home a quarter of his earnings. Reflecting later on this moment, Coler recalled that "Right then and there we started a reorganization and audited bills began to come in from everybody for services rendered to the city by private corporations," leading him to uncover a number of fraudsters.

Combining an accountant's scruples and a crusading detective's brashness, Coler was soon upending how the city monitored charity and ran its welfare programs. Early in his tenure, he worked with DA Banton and the city magistrates to require any street solicitors to first obtain a license from his office. It was not as comprehensive as Swann and Kilroe's congressional bill, but this one actually passed and Coler used it to clean up the streets of pencil and button sellers, benefit promoters, and hawkers of heartwarming causes. When he suspected criminal activity, Coler gathered what information he could and referred the case to Banton for prosecution, delighting in every swindler he put behind bars.

"We sent a man to jail the other day for collecting money for wounded soldiers," Coler boasted to an audience who gathered to hear him speak at the Hotel Astor. "Nowadays it's a good business, collecting for the 'poor soldiers.' All a person has to do is to get a tin can and go out on the streets. It is possible to make a pretty good living if you don't get caught."

Many of Coler's targets were the excessive parties aimed at raising funds for charity, a practice that grew every year. The 1920s were a time of extravagant displays, parties, and festivals such as the association's New Year's Land. Citywide gatherings like the Coney Island Mardi Gras and Tree of Light ushered in a new era of civic festivity, but the 1920s saw these celebrations grow in frequency and magnitude. Ostensibly held to strengthen bonds between church members or promote a cause, the parties soon became bonanzas for bootleggers and gamblers. "The first idea of the community party was admirable," *Times* editors wrote in 1923, but they fretted it had degenerated into "a sort of unlicensed dance hall." Coler followed the same strategy he had with street solicitors, working to set a permit requirement on all street parties.

He made waves in his first years but, as was his nature, he also made enemies. Coler earned headlines for shutting down blatant frauds but also didn't hesitate to accuse established charity drives for the Red Cross, United Hospital Fund, and New York Tuberculosis Association of "robbing orphans" or tangle with the Salvation Army over its politics. Rather than allying with the Charity Organization Society, Coler more often approached it as an adversary. At the start of his tenure, the commissioner withdrew more than $100,000 in funding that was promised to the City Home Hospital, leaving the society and its partner, the Association for Improving the Condition of the Poor, no choice but to relocate the tubercular patients convalescing there. When they complained of his stringent approach, the commissioner declared that "There are people in the Charity Organization who, I believe, would like to see deaths and accidents . . . to prove us in the wrong."

Perhaps because John Gluck respected Coler's battle with the COS—his own enemy—or that he hoped to keep the hard-charging

Despite Gluck's frequent criticism of city charity work, he made attempts to flatter the tough new public welfare commissioner with gestures such as this photo in the SANTA CLAUS ANNUAL.

commissioner from coming after him, Gluck made an effort to stay on Coler's good side. "Mr. Bird S. Coler: Not associated with the Santa Claus Association but intimately connected with Santa himself," read the front page of a *Santa Claus Annual* at the time, under a photo of the commissioner, sporting a bow tie. "Mr. Coler has some interesting ideas with reference to professional charity."

But as the exhausting 1923 Christmas season came to a close, Coler realized he could not keep doing all this work on his own. His Christmas dinner basket program, which proved a success in reducing duplication, had allowed him to mend some connections with the city's private charity organizations. Fatigued from going after all the "charity adventurers and adventuresses" himself, he thought of an idea: the creation of a committee to "act as a sort of Bradstreet's of charities." It would include representatives from the Chamber of Commerce, local business organizations, and of course himself. Members could collaborate to set citywide standards on any charity effort. But to make this scheme work, Coler would have to do something that did not come natural to him: play nice with others.

Street begging, noisy public parties, and the threat of moral corruption—the concerns that drove Bird Coler's crusade had also weighed on the men who helped invent Christmas in America. In New York, the holiday originated in the streets, with the lower classes carousing from Christmas Day to New Year's Eve—singing, playing music, and shooting guns—while the upper classes waited until New Year's Day to go about their more dignified visits to friends. Newsboys, laborers, and complete strangers knocked on doors demanding tips and gifts from the wealthy—their interpretation of Europe's centuries-old "customs of outlawry, role reversal, and colorful mockery of the existing order," as historian Penne Restad describes it.

But growth in immigration and urbanization at seaport cities led the patricians at the top of the social ladder to lose patience with those on the lower rungs. Just as the mushrooming street solicitors and block parties had forced Coler to take action by the 1920s, street begging and drunken revelry—most excessive during Christmastime—finally reached a breaking point for New York's elites by the 1820s. As John Pintard tried to rest on the night of December 31, 1820, looking forward to his genteel New Year's Day calls, he was interrupted by a band of carousers playing their drums, fifes, and whistles down Wall Street. The noisy revelers "interrupted all repose until daylight, when I arose," the frustrated Pintard wrote to his daughter. The man who helped introduce St. Nicholas to America was expressing a frustration common among his high-class set. But again, it would be his friend Clement Clarke Moore who would strike on the solution to make Christmas work for everyone.

In devising his version of Santa, Moore dropped the ecclesiastical garb in Pintard's woodcut and imagined him as a merchant. He gave him not the long, upper-class pipe common in Washington Irving's *History of New-York*, but "the stump of a pipe," associated with a rougher sort. Indeed, at first St. Nick and his noisy arrival frightens the narrator, as the rambunctious revelers often did the city's wealthy during the holidays. But then Santa reveals himself to be cheerful and "nothing to dread"—not here to ask for money but to provide gifts. "A Visit from St. Nicholas" relieved the fear felt by elites at this changing time—and it also assuaged their guilt. By shifting the focus of Christmas from the streets to the home, Moore removed anxieties about failing to fork over holiday tips and gifts to the neighborhood vagabonds. The social inversion long associated with the holidays remained, but instead of the rich providing gifts to poor, adults now gave to kids.

This was a new way to celebrate Christmas: neither a noisy party on the street nor a dignified visit to friends, but rather a family holiday, overseen by the good-natured spirit of Santa Claus. Moore's conception of Christmas filled a budding need and once introduced, this domestic version of the holiday spread fast. Merchants eagerly promoted it, seeing the obvious profit to be made in this peaceful, present-filled holiday. Domesticated Christmas became the "real Christmas" in newspaper reports, while the drunken street carousing was soon rebranded as "crime" (New York City created a professional police force in 1828, replacing the private watchmen who had protected the city previously). "More than any other text, it was Moore's poem that introduced the American reading public to the joys of a domestic Christmas," says historian Stephen Nissenbaum. The modern celebration of Christmas began and spread by moving it into the private space, honoring the home as a refuge from the clatter and criminality of the world outside.

But a century later, Coler was dealing with a more sophisticated update to the holiday revelers Moore had helped banish. These men did not request coins to help pay for a meal; they wrapped their appeals in grand, inspiring causes. They did not bellow their pleas from street corners; they used newspapers, mailers, and movie stars to tell their tales. The trappings of domestic celebration and Santa Claus himself no longer kept these grifters out; the Christmas spirit gave them entry anywhere they liked.

Gluck's latest humiliation from the Samaritan Hospital failed to slow the Santa Claus Man's moneymaking schemes. Just as during the war he had tapped into fears about German spies while simultaneously raising money off sympathy with Germans living in New York, he also played both sides of the Prohibition debate. While he published a tract against the outlawing of alcohol, at the same time he launched a campaign from his Knickerbocker office called the "Crusade against Illicit Traffic in Narcotics."

"In the state of New York we do not propose to wait for any international agreement with reference to the illicit traffic in narcotics," Gluck wrote in a letter sent to the New York State Assembly. "We cannot afford to wait. We cannot have thousands on our streets addicted to the use of narcotics. We must take them off the highways of our cities, for each one is a unit to spread this scourge." Gluck explained that his group was preparing a bill to introduce to Albany, setting forth "severe penalties for criminal narcotic trading." All he needed to run the campaign was donations from concerned citizens.

To give the group credibility, on its stationery and communications he began adding "endorsers" for the group. History repeated itself as the individuals revolted as soon as they learned of the misappropriation of their names. Nathan Jonas, president of the Manufacturers Trust Company, went to the *Times* with his complaint. Just as with the USBS, when word got out about the deception, others came forward: One businessman after another asked that his name be dropped, unsure how he had gotten on Gluck's list.

He created a society to promote an odd new product for toddlers cooped up in cramped apartments: Boggins' Window Crib. The glass-and-metal box, secured on the outside of an apartment window like an air-conditioning unit, was supposed to serve as a sort of window box for kids—providing the infant with sunlight and fresh air while they gazed out the slatted side to the street, many stories below. It's impossible to say how much money Gluck made on the venture, but he dubbed himself "Chairman of the Window Crib Society."

CAPITAL & LABOR BUREAU
ECONOMIC RESEARCH Inc.

PHILADELPHIA   NEW YORK
John Duvall Gluck, *President*

MAKES private, confidential, surveys and reports on Charity Organizations, not connected with church, no matter how large or small. We have just completed a survey and report containing 300,000 words, twenty charts and 291 photographs, together with several actual test cases, over a period of one year. It is the only report of its kind ever compiled in the United States.

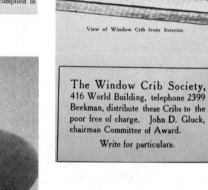

View of Window Crib from Interior.

The Window Crib Society, 416 World Building, telephone 2399 Beekman, distribute these Cribs to the poor free of charge. John D. Gluck, chairman Committee of Award.

Write for particulars.

Throughout the 1920s Gluck launched one organization after another, promoting disparate causes, and fund-raising off of them. SANTA CLAUS ANNUAL.

Gluck invented the Capital & Labor Bureau for Economic Research. It appeared to be something of a catchall for many other interests and projects, illicit or otherwise. An ad for the group in the *Santa Claus Annual* summed up its numerous responsibilities, including publicity campaigns, investigations, motion pictures, biographies, factory bulletin service, press clippings, and government tariff surveys. Mostly it seemed to serve as a platform from which he could criticize the Charity Organization Society and others that might question his style of "relief work."

The Santa Claus Association returned to prominence in part because Gluck lowered his profile in the group. But his hiatus proved short-lived. Once his injured ego healed and the threats kicked up by the USBS dissipated, his self-aggrandizement came roaring back, rising higher than the Woolworth's roof: "Mr. J. D. Gluck, of course, is so thoroughly versed in all matters of charity, so experienced, so strong an executive, so keenly alive, and so absolutely sure of the right of what he is doing, that we have been able to rise above the undertow and subterfuges resorted to by those who might wish to corner the market on philanthropy," he wrote in the *Annual*. Since most of the papers had lost interest in Gluck's clever ideas about philanthropy, the *Annual*s became the main outlet for the Santa Claus Man to toot his own horn.

These organizations hardly enjoyed the public interest and staying power of the Santa Claus Association, but each one helped him gather more names and addresses of potential donors and supporters, all of which he added to his growing mailing list. Should a group be exposed, Gluck would take the names and information and move them to another of his schemes. The complexity of these groups, the opacity of what exactly they did, and the identification of real members made it difficult for watchdogs to fully wrap their arms around it all, let alone gather enough evidence to intervene.

Gluck's catalog of organizations and campaigns floated around law enforcement groups like a swarm of fast-moving flies. One could be swatted, but before you could check if it had been terminated, another caught your eye. The Window Crib Society, Defense Reports Committee, Crusade against Illicit Traffic in Narcotics, Serum Control of Cancer, Anti-Prohibition Group, and of course the Santa Claus Association—all continued to exist in one form or another, accomplishing little but boosting Gluck's profile and fattening his pocketbook. All followed the same strategy he learned in the US Boy Scout and perfected at the Santa Claus Association: draft a letter that touches a deep emotion, buttress it with a long list of impressive names and claims, send it far and wide using the growing list of donor names, and wait for the checks to roll in.

But reviewing Gluck's activities during this prolific period in the 1920s, it is hard to conclude he cared only about money. What was driving him more than profits was his continued desire to elevate himself to greatness. In the 1923 edition of *Herringshaw's American Blue Book of Biography*—the bible for those seeking to present themselves in a favorable light—he dubbed himself "a Business President and a Sociologist." Despite the fact that he had received only a high school education, Gluck's credentials included that he had been "educated in private and public schools, the Lincoln Academy, the Columbia University, and studied international law at Cambridge and Heidelberg." He never attended any of them. In the 1924 *Who's Who in New York City and State*, he refused to accept the mundane title of "managing editor" at the *West Hudson Record* and instead called himself "special representative of newspapers" and replaced Cambridge with Oxford. In the 1925 *Santa Claus Annual* he is not a "customs broker" but a "famous tariff expert and investigator." More strangely, at this time, he also added an extra "l" to his middle name, becoming "John Duvall Gluck Jr." Just like "Esq.," this addition seems to have just appeared one day in his signature and remained there.

Gluck wanted to be a man of consequence. He expanded his wardrobe of three-piece suits and stylish hats, and put on increasingly elaborate airs as if trying to convince the world and himself that he was doing important work. He put himself forward as a writer, editor, charity expert, Ivy Leaguer, lawyer, sociologist, publicity man, Duval, and Duvall; Gluck could be any and all of these when the opportunity suited him. But while this dilettantism allowed him to pretend to be a man of importance, it led to sloppiness in his running of the one organization that still served an important purpose in the city.

Although Gluck put great energy into juggling his various schemes and identities, he let much else about the association slide. Since the

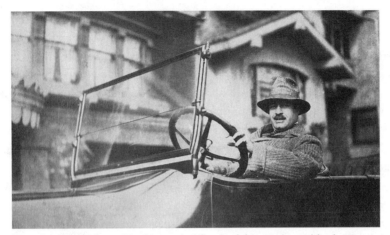

Money rolled in from Gluck's myriad fund-raising work, and he kept up appearances with new clothes, a stylish automobile, and more.
COURTESY OF FRANCES GLUCK.

end of the US Boy Scout had wiped out his investigative team, he had simply stopped doing any follow-up on questionable Santa letters. At the same time, the group's overhead costs had somehow ballooned, with Gluck claiming to those who asked that there were at least a dozen directors pulling salaries, despite maintaining in the press that the association was entirely volunteers. While thousands of dollars rolled into the group through fund-raising, it seemed there was never enough to cover the costs of postage. Gluck's driving concern was pulling in funds, positive press coverage, and high-profile endorsements. Gone was his concern about running an exacting, effective system, and in its place he had embraced the very excesses, inefficiencies, and lies he once claimed the Santa Claus Association remedied.

This was clear to any volunteers who stuck around the headquarters long enough. The end of the 1925 season saw a mass exodus of officers. Samuel Brill stepped away from his position as honorary president. The entire Finance Committee vanished from the masthead, and in its place Gluck named himself secretary (along with his title as president of the Capital & Labor Bureau, Inc.). The Brooklyn chapter was dissolved.

Gluck replenished the list of honorary vice presidents in the face of these departures. He sent out mailers to members of Congress, political leaders, and postmasters, asking them to accept the position "in the interest of poor kiddies," explaining that "This organization permits no drives for money and it has never had a financial deficit." For most, this was enough to agree to the honorary position. Some expressed concern, asking why the association contacted them specifically. When Harvard social ethics professor Sheldon Glueck made such an inquiry, he was assured that while most of the names on the list were known personally by the group's founder, "When our committees are depleted through death from time to time, we have a time honored custom of drawing the last name" of a new member at random, who is usually "a stranger to our committee." In fact, almost all honorary officers were strangers to Gluck.

Most of the Santa Claus Association officers had lost faith in their leader, but his tall tales still proved charming to at least a few appreciative listeners. In 1926, Gluck married Gertrude Avery. Two decades his junior, just as Symona Boniface had been, Avery was a graduate nurse of Beaverton, Ontario, who had moved to New York City several years before. It was a relatively subdued marriage ceremony, taking place in the Manhattan Municipal Building—the same structure that housed Coler's office. Three times would be the charm with Gluck's marriages. By all accounts the two were well matched. She dressed impeccably, laughed easily, and wore fragrant perfume. Several inches taller than he, she had a sense of humor and flair to compete with the Santa Claus Man, and she was totally smitten. "She thought he was the moon, the sun, and the stars," Gluck's niece Muriel recalled of their relationship. "She could hear the same joke fifty-thousand times and would still laugh like she'd just heard it the first time." Unlike his first two short-lived nuptials, this one would last decades.

But joyous as the event was for Gluck and the new Mrs. Gertrude Gluck, his timing was surprising. For a man born on Christmas Day, who took holidays seriously, their wedding date drew some surprise: as one newspaper headline stated, "Santa Claus Marries on Friday the 13th." Gluck and Avery were one of just sixty-one couples who received their marriage license in New York City on Friday, August 13, 1926—the average number for a weekday wedding was about 150 couples. But this just put a greater spotlight on the Santa Claus Man. "J. D. Gluck, 'Santa Claus,' Is One of Those to Defy Superstition," read the *New York Times* headline, mentioning just one other individual—John Davis Dun, editor of the *Toledo Times*—as among those marrying on that date.

While Gluck would prove lucky in love on this third, final wedding, his luck in most other matters was about to run out.

In January 1926, Jimmy Walker ascended to the position of New York City mayor, and Coler's political future was thrown into question. Though a Democrat like Coler, Walker was a bon vivant embodiment of Jazz Age New York and could not have been more different in temperament and style from the dour public welfare commissioner.

But while he swapped in his own men for many of Mayor Hylan's appointees, the "Playboy Mayor" held on to Coler. After eight years in the position, the commissioner lived up to his promise as a sharp guardian of the city's spending. Beyond trimming New York's bloated welfare apparatus and exposing fraudulent charities, Coler had made substantial reforms in the city hospitals. He instituted citywide standards from the American College of Surgeons and demanded that hospitals carry thorough case records to ensure they were not covering up mistakes. Two years after implementing these standards, Coler was able to report that all hospitals under his department had attained Class A in their inspections—the top level.

But soon into his tenure, Walker set about implementing his own program for the improvement of the hospitals, allotting almost $6 million over three years to be spent on improving Brooklyn's Kings County Hospital, which Coler was to oversee. The overcrowded and dilapidated medical center was in desperate need of a new surgical pavilion and maternity ward, where almost six hundred patients would cram into a space meant to hold half that. The mortuary got so crowded that bodies had to be placed on the floor. But instead of simply alleviating the congestion by buying up more beds and equipment, Coler applied the funds to something more ambitious: a seven-story, state-of-the-art laboratory to be used as a research facility by students of Long Island College. He sought to leave a legacy of elevating New York City to a paragon of medical education. This was not what Walker had asked the commissioner to do. But since the mayor paid only intermittent attention to the activities of many of his officials, Coler got far along in his transformation of the hospital before Walker was made aware. When he learned Coler had been spending millions of dollars on his own plans, the mayor grew furious.

Walker confronted Coler at a Board of Estimate meeting when the money was being discussed. The dapper mayor looked about the chamber and, seeing that Coler had not shown up, began to speak as if censuring a disobedient child: "I do not see the Commissioner of Public Welfare," he called out. "The Commissioner had better be here at a time like this. A matter of $5,820,000 does not push itself. There should be somebody here to advocate this expenditure and inform us how the money already allocated is being spent."

One of Coler's subordinates, seated in the audience, sheepishly ducked out and called his boss. In fifteen minutes the commissioner rushed in, flustered. The mayor gave Coler a brutal dressing-down. "You are pushing this laboratory to completion for the benefit of a private institution, and with city money which is sorely needed to provide beds for sick patients and adequate and sanitary facilities for surgical and maternity cases," Walker went on. In the end, the Committee of the Whole voted to appropriate $60,000 to modify the laboratory Coler had labored over so that it could be converted to a surgical pavilion. While the papers openly discussed whether this would be the end of Coler, the commissioner continued in his post and assured reporters, "I have not been asked to resign, and I do not intend to resign."

But in July, two months after the disastrous Board of Estimate meeting, Walker announced that he would unify all the city hospitals into a new Department of Hospitals—bringing together all twenty-seven institutions operated by the Public Welfare Commission, Health Department, and Board of Trustees of Bellevue and Allied Hospitals under one department head. The move aimed to bring greater consistency to the city hospitals but, as the *Times* put it, "If the Mayor is intent upon getting rid of Commissioner of Public Welfare Bird S. Coler . . . a new city department would give him an opportunity to do so." The *Brooklyn Daily Eagle* was pessimistic about the department's future and reported that "if these services are to be taken away, according to the views held at City Hall, the once important department will be relegated to the position of a minor bureau."

It was a major blow for a man who had made great strides in raising the standards of care in the city. Coler moved to at least consolidate his power over charities, and in the process grew closer to the Charity Organization Society. Working together, they developed the Welfare Council, charged with coordinating two thousand of the city's charities, which together brought in some $80 million each year for relief efforts. The same month Coler and the COS bolstered the work of the Welfare Council, the two drafted a bill that would further restrict street solicitations. It extended the license requirements New York City instituted all across the state, demanding any charity seeking funds get an annual license approved by the State Board of Charities and the local charity commissioner. "Business people throughout the State, and still to some extent in New York City, are daily harassed by so-called charitable appeals which have no legitimate organizations that need and deserve help," Coler explained. He was taking his charity-fighting crusade statewide.

Working closer than ever with the COS, Coler was finally tipped off about a group operating under one charismatic man—a group that used to drive a lot of public interest but was now just a scattershot scheme to rake in money. Coler's interest was piqued, and he determined that the next Christmas, he would add the Santa Claus Association to the top of his "to do" list.

CHAPTER 14

Spectacle on 34th Street

Are we living in an age when one may be destroyed overnight without trial or the presentation of a complaint?

—John Duvall Gluck Jr.

Gluck had a new scheme. This season, he gathered in his Knickerbocker office the handful of volunteers who continued to offer their help to the Santa Claus Association. Though his assistants numbered hardly more than one dozen, he told the press that for 1927 he had the help of six hundred clerks and one hundred district captains to help him do Santa's work. But while he inflated these numbers, Gluck's big innovation this year was not a newly exaggerated claim about the association's accomplishments or an elaborate new publicity stunt. For 1927, as Gluck explained to his volunteers late in November, the major change to the group would be what it asked from its donors.

Unlike in years past, this season they would not wait for the Post Office Department to send the children's Santa letters. It may have been that donations were not flowing as they once had, or that Gluck's wants had grown so far beyond what the association's usual methods could generate that he decided to get more aggressive in his fund-raising. This season, Gluck informed his helpers that they would begin sending out solicitations before the postman delivered a single Santa letter to the Knickerbocker. The association's 1927 appeals would not include a Santa letter with each request for assistance. They would not ask recipients to answer Santa letters at all, nor would they request volunteers help the group. This year, the association would only ask for checks, made out to the association and sent as soon as possible, if they were to help spread Christmas cheer in the city.

Gluck had come a long way from his assertion to Edward Marshall fourteen years earlier that what differentiated the association was its "direct service, not rendered through the medium of a charitable association whose operations would eat up a portion of the proceeds." Now his association was promising to buy the gifts itself, eating up more than just a "portion" of the proceeds in the process.

With no time to lose, the helpers got to work typing, stamping, and mailing hundreds of fund-raising letters. In the midst of their furious activity, Gluck could have watched from his eighth-floor office at Broadway and Forty-Second Street a most impressive display in progress on Thanksgiving Day.

Thursday, November 24, 1927, officially marked the beginning of the Christmas season in New York City. A few decades before, merchants held their holiday opening at the start of December at the earliest, advertising in newspapers the final week or two, and staying open late on Christmas Eve. But by 1927, the sales season had lengthened. What helped lock in this commercial jump start was a practice begun four years earlier, when R. H. Macy & Co. officially began "Welcoming Santa Claus to New York," as its newspaper ads promised. When the department store expanded in 1924 to take up an entire city block, with a southeast corner opposite the Hotel McAlpin in Herald Square, it sought a way to set itself apart as Santa's standard-bearer. Under the direction of master puppeteer Tony Sarg, the merchant launched its eye-popping inaugural Macy's Christmas Parade (it would not be called "Macy's Thanksgiving Day Parade" until 1935).

It was an exciting novelty in its first iterations, but by the year Gluck sent out flagrant requests for checks, Macy's Christmas Parade could be considered a New York City tradition. Gluck could see thousands gathered on the streets below as a series of floats displaying nursery-rhyme and fairy-tale characters—Red Riding Hood and the Wolf, the Little Piggies That Went to Market, and Robinson Crusoe preceded by a forest of walking trees—traveled south from their starting point at 110th Street. While from the eighth floor, Gluck would just barely make out the tiny members of the three bands providing the parade's score, he would have no trouble identifying the truly spectacular additions to the parade this year. This was the year the event took on the appearance of the Macy's parade we know today, with the introduction of giant inflatable character balloons, produced in partnership with the Goodyear Tire & Rubber Company (they would begin filling the balloons with helium the next year).

Among the creations being marched down Broadway was a twenty-foot-long dachshund and sixty-foot-long, smoke-breathing dinosaur escorted by a group of cavemen. Next came an even more striking figure. Towering over the police vanguard and festival volunteers was the twenty-one-foot-tall "human behemoth"—a giant man, who stood above everything else in the parade, and seemed to peer into second-story windows as he passed. So tall was the figure that it had to be tucked under the elevated train line at Sixty-Sixth Street and Broadway to continue the route. Impressive, commanding, and the center of attention—there was much about the character Gluck could envy.

Closing out the procession, behind a giant Yule-log float towed by a dozen woodsmen, Santa himself rode atop his own conveyance—the cockpit of an airplane. After crossing Forty-Second Street and slipping out of Gluck's view, the float stopped in front of Macy's newly expanded Herald Square store. Parade workers helped St. Nick ascend a series of red-carpeted steps to a throne, set on the marquee over the store's Thirty-Fourth Street entrance. There he assumed his post for the Christmas season. Seated, his fur hat was removed and in its place a crown set, officially dubbing him "King of the Kiddies."

Combining elements of immigrant culture with civic celebration, wrapped in a bow of opulent 1920s commercialism, the parade was the pinnacle of the new, public, extravagant form of Christmas. And it was here to stay. A century before, John Pintard had failed to install the moralistic St. Nicholas as the patron saint of New York City. But in the intervening years Santa had grown fat and jolly, abandoned his birch switch, and become less interested in punishing naughty children than in distributing goodies with ever-grander largesse. He had escaped the confines of the city's insulated homes and transformed into a beloved public figure embraced by merchants and marketers. By 1927, Santa Claus had metamorphosed into a character completely unrecognizable from Pintard's 1810 ideal—and was now finally ready to take his seat on Gotham's throne.

While the Macy's parade is now a staple of the holidays throughout the country, it was not until the late 1940s that those outside New York City could vicariously experience it through 1947's *Miracle on 34th Street*. The film follows Kris Kringle as he anchors the parade and enchants visitors to Macy's but struggles to convince jaded New Yorkers that he is in fact the real Santa Claus. In the film's climax, Kringle is put on trial and Judge Henry X. Harper demands that some "competent authority" affirm he is Santa or else face commitment to an insane asylum. This proof comes from a Post Office Department mail sorter, who enters the courtroom and declares that the dozens of mailbags full of letters addressed to Santa, abandoned in the Dead Letter Office, belong to the defendant.

Fred Gailey, Kringle's defense attorney, points out to the judge that the Post Office delivered all these letters, and that therefore the Post Office—part of the federal government—recognizes Kris Kringle as the one and only Santa Claus. Judge Harper, pushing aside the mountain of letters just dumped on his desk, concedes the point. Kringle embraces Gailey, shakes Judge Harper's hand, and the world can again believe in Santa Claus.

Commissioner Coler was not as easily persuaded as Judge Harper.

Under crushing pressure from Jimmy Walker and more eager than ever to flex what power he had left, Coler was on the lookout for dubious charities he could pound, as long as he had the evidence to take them on. The Santa Claus Association had for years avoided Coler's questioning eye, thanks to Gluck's claims that it was not a charity at all but simply facilitated Christmas generosity, asking only for time and gifts, not money.

But through Coler's work with the new Welfare Council and his warming relations with the Charity Organization Society, that began to change as he learned more about Gluck, the association, and their

Mayor Jimmy Walker presented the Santa Claus Association with the key to New York City in 1926. SANTA CLAUS ANNUAL.

penchant for exaggeration and misdirection. Excessive Christmas giving remained one of his bugbears. His 1927 holiday guidelines urged anyone feeling generous to direct their donations not to any secular charities, but to "the federation of your own creed"—the Catholic Charities of Brooklyn, Federation for the Support of Jewish Philanthropic Societies, or Federation of Agencies for the Caring for Protestants.

While Coler was hardly charmed by the Santa Claus Association's mission, its high profile attracted him. It remained the only group in the city charged with answering letters to Santa, and exposing its dubious practices was sure to generate headlines—an important concern for a commissioner struggling to demonstrate his relevance. The bow on top would be the rebuff it offered to Jimmy Walker. The year before, the unscrupulous mayor, always up for a playful public event, invited members of the association to City Hall, where he personally presented them with a key to the city. Investigating an organization the mayor personally endorsed could make a satisfying distinction between Coler's rigor and Walker's recklessness.

What the commissioner lacked was hard evidence of fund-raising malfeasance—something from which he could launch an investigation. But in 1927, as the days of December ticked by, the commissioner's contacts at the Charity Organization Society passed along a mailer that had been forwarded their way that they thought he might find interesting. Unbeknownst to Gluck, his new cash-grabbing campaign had inadvertently handed Coler just the weapon the commissioner needed:

The Santa Claus Association is the clearing house of little children's letters written to Santa Claus. The post office turns over these letters to us and after investigation we find means of bringing happiness to the deserving children, who would otherwise be neglected. In these letters their little hearts are poured out to the performer of miracles, Santa Claus. The Santa Claus Association in so doing brings happiness to the thousands of little children living in homes too often devoid of any cheer.

May we, dear Mr. ___, ask you to help us distribute Christmas cheer by donating $100? If so, please make your check payable to the Santa Claus Association and send it to the Knickerbocker Building.

Merrily yours, Santa Claus Association.

Despite all of Gluck's public assurances that the organization sought no money—only donors to provide the gifts themselves—here in black and white was an official solicitation for funds, with no child's letter and not even a request to buy a toy. And this was not asking for a few pennies to cover postage stamps, but $100—more than $1,300 in today's value. It was a blatant cash grab that gave the lie to Gluck's promise this was a unique sort of philanthropy. It also gave Coler the leverage he needed to look into how exactly the association was spending this money it raised. In the midst of another busy season for the Public Welfare Commission, the commissioner knew an opportunity when he saw it. He launched an investigation into the association, or, as the *Daily News* put it, "Bird S. Coler wants to know if there is a Santa Claus."

On Thursday, December 22, 1927, as Gluck was in the thick of association operations, Coler summoned him to his office. Receiving the summons, it likely struck Gluck as a mild annoyance. He had been investigated by at least a half dozen agencies and officials, none of whom had been able to definitively prove anything amiss about the group. His biggest concern was that this was the most important week of the year for the association, with checks and gifts coming in fast. But it was not a request he could ignore. So Gluck donned his expensive trench coat and bowler to protect him from the chilly winter day and made his way to the Manhattan Municipal Building. He wore round spectacles, gloves, black shoes, and spats, and he sported an impeccably waxed mustache.

Coler invited Gluck in and offered him a seat. Unmoved by Gluck's usual gestures of bonhomie, the commissioner wasted no time on niceties. He had a long list of questions and other business to handle this Christmas week and he was sure Gluck did as well, so he got down to business. The commissioner explained that he had concerns about the Santa Claus Association's finances and fund-raising, and he hoped that the group's founder could illuminate the workings of the group. With that, Coler began.

How much money is the Santa Claus Association generating from all these fund-raising letters? Gluck could not say. *Can you name the group's officers?* Gluck could not name them all offhand, nor did he know exactly how many were employed to investigate letters or buy the gifts. He would have to check back at headquarters. *Could you name the members of the board of directors?* He'd have to get back to Coler on that question. *Can you at least tell the Commission how many officials receive salaries?* He could not. *Well, then, who is in charge of the group's finances?* Gluck admitted that at the moment, despite his inability to answer the man's most basic financial questions about the association, he alone oversaw the group's finances.

Astounded by Gluck's stonewalling, Coler switched lines of questioning. *How many names are on the group's mailing list?* Gluck had no idea. *Well, where did you get their information?* From the Capital & Labor Bureau for Economic Research. *Who can we contact at this bureau for more information?* Well, he explained, as the founder and president of the Capital & Labor Bureau for Economic Research, Gluck himself would probably be the best person to ask, but he did not have access to the list at the moment. *With what other organizations are you associated?* Promotion and investigation were "his life work," Gluck explained—he could hardly list *every* group he organized or assisted when put on the spot like this.

The stalling, dissembling, and nonanswering continued for two hours. It became plain to Coler that Gluck could not, or almost certainly more likely *would* not, provide the information he sought. His obfuscations made it difficult for the Public Welfare man to even understand how the group ran, let alone where all the money went. He demanded Gluck provide him with the organization's documents, including a full list of the donations received and gifts distributed. Gluck protested: doing so would be an enormous inconvenience for the association at the moment, right in the midst of its busiest week. He described for Coler the vast operation he was running, painting a picture reminiscent of the group's massive second and third years: hundreds of volunteers rushing through the association headquarters, ladies in floral hats addressing envelopes, and celebrities dropping by. But instead of providing his much-needed help to these activities, Gluck was stuck in the municipal building, answering questions.

"It would interfere with the organization" mere days ahead of Christmas, he complained. Irritated, the commissioner threatened to get the district attorney involved. This threat did not worry Gluck. He had gone toe-to-toe with the DA a decade earlier and knew that he was operating, if barely, within the city's laws. He demanded that, unless Coler had any more evidence against him, the commissioner let him get back to the more important work of fulfilling the city's Christmas wishes. Knowing he had pulled all he could from Gluck for the time being, the commissioner reluctantly thanked him for his time. As soon as the Santa Claus Man left his office, Coler discussed with a few of his trusted advisors how to proceed. If Gluck refused to bring his books to them, he decided, they would get them from him.

The day after the acrimonious meeting at the Public Welfare office, Coler sent auditor L. Maltha to the Knickerbocker Building's eighth floor to have a look at the association's accounting. Gluck grudgingly allowed him inside, where the auditor noted tables that were indeed piled high with envelopes and notes being answered. But instead of the throng of volunteers and officers Gluck had described to Coler, on this afternoon just two days before Christmas, only five people sat in the quiet office, opening, sorting, and mailing the letters.

Gluck told the auditor that they were simply too busy with the Christmas traffic to deal with the commission's request and asked Maltha to go. He left empty-handed. Coler's third deputy commissioner, James W. Kelly, was mystified: "If the organization has nothing to conceal, we should be permitted to examine its finances," he said.

Gluck provided his own reason: "We think this whole matter is very unfair to us. It is remarkable that we have been permitted to operate without interference for thirteen years and suddenly be suspected. . . . Everything connected with the conduct of this Association is open to public scrutiny and entirely above board." He added that "the list of persons who have been willing to associate their names with the organization as the sponsors ought to place it beyond all suspicion."

Despite the "Esq." he liked to write after his name, Gluck recognized it might be wise to hire a real lawyer. He secured the services of Sidney Forscher, with offices just a block north of the Knickerbocker, in the Paramount Building at Forty-Third Street and Broadway. Gluck and Forscher pushed back against Coler's accusations, meeting with reporters the same day Gluck kicked the auditors out of his office. He attempted to use the public's sympathy as a weapon, a tactic that had served him well in the past. "All I ask is that people don't sock it to us this time of year and spoil the faith of little children," Gluck said. "Give me a chance to show I am fit enough and if I'm not, then quietly remove and replace me. I have yet to see any specific charges and wouldn't allow anyone to see my books today. That is looked upon with suspicion, but I did it under the direction of counsel. The least I have done is to dignify my movement with the names of great persons, from the President of the United States down to some in ordinary walks of life."

After making this statement, he handed each reporter a copy of the 1927 *Santa Claus Annual*. The *Times* noted the page with the picture of Jimmy Walker handing the association the key to the city. The *Daily News* ran a photo of Gluck exiting the municipal building under the headline "Charity Head Defiant" and took a critical tone to Gluck and his work. "The scope of many of the organizations this promoter-extraordinary, a stocky aggressive man with a waxed mustache who can and does speak appealingly for whatever interest he takes up, is nation-wide," wrote reporter Jack Kenny. "The usual mimeographed appeal the society mails with a letter to Santa Claus from a child or poor family contains this paragraph: 'If you are too busy, send us your check and our shopping committee will attend to the case for you.'"

But while Gluck was back on his heels, when reporters pressed Coler about whether he had received any formal complaints about the group, he had to admit he had not. The commissioner explained that the investigation had been launched on the basis of "inquiries as to the nature of the organization" but gave no further details.

Charity Head Defiant

(By Pacific & Atlantic)
John Duvall Gluck of the Santa Claus Association Inc., leaving the office of Bird S. Coler, commissioner of public welfare, after quizzing about his organizations affairs.

'Santa Claus' Closes Accounts to Prober

Gluck leaving Coler's office after their acrimonious meeting. The *New York Daily News*, which ran this photo, quickly became one of Gluck's most vocal critics. PHOTO BY *NEW YORK DAILY NEWS* VIA GETTY IMAGES.

Gluck and Forscher spotted an opening. "We would like to know either from Commissioner Coler or from anybody else who may be attempting to investigate the affairs of this association what this investigation is about and what improper act or acts, if any, this association or any of its officers have committed," the lawyer stated to the press. "To all well-wishers in the past, and to those who are not swayed by mere accusations the association desires to state that there is nothing it has ever done in its entire existence of which it is not proud, and there has not in the past, or now, been any improper act or acts." Both men blamed "charity forgers and pirates"—veiled references to the COS—for jump-starting the investigation in the first place. Gluck added that the *Daily News*, responsible for the most negative recent press about the group, had in fact referred 810 Santa letters to the association that season. "If the post office authorities didn't think we were responsible people, they would not have kept turning over the Santa Claus letters for us to handle during the last fourteen years."

New York postmaster John J. Kiely did not offer much assistance to either side. Named an honorary vice president of the association, he acknowledged to the *Times* that the letters were turned over under a provision of the law that allowed him to give the letters to any charitable organization deemed worthy. When pressed to explain whether he remembered giving the group permission to use his name, he admitted that he could not say for sure without looking at the correspondences in his files. In any event, he would not have time to get to the bottom of it before the end of the year.

Coler had to concede. Just as District Attorney Swann had found, the city had limited legal power to force an audit of Santa's Secretary. Gluck's behavior was suspicious but, without a formal complaint and evidence of wrongdoing, he could not raid Santa's offices. He would have to hold off his investigation. "[T]he inquiry," wrote a reporter for the *Herald-Tribune*, "is gradually subsiding."

On Christmas Eve, Gluck gathered the volunteers who were left in the Knickerbocker headquarters to make an announcement. From the same place in front of the window where he would have watched the floats and masked characters march down the street exactly one month earlier, he proceeded to deliver a sputtering, 3,400-word lecture that sounded at times lucid and other times a bit crazy.

"The first Christmas was nearly two thousand years ago. That night Three Wise Men in robes of crimson silk rode silently from the East into the West, each carrying on his saddle-bow a finely wrought casket." From that launchpad, Gluck digressed into Christmas's important role in promoting gift giving, kinship, and charity; the effectiveness of the association's approach to philanthropy; and the many institutions the group had helped to reach needy children—Wanamakers and Macy's, the Tuberculosis Association and the Red Cross.

He described some of the group's unusual cases: "The latest, Mickey, the Irish lad whom the clerks of a New York Bank have adopted as their Christmas present. It took us two weeks of hard digging to meet the requirements necessary for a visit of this very exacting Santa, but we got the order and nothing ever pleased me more. I claim that Mickey has the makings of a second [New York governor] Al Smith. Although I am a Republican, I am sure Mickey will be a Democrat and a great one, too."

Gluck cataloged his various enemies. "It is a matter of record that the *New York Daily News* sent us nearly five hundred families during a period when they were publicly attacking us," he declared. "To my mind the most remarkable example of newspaper jurisprudence that this city has ever witnessed." He criticized the Charity Organization Society, or as he called it, "certain professional charities today [that] have drifted from the hands of those who are the children of love . . . [to] the gold-rimmed spectacled professor, in a dungeon in the midst of a perfect labyrinth of scientific fungus, whose knowledge of human need doesn't extend beyond the bounds of the narrow confines of his den." And then: "These scientific sleuth-hounds; these emissaries of fat secretaries of clandestine information bureaus maintaining their suites in the highest-priced rental spaces in the world, surrounded by an impenetrable wall of impeccable and impervious meddlers."

And of course he went after the public welfare commissioner, who "failed to act in a conservative, dignified, legal manner. . . . We were the victim of St. Toogood, who talked so loud he broke the dishes."

After such an expansive rant that must have left at least a few of his listeners exhausted, confused, or perhaps inspired, Gluck concluded with a dramatic flourish. "It is Christmas Eve. Tomorrow will be my birthday. All of you like myself need to leave as early as possible. The halls and offices are crowded. People are standing on all the desks and the main hall in the Knickerbocker Building is jammed with good friends and well wishers. I thank you all for this demonstration of loyalty and good will. A merry Christmas to all and to all a goodnight!"

CHAPTER 15

Dead Letters

Now I must get back to work. Good-by, Good-by.

—Santa Claus

Gluck had survived Coler's scrutiny. But the public welfare commissioner was not about to give up. The first week of the new year, Coler's third deputy commissioner James W. Kelly again demanded the books of the Santa Claus Association. Gluck's excuses of being too busy with the holiday season no longer applied. If Coler could not subpoena the association, he was willing to publicly embarrass them until Gluck coughed up details. The Santa Claus Man decided the best way to pacify the commissioner was to give him something.

He called reporters to his Knickerbocker office on January 10 and handed each a sheet of paper. The heading read "Statement of Receipts and Disbursements, 1927." "I have never tried to avoid making this report," he told the group jotting notes as he spoke. He had provided the same paper to Coler's office, he explained. "It was not requested until December 23, and at this time of year it is difficult to obtain auditors in the first place. However, they have been working." He promised that anyone reading the statement would see how the association had done nothing but "brought rich and poor in closer contact and taken the sting out of charity." Gluck invited "any man or woman in the City of New York to call on me personally and file any complaint against the conduct of the office" and promised to keep the Knickerbocker headquarters open for ten additional days, just in case there were any such requests. He added that he never received compensation for his work, that he was an annual contributor to the association himself, and that no one had complained in all the years he ran the organization.

On the surface, Gluck's "Statement of Receipts" appeared to fulfill Coler's demands, with a list of earnings and expenses along with estimates of spending by the many donors who purchased gifts for the "kiddies" without using the association as a broker. The reporters accepted the document at face value. Coler did not.

The audit was not what Coler requested, and it irritated him that Gluck would insult him with such a ploy. In the association's apparent show of transparency, the commissioner saw that Gluck was answering the questions he wanted to answer. Rather than allowing the Public Welfare office to review his financial records, Gluck had tapped his own accountant, Eric Pusinelli, to prepare the statement and provided no supporting details or receipts.

It reported that the total spent on the association's efforts for the year, including the gifts that donors bought and delivered on their own, came to more than $106,000 according to Gluck's own calculation (about $1.4 million today), but he claimed only $4,400 came in the form of cash disbursements sent directly to the group. None of the rest of the money was supposed to be handled by the association, but none of it was accounted for either. Tens of thousands of dollars could be going anywhere, and because it was impossible to find another member of the group's leadership who could shed light on the operations, it seemed unlikely it was going to anyone but Gluck.

But even in such a specious document, the commissioner found other evidence of waste and dubious accounting. The total receipts by the association from the first of January 1927 through the seventh of January the next year amounted to $19,800, in addition to the balance of $2,730 on hand prior to the first of the year. Just $9,879 of that was alleged to go to relief work, with the rest covering salaries and other expenses. This contradicted Gluck's claims that the work was done entirely by volunteers. Coler looked at the numbers from the group's previous years. Every season, the cost of salaries ballooned—$126 in 1919, $3,695 in 1924, $4,265 in 1927.

The cost of "personal shopping" followed the same pattern—$2,341 in 1921 (the first year for which it was accounted), $7,612 in 1926, almost $10,000 in 1927. All of this was unsupported by any backup documents. Whoever was doing the shopping could easily be buying themselves a sizable share of the gifts. Even though Vincent Astor allowed the association to use the Knickerbocker Building for free, $1,662 went to rent in 1926. A $10,000 fund from 1924 that was to remain "untouched" according to that year's audit disappeared from the books two years later.

Then there was the mailing list. Gluck kept painstaking records of each individual who had been inspired enough by the Santa Claus Association to reach out to them. To that ever-expanding list, he added names gathered from fund-raising for the Citizenry Secret Service, the United States Boy Scout, and every other patriotic or charitable impulse he had tapped in the past decade and a half of promotion. Many of the groups had been shut down or discontinued, but the mailing list only grew. Under pressure, Gluck allowed the commission a brief look at this list. While Coler expected that Gluck's information resources would be significant, even he was startled by the list the Santa Claus Man had accumulated: seventy-six thousand names of New Yorkers, gathered one by one over fifteen years. Coler's deputy commissioner Kelly described it as the largest list of names he had ever seen and "one of the largest in existence."

But with Coler unable to take any further action due to the limits of the city's regulations on charity, Gluck could still claim victory. He stated that he had been exonerated of all charges against him, pointed to the wide support he received from other public officials on his "honorary vice presidents" list, and cockily told the papers that all the commissioner's inquiry had been able to prove was that he "possessed a waxed mustache." The *Bridgeport Telegram* ran with that crack for its headline, "New York Probe Proves Gluck Waxes Mustache."

Once again, Gluck seemed to have slipped from Coler's grasp. The commissioner soon got caught up in pursuing other charities and clinging to his job. He spent much of the summer and fall stumping for Governor Al Smith, a fellow Democrat as well as a fellow Catholic, in his run for the presidency against Herbert Hoover. His efforts made little impact.

Smith eventually lost, with just 87 electoral votes to Hoover's 444. The Friday before the election, with Smith's loss all but ensured, Coler paused the proceedings at an annual dinner of the Cumberland Hospital Alumni Association, held at the Montauk Club in Brooklyn. He wanted to make an announcement of his own.

"There comes a time when a man of long experience must give the benefit of such experience to others," Coler said. "And outside the department I may be able to talk more freely than I have inside. At the present time a fight between two interns who may hit each other gets a column in the newspapers. But the constructive work which the department is doing is lucky if it gets a 'stick' in the news." Early the following year, he explained, he would be stepping down from the position of public welfare commissioner. Though he did not say it, key to his decision was that Mayor Walker was pushing through his bill to create the new Department of Hospitals. It was sure to pass, removing a large portion of Coler's responsibilities starting February 1 the next year. Meanwhile, the commissioner's bill to bring his charity reforms statewide had floundered. The bureaucracy and thanklessness of his work had finally worn Coler down, and he urged the city to provide more support for the department's workers, even if he would no longer be around to benefit from it.

The battle with the public welfare commissioner had rattled Gluck, more perhaps than the implosion of the US Boy Scout. But now Saint Toogood was leaving his post. He would likely be replaced by one of Jimmy Walker's cronies, and the Santa Claus Association would be free to continue its work undisturbed. Gluck had survived another tangle with the authorities. He had seen before that New York City's public had a short and forgiving memory, especially when it came to Santa Claus. Just weeks after the group's confrontation with Coler, the *Times* ran a typically cheery story about the organization, explaining that "The Santa Claus Association, devoted to the care of needy children, takes charge of many [letters to Santa] each year." Things were getting back to normal. Gluck resumed his fund-raising and promotion of the group, speaking at the association's old headquarters of the Hotel Astor before the Convention of the New York City Federation of Women's Clubs. But as he took a victory lap, Gluck did not realize that Coler was a few steps ahead of him. The commissioner had one last arrow in his quiver, and this one would prove fatal.

———

In December 1928, New York City postmaster John J. Kiely, like his predecessor Edward Morgan, braced for a record-breaking year of Christmas mail. Although Morgan had faced several million pieces of mail, fifteen years later Kiely, working from his office in the elegant General Post Office, expected ninety million pieces. He hired three thousand extra mail clerks for Manhattan alone and more than tripled the number of delivery trucks. But the influx in mail was hardly as newsworthy as it had been on Morgan's watch. The parcel post had long been common practice; the sending and receiving of enormous numbers of holiday packages and the record-breaking spending on Christmas gifts was now unremarkable.

In the midst of this predictable frenzy, Kiely got a call from First Assistant Postmaster General John H. Bartlett. He wanted to discuss Santa letters. It was fifteen years almost to the day since another assistant to the postmaster general had called Morgan to tell him about a publicity man with some creative ideas about handling New York's Santa mail. As it happened, this call concerned the same clever fellow but had a less cheery purpose. Bartlett was checking to confirm that the postmaster had seen the order in the December 6 *Postal Bulletin*. It contained the first revision the Post Office Department had made to its policy of Santa Claus letters since permanently releasing them in 1913, sparked by blatant and long-running abuse of the policy by one individual—a New York City man within Kiely's territory. Bartlett was confirming the postmaster would act on the order immediately. Kiely said he would.

Contrary to what Gluck believed, Coler was not going to leave office without making a final push to end the Santa Claus Association. In his joust with the Santa Claus Man the previous Christmas, he had eventually ascertained the limits of his authority. Coler had no power of subpoena. He could pass the case to the district attorney, but the previous man who held that position, Edward Swann, and his assistant Edwin Kilroe had already taken a crack at Gluck and his phony charities, and he had slipped through their grasp. The Charity Organization Society and its leaders, going back to Barry C. Smith and W. Frank Persons, had tried to raise awareness of how Santa letters and the groups that answered them exploited the public's emotions and generosity, but the public ignored them and hailed the association as a wonderful, worthy cause. Bureau of Investigation agent J. W. Kemp had gotten the most comprehensive view of the Santa Claus Man's double-dealings but was only interested in spies, not crooks, so he left Gluck alone. Chief scout executive James E. West had inflicted the most damage on Gluck, toppling his lucrative US Boy Scout scam, but in the magnanimous 1920s, the Santa Claus Association soared back stronger than ever. Gluck's Citizenry Secret Service and Crusade against Illicit Traffic in Narcotics had been shut down, but Santa continued to stand tall.

So many strikes made on Gluck from so many angles, but the Santa Claus Association survived every one. What had these others missed that Coler might use against the group? The commissioner, relentless when he found a quarry worthy of his energy, would not step down without first toppling this blatant fraud. So it came as a thrill to the public welfare commissioner when he struck on a tactic that it was hard to believe nobody had tried before. It seemed so obvious: the key to the Santa Claus Association's undoing was in the US Post Office.

After his initial surprise the previous season when Coler asked him about the Santa Claus Association, Postmaster Kiely had since done some investigating and found that—unlike many names on Gluck's list—he had indeed given the group permission to use his name as an honorary vice president. "The Association had written me previously asking the use of my name, and when I saw the list of men who were honorary officers I said all right," he explained.

The support and original endorsement of the association by his respected predecessor Edward Morgan likely also played a role in Kiely's backing of the group. In fact, the relationship Gluck cultivated with Morgan, including positive mentions in the press and twenty-five-pound plum puddings, was no doubt key in keeping the post office from seriously investigating the organization since it had earned the privilege to answer Santa letters in the first place. It allowed Gluck, at first a stickler for following his detailed process, to over time give up any pretense of propriety. But now, learning that the group had grown lackluster in its methods, and uncomfortable with Gluck and his lawyer citing Kiely's name on the masthead as evidence of support from the postal department, the postmaster asked that his name be withdrawn.

This was a start, but Coler knew he would have to take his case further. He brought his findings to Charles H. Clarahan, head of the postal inspection service for New York City. He laid out what he had learned about the Santa Claus Association and what Gluck had refused, after repeated attempts, to tell the Public Welfare Commission. Clarahan contacted Gluck himself and demanded what records he had. Looking over the paucity of information provided, he determined that despite all of Gluck's grandiose claims of celebrity endorsements and hundreds of clerks and volunteers, "the Santa Claus Association is a one-man organization." Further, "the names of many prominent persons are listed on its letterhead, but they take no actual part in its administration. It has no treasurer. John D. Gluck is the whole organization and handles the moneys."

This was a conclusion at which others, including Coler, had arrived. Gluck's schemes were now common knowledge among authorities—with one investigation after the next and the Santa Claus Man's own contradictory statements to the press exposing the real beneficiary of Santa's generosity. But as Coler realized when passing the case to the postal inspector, Clarahan had an additional weapon that these investigators did not: the mail. Clarahan presented his findings to Kiely as well as Brooklyn postmaster Albert Firmin and First Assistant Postmaster General Bartlett. Reviewing Clarahan's findings, they had to agree: The group was untrustworthy and it was hard to characterize the association as anything but the moneymaking scheme of one man. It was a startling realization: the Post Office Department had for years been enabling a huckster, passively endorsing his campaign to line his own pockets with the city's Christmas generosity. That the malfeasance had been happening for years with the post office's support spurred Bartlett to move quickly to formally distance the department from Gluck's shenanigans. On December 6, he released the first formal change to the post office's Santa-mail policy in fifteen years:

As a result of a recent investigation by post-office inspectors the depart-ment is convinced that "Santa Claus letters," which postmasters under authority from the department are accustomed to turn over to charitable organizations and individuals for philanthropic purposes, have been used by certain organizations and individuals for purposes of private gain.

Postmasters are therefore cautioned in distributing such letters this year to deliver them only to established and well-known charitable organizations and individuals who are approved by the local associ-ated charities, community chest organizations, or municipal agencies charged with supervision of matters of this character. In other words, make absolutely sure that your "Santa Claus letters" are not given to some one who will use them for selfish purposes.

Every precaution should be taken to the end that the Postal Service does not lend its prestige nor become party to any scheme wherein the appeals of the needy or the charitable impulses of philanthropic persons are exploited for private gain.

With the formal ruling in place, it was up to the city postmasters to execute the rule. Bartlett called Kiely and Firmin to ensure that they did. On December 9, the postmasters publicly and definitively withdrew sup-port for the Santa Claus Association. "Fake Charity Caused Post Office to Change Disposals System," the headlines blared.

It was the first Gluck heard about it. He'd already received a few deliv-eries of Santa letters for the year, and he and his few remaining volunteers busily addressed and mailed fund-raising appeals from the Knickerbocker Building when the news arrived. Gluck was stunned. For the first time since the group had launched fifteen years earlier, a December day came and went with no mail for Santa. But Gluck's delivery did include an envelope from the office of the first assistant postmaster general. It was a copy of the December 6 *Postal Bulletin* along with a letter from Bartlett himself, advising Gluck that after reviewing the evidence with Clarahan and the postmasters of Brooklyn and Manhattan, they had decided: "We will stop your mail."

Gluck refused to believe it. He'd been doing this for a decade and a half, and survived lacerations in the press, the COS, and the Bureau of Investigation. How could the post office arbitrarily make such a decision now? Who would do a better job? Speaking from the group's headquarters, Gluck downplayed the decision. He promised that this was a small setback and the group would carry on. He pointed to several hundred letters he had just received from the Board of Child Welfare and plenty of other letters that had been sent directly to the Santa Claus Association, rather than through the postal service. He blustered that the group had been so successful that only a small percentage of letters even went to "Santa Claus" anymore—kids knew it was his association who would answer.

Coler was not going to let this slide if he could help it. As soon as he heard Gluck's statement about receiving letters from the Board of Child Welfare, the commissioner reached out to its leaders to tell them how the association did not foster the Christmas spirit, but preyed upon it. The board severed all connections to the group, and Gluck was forced to return their letters. Coler continued his phone calls, spreading the word to the lengthy list of famous names on the group's masthead. Reverend S. Parkes Cadman, the famed Christian writer and broadcaster who was the latest honorary president of the association (and the man who had dubbed the Woolworth Building the "Cathedral of Commerce"), publicly resigned amid the embarrassing headlines.

As the flow of mail to the headquarters slowed, Gluck, still constitutionally unable to recognize when he had been bested, desperately tried to keep it going. He called in every favor he could with his long list of press contacts but was rebuffed at every turn. The story of Santa's downfall was much juicier than another roundup of childish scrawls. The papers that had fueled his rise were now celebrating his collapse.

Gluck soon learned that the Knickerbocker would not be available to him the next year. By Christmas, the letters coming into the office and the public's support of the group evaporated. Without the endorsement of the US Post Office Department, the association lost its logistical ability to collect letters to Santa. But more importantly, it lost the city's faith. Like a reversal of the climax of *Miracle on 34th Street*, the letters to Santa on which Gluck prided himself were taken from him. His right to claim the title of

Santa's Secretary had been revoked as the postman literally walked into his office and removed the missives delivered to Gluck days before. Fred Gailey's defense argument held: Santa's power lay in his letters. When the Post Office recognizes a man to be Santa Claus, he is. But when the post office revokes his mail, the right to play Santa Claus is likewise withdrawn. The effort to which Gluck had dedicated fifteen years, which had filled him with a sense of purpose and importance, was taken from him, thrown in the Dead Letter Office, and destroyed.

—◆—

Without a reputable New York City Santa Claus to handle the North Pole mail, the Post Office Department was left with little choice but to send the letters back to the Dead Letter Office. The newspapers continued to print the children's notes, and scattered individuals stopped by the General Post Office to answer one here and there. But without an organization to take over the work left by the Santa Claus Association, to help remind the city of the existence of the missives, most of the letters were destroyed—unanswered.

Over the next years, Gluck made sporadic attempts to keep the group alive without the Post Office Department's involvement. As difficult as it was to generate interest in the association in 1928, when Coler was spreading the word about its corruption, the next years only got harder. The press and civic-minded people that had built Gluck into a modern St. Nick abandoned him. Worse, the stock market crash of October 1929 shattered the economic optimism that fueled the robust giving of the preceding decade. Production and employment collapsed. The American public's unqualified confidence in the market and deification of businessmen were revealed as myths just as desirable, but ultimately unreal, as that of Santa Claus himself.

In the winter of 1931, as unemployment climbed and the country entered a deflationary spiral, Gluck tried, as he had successfully done so many times before, to turn misfortune into opportunity. He went to his typewriter and drafted a letter.

"Your Excellency," he began his correspondence to President Herbert Hoover, written on one of the remaining pieces of Santa Claus

Association stationery. "Five Presidents of the United States have sent Christmas greetings to the children of America, through this Organization." He continued:

The writer has been a student of Christmas celebrations for a period of over thirty five years. In his humble opinion this Christmas is in a class by itself. WE NEED SOMEONE TO ORDER OLD MAN SANTA TO DO SOMETHING.

Why not inaugurate a national "Smile Week"—from Christmas Eve, December the 24th, until January the 2nd, 1932. Call it "Good Humor Week."

He asked Hoover to send a telegram suggesting that Americans "leave a note on all chimneys that the children of America ask their parents to smile during 'Good Humor Week.'" It was a letter much like those he had sent asking for prominent endorsements, benefit shows, a Christmas armistice, and for permission to answer Santa's mail in the first place. For years it seemed that some spirit had seen to it that Gluck's Christmas wishes were answered, but the holiday magic had since abandoned him.

George Hastings, Hoover's administrative assistant, forwarded Gluck's request to the National Information Bureau. The organization had grown out of former COS executive Barry C. Smith's National Investigation Bureau of War Charities and now served as auditor of the country's relief groups (characteristic of Hoover and his "associationalism," he put his faith in the private sector to assist in a government matter). The group had recently added to its roster of directors none other than Boy Scouts of America chief scout executive James E. West. Needless to say, Gluck's request did not receive a sympathetic response from this collection of enemies.

"When he first formed the Santa Claus Association, Mr. Gluck claimed that his only activity was to put donors directly in touch with children in need," wrote back the group's secretary and director, May H. Harding, in a page-long summary of the association and its dishonest practices. "In recent years, however, he has been flooding New York and vicinity with letters asking for checks and cash to be sent to him." The next paragraph of the letter, Hoover's assistant circled in blue pencil: "So far as we know, no satisfactory accounting of the books of the Santa Claus Association and the money sent directly to Mr. Gluck has ever been made. The Post Office authorities have, in recent years, made so thorough an investigation of Mr. Gluck and his activities, that they are no longer turning over to him the letters to Santa Claus which pass through their hands."

"On the basis of present information," she concluded, "this Bureau is unable to approve the Santa Claus Association." Hastings took the bureau's advice and pointedly declined Gluck's idea. "I am directed to inform you that the President does not wish to proclaim any special week at this time." The president, the country, and New York City were no longer receptive to Gluck's Christmas wishes.

———

Coler had won. The final undoing of the Santa Claus Association could not have been a more delightful note for him to end his up-and-down career as public welfare commissioner on. He took great pleasure in halting the efforts of a man who played on the emotions of the public, who exploited their naïve generosity for anything involving Christmas and children's welfare. It was a small victory in a decadelong crusade against such sneaky solicitors, but a deeply satisfying one nonetheless.

Coler's rout of the association was one of his very last acts as commissioner. Days after Gluck lost his right to play St. Nick, Coler's decade as charity sheriff neared its end with a retirement celebration in the glitzy ballroom of Brooklyn's Hotel Commodore, as the leaders he worked alongside for years gathered to honor his work. Many of Coler's ambitions had been thwarted, and he left the position with a sense of frustration that there was much more to be done. But he could take solace in the reforms accomplished.

Five hundred board members of the city hospitals and organizations that, at least for a few days more, still fell under the Public Welfare Commission's jurisdiction gathered in the Commodore. They were there for what the *Brooklyn Daily Eagle*'s editors described as a cheery and too-rare tribute to "a long term of distinguished service of which the general public has but little knowledge." After breaking the ice with a joke, wondering how men connected with city government could afford the $600-a-person tickets for the dinner, toastmaster Orrin S. Wightman, former president of the Medical Society of the State of New York, sounded a note of sincere gratitude. "I feel that the tribute we pay Commissioner Coler tonight is more than ordinary lip service, and I know the Commissioner feels that the tribute is one from the heart—in addition to a response from the pocketbook."

Over the next two hours, a string of doctors and city colleagues teased and praised Coler's long, often unglamorous career. They celebrated the length of his service to the city. They toasted how he changed public perception of Blackwell's Island by championing its name change to Welfare Island, helping remove the stigma surrounding the strip of land and services available there. He was applauded for being "an unrelenting foe to every form of trickery and every imposition in the name of charity that from time to time would be foisted upon a too gullible public." The speakers testified to Coler's character as a principled man less interested in pleasing people than doing what he believed to be right—a commissioner who spent this last decade embroiled in fights with charity groups and city officials often far more popular with the public than he, who preferred telling hard truths rather than delightful fairy tales. The heartfelt tributes from some of the city's and country's most respected men must have provided solace to Coler, a man unused to receiving public accolades.

After this string of speeches, Coler himself took the podium. He expressed gratitude for the kind words, but as was his nature, celebrating soon gave way to discussing business. He talked of frustration that the projects on which he worked did not get the attention they deserved, that the men working for him were making a fraction of what they ought. He could not resist another mention of the Kings County Hospital he once tried to build, with "every possible convenience and facility of the highest type for the care of the sick," which was not to be. But in the midst of his imaginings, Coler stopped himself. "Gentlemen, I could talk all night on other phases of this subject," and with that he wrapped up his speech. As a final gesture of thanks, Toastmaster Wightman strolled to the lectern and presented Coler with a small case. Inside was a Tiffany watch with cigar fob that reflected the Hotel Commodore's lights into the commissioner's tearing eyes. He had not expected such a gift. But before handing the trophy of gratitude to Coler, Wightman delicately turned the watch over in his hand and, in part to give the commissioner a moment to collect himself, read the engraving on the back.

"Presented to Honorable Bird S. Coler, December 14th, 1928, by the combined staffs of all the Hospital Medical Boards of the Department of Public Welfare as a tribute to his devotion to Public Service, in raising the standards and caring for the sick and helpless of a great metropolis." Coler was for a moment speechless, struck by a wave of emotion and gratitude. He gathered himself. "I appreciate this gift more than I can express," Coler told the cheering crowd. Then, ever the pragmatist, added, "I will take it home and get an insurance policy out on it tomorrow."

The good cheer of the dinner buoyed him for days. Having spent a decade curbing inefficiency and exposing phony charities, Coler was relieved to take his last Christmas as public welfare commissioner at a more leisurely pace. Instead of his more typical holiday activities of shutting down fraudulent fund-raisers and warning the public against imprudent giving, he helped organize events for the New York Cancer Institute and the inmates of Welfare Island's penitentiary.

Three days after his own fete, he attended a Christmas dinner for the young patients of the city's hospitals. More than three hundred disabled and destitute children were bused to Central Park, where they took a ride through the tree-lined paths that many, coming from the outskirts of Staten Island, the Bronx, and beyond, had never seen. From there they headed to Drake's Restaurant on West Forty-Second Street, not far from the Knickerbocker Building, where owner William Richters sprang for the cost of a massive turkey dinner for the assembled unfortunates. A mountain of Christmas gifts sat in one corner of the restaurant, the donation of wealthy businessman S. S. Rosen, who for years helped pay for cheery celebrations for the city's hospitalized children.

Vaudevillians and singers entertained the gathered group, and each child got his or her own folded-paper hat as part of the festivities. Getting into the spirit of the evening, the commissioner snatched up a hat of his own and popped it on his head. He joked with a few of the children and sang along to the Christmas tunes. When the time came, Coler began handing out toys, candles, and dolls to the eager kids, first one at a time, and then by the armful, unable to hide an uncharacteristic grin on his face as the invalids laughed and shouted with every new gift he gave away. For all his high-level reforms, improvements to efficiency, and exposures of charity frauds, the commissioner could not deny that sometimes it just felt good to play Santa Claus.

EPILOGUE

Operation Santa Claus

Soon after the unraveling of the Santa Claus Association, Gluck and his wife, Gertrude, left New York altogether. They moved to Miami, where, after some struggles, he found steady work as a real estate broker. He would never run another charity, perhaps because he had learned his lesson in New York or because the reforms and regulations instituted in the wake of the Great Depression made it harder for a man to fund-raise on little more than a worthy cause and a charming story.

Whatever the reason, this chapter of his life had passed, and Gluck rarely spoke about his time playing Santa Claus after leaving Manhattan. But his colorful personality remained intact. His niece Muriel recalled how "John would tell these wild stories about foreign potentates and India" and was always the person she would want to sit next to at dinner. His marriage to Gertrude was a happy one. It probably did not hurt that she never failed to laugh at his jokes. They remained together until his death in 1951, at the age of seventy-three.

Gluck never got his Santa Claus Building, but Coler's relentless efforts to reform the treatment of New York's poor were honored in 1952 with the opening of the Bird S. Coler Memorial Hospital on Welfare Island. Among his proudest successes had been to rename Blackwell's Island, notorious for its miserable conditions, to Welfare Island. He got the name changed, even if the name itself did not prove lasting—in 1971 it would again be rebranded, this time to Roosevelt Island. The hospital named after the hard-charging public welfare commissioner continues to provide long-term and rehabilitative care for the city's needy. Though it offers a great view of Manhattan, the quiet, tree-lined, nearly car-free island feels insulated from the city's clamor. A sense of order and peace pervades the place that would no doubt please Coler.

Gluck received no such legacy. His and the Santa Claus Association's work occasionally appear in holiday books and articles. A two-page magazine ad for Seagram's V.O. from 1976 offers a roundup of "eight old Christmas Classics"—individuals who impacted the celebration of the holiday, including "Yes, Virginia" respondent Francis Church, Christmas card inventor Sir Henry Cole, and St. Nicholas himself. Among these innovators is "Gluck, The Preserver," complete with illustration of the Santa Claus Man in suit, tie, and mustache, with no mention of his disgraceful end.

If Gluck has a legacy, it is that once he moved the children's wishes out of the Dead Letter Office, it proved hard to send them back. For years, the Post Office Department continued to offer the letters on an informal basis, with occasional help from private charity groups. In the early 1930s, clerks in the money-order division of the New York Post Office raised money to buy toys for the poor letter writers. In 1962, the New York City Post Office formalized the process of answering Santa letters under the program Operation Santa Claus, which got a boost from Johnny Carson as he would read a few letters each December on *The Tonight Show* and urge viewers to take part in the program. In 2006, "Operation Santa Claus" went national, along with an official set of guidelines for each postal employee.

Today, hundreds of local groups handle the routing and answering of Santa letters across the country under the umbrella of Operation Santa Claus. In New York City, the postal department employs a "chief elf" (a friendly man named Pete Fontana, who works from the same Midtown headquarters to which Postmaster Edward Morgan and his men moved in 1914—now called the James Farley Post Office). Fontana has refined the system over the past few years to ensure the privacy of the letter writers. Now, each letter is photocopied and assigned a number, and the children's names and addresses are blacked out. People wishing to answer a letter present photo identification and head to the Operation Santa Claus headquarters (the northeastern corner of the vast Farley Post Office) where they can sort through stacks of Santa letters, ten at a time, until they find the one that touches them.

Gluck, with his wife Gertrude at his side, leaving his cares behind. COURTESY OF
DAN PALMER.

    Gluck's public persona dissipated as soon as the Post Office Depart-
ment withdrew the Santa letters. He had sought escape, to add excitement
to his life and transcend his narrow existence. In some ways he succeeded:
during the 1910s and 1920s he rubbed shoulders with celebrities, saw
his name in print and on theater screens, and enjoyed adulation from the
press and public. But this all proved fleeting and vanished with the Santa
letters. In Miami, he turned his focus inward. His house became known
as a fun place usually filled with his laughter and that of his wife. He kept
up a regular correspondence with another niece of his—my grandmother
Emy, who saved many of his joking letters and postcards. For Labor Day
Gluck created his own booklet, with photos and captions of him and
Gertrude reclined in chairs outside their home, enjoying the lush grass
and palm trees. As always, they had glints in their eyes as if they had just
stopped laughing long enough for the photo to be snapped. The warm
weather seems to suit him, as if he found the escape he'd been seeking.
Another photo sent to Emy, from 1939, shows Gluck on a boat belonging to a friend, whom he cryptically refers to as "the son of the Spaghetti

King." He looks back at the mainland through a pair of binoculars, his arm around Gertrude's shoulder as she grins at the picture taker. Gluck strikes a mock-triumphant pose, a beret atop his head and his mustache waxed as always (and still a youthful brown thanks to a regular dye regimen). "I am observing the looks of panic on the faces of the bill collectors lined up on the shore," he noted slyly to my grandmother on the picture's back. "There must be five thousand."

Acknowledgments

Thanks to my agent, Michelle Tessler, for her constant support with this project and guidance throughout the process. Thanks to the team at Lyons Press for helping to ensure this book was as good as it could be, including Eugene Brissie, Jon Sternfeld, and Keith Wallman.

Big thanks to my uncle Dan Palmer, who tipped me off about the colorful character in our family tree and provided me with great material and support throughout the years of researching and writing this book.

I could not have written this book without the help of Gluck's nieces, Frances Gluck and Muriel Johnston, who were so generous with their time and memories of John. Sadly both remarkable women would pass away before this book reached publication. I am sad not to have known them sooner but will always be grateful to have had the chance to get to know two such wonderful people whom I can now consider family.

While direct and extended family members provided much of the original documents, a wide network of institutions and individuals helped to fill in the rest of the essentials. The New York Public Library and its microfilm room were my second home for more than two years. The NYPL's Archives and Rare Books Division's collection of McAlpin Papers was helpful.

The Smithsonian's National Archives, as well as the National Postal Museum and its branch librarian Baasil Wilder and curator of philately Daniel Piazza helped me piece together the history of Santa Claus letters and Post Office Department. Mark Leutbecker and Vicki Killian of Nicklason Research helped me sort through the National Archives. And thanks must also go to the US Postal Service's own chief elf officer Pete Fontana, who showed me how Santa letters are answered today. The New-York Historical Society offered up the fascinating history of Santa Claus, as well as materials on Washington Market and NYC hotels. NYHS's library director emerita Jean W. Ashton was especially generous with her time and insight into how Santa was invented in New York City. The

National Scouting Museum and its archivist, Steven Price, were invaluable in helping me piece together the history of the BSA, the USBS, and the battle between the two.

A special thanks to the Rare Book & Manuscript Library at Columbia University, where I gathered much of my information on the Charity Organization Society and its fight against Santa letters. The New York City Municipal Archives, Brooklyn Public Library, Brooklyn Historical Society, Herbert Hoover Presidential Library, and Harvard Law School Library also helped with background research or to fill in essential pieces of the narrative.

Researching this book, I got the chance to meet my extended family, but it also gave me a chance to meet the families of others connected to this story and learn a bit of their fascinating histories. Bird Coler's grandsons Bird Norton and Todd Coler helped me understand the public welfare commissioner. Laurel Brill Swan offered helpful details about her great-granduncle Samuel Brill. Nik and Marienka Sokol provided great info about their grandfather, the sculptor Joseph Kratina, who created the association's bust made from five thousand Santa letters (and who, it turned out, lived across the street from my apartment in Brooklyn).

Dave Herman and the Brooklyn City Reliquary helped me tell this story first in 2012 with an exhibit at their amazing space in Williamsburg. Thanks to their early interest in this story—and to Dave for several late nights of cutting and pasting photos for the show, which turned out to be a lot of fun.

Thanks especially to my friends and readers: Alexandra Ravenelle, Brian Kennedy, and Bess Lovejoy for their help in the early stages; Ryan Joe, Vincent Alonzo, and Sean McKissick for their valuable input during the later stages. Special thanks to my brother Nick, who read every version and joined in plenty of venting sessions, always offering spot-on suggestions for how to strengthen the story.

Thanks most of all to my wife Jennifer McCartney, who was there the night I first heard the story of John Gluck and has been there to discuss, revise, stress over, and celebrate the completion of this book. Not only is she an incredible editor, she has graciously tolerated the piles of Santa books taking up space in our small apartment.

Appendix

Timeline of Santa Claus in New York City

1804—John Pintard and ten other city elites found the New-York Historical Society. The group aimed to preserve important documents, as well as to reignite the "virtuous habits and simple manners" of Gotham's forgotten Dutch culture, including the veneration of St. Nicholas.

1809—Washington Irving publishes *A History of New-York* under the pseudonym "Diedrich Knickerbocker." A satire, it adds comical overtones to the ecclesiastical St. Nicholas.

1810—Pintard commissions a woodcut of St. Nicholas, the first known depiction of the character in the United States, and distributes it at the New-York Historical Society's first annual St. Nicholas Day dinner.

1821—William Gilley publishes *The Children's Friend*, the first known depiction of Santa with reindeer (though in this picture book he only has one).

1822—Clement Clarke Moore composes "A Visit from St. Nicholas," drawing together elements from Irving's book, Pintard's woodcut, and *The Children's Friend* to create a cheery, mercantile character. The poem is published the next year in the *Troy Sentinel*, and this version of Santa, and of domestic Christmas, quickly takes off.

1851—Mark Carr opens the first Christmas tree market in Washington Market. Many additional markets follow, helping spread the popularity of Christmas trees in the home.

1863—Thomas Nast publishes his first illustration of Santa Claus for *Harper's Weekly*. It begins a hugely popular annual tradition that will establish his version of Santa Claus, complete with workshop and assistant elves, as the definitive version of the character.

1870s—Earliest reports by newspapers of children using the Post Office Department to send letters to Santa.

1897—Eight-year-old Virginia O'Hanlon sends letter to the *Sun* telling of her friends who don't believe in Santa Claus. Editor Francis Church confirms that "Yes, Virginia, there is a Santa Claus."

1907—The United States Postmaster General releases Santa's mail for one holiday season but cancels the practice the following year.

1911—The new postmaster general again releases Santa's mail. The practice is made permanent two years later.

1912—New York City holds the first city-sponsored public Christmas tree gathering, in Madison Square Park. At least fifty more cities will adopt the practice the next year.

1912—Christmas giving becomes so excessive that concerned citizens, including Teddy Roosevelt, form the Society for the Prevention of Useless Giving.

1913—The new parcel post law allows for packages to be sent more cheaply and efficiently, opening floodgates of Christmas gifts. John Gluck launches the Santa Claus Association.

1924—Macy's hosts the first "Christmas Parade."

1933—The New York City Christmas-tree lighting moves to Rockefeller Center, the same year the Radio City Music Hall Christmas Show begins (which would grow into the Radio City Chirstmas Spectacular, featuring the Rockettes). While the first lighting occurred at Rockefeller Center in 1931, when demolition workers at the site erected a twenty-foot balsam fir, 1933 was the year the official event left Madison Square Park.

1939—Robert L. May writes *Rudolph the Red-Nosed Reindeer*, which is published and distributed by Montgomery Ward. A decade later, May's brother-in-law Johnny Marks, working from New York's Brill Building (named after Santa Claus Association honorary president Samuel Brill's clothing store on the ground floor), would adapt the book into a song.

1947—Fox releases the film *Miracle on 34th Street*.

1962—New York City Post Office launches Operation Santa Claus, a formal program to answer the letters Gotham children send to Santa.

2006—Operation Santa Claus goes nationwide, with branches throughout the country.

Endnotes

PROLOGUE: AN ARREST IN CONEY ISLAND

viii. *At 9:30 p.m.:* "Weather Forecast," *Sun*, September 9, 1913, 13.

viii. *It was New York City's:* "Outdoor Amusements," *New York Times*, September 7, 1913.

ix. *At such an exhilarating time:* David Nasaw, *Children of the City: At Work and Play* (New York: Anchor Books, 2012), 115.

ix. *Henkel sold tickets:* Advertisement, *New York Times*, September 7, 1913, 7.

ix. *Gluck could barely:* "Coney's Mardi Gras Opens in Splendor," *Sun*, September 9, 1913, 4.

ix. *Among the audience:* John F. Kasson, *Amusing the Millions: Coney Island at the Turn of the Century* (New York: Hill and Wang, 1978), 88.

x. *Coney was a place:* Jeffrey Stanton, "Coney Island—Second Steeplechase Park (1908–1964)," *Coney Island History*, May 20, 1998, www.westland.net/coneyisland/articles/steeplechase2.htm.

x. *If You Can't Break:* Kasson, *Amusing the Millions*, 59.

x. *The crowd was especially:* "The 'King' of Coney Island Dethroned at Luna," *New York Times*, September 11, 1913.

x. *It fueled the horde:* Patrick Amsellem, "Steeplechase, Luna Park, and Dreamland," *Brooklyn Museum*, January 16, 2008, www.brooklynmuseum.org/community/blogosphere/2008/01/16/steeplechase-luna-park-and-dreamland.

x. *The shop girls:* "Cops Best Actors at Coney's Bullfight," *Sun*, September 10, 1913, 3.

x. *And there is no reason:* "Coney's Mardi Gras Opens in Splendor," *Sun*, September 9, 1913, 4; the article refers to Gluck as "an excited press agent."

x. *The crowd knew this man:* "Man Who Fights Bulls Is with Us," *New York Times*, July 17, 1913.

xi. *Robles and his retinue:* "Man Who Fights Bulls," *New York Times*.

xi. *When the authorities:* "Bullfight Stopped, Crowd Burns Arena," *New York Times*, June 6, 1904.

xi. *A 1911 letter:* "A Spanish Bullfight," *New York Times*, August 22, 1911.

xii. *The doctors signaled:* Gluck would later deny the matador smacked the bull, and news accounts would vary, but the animal's reaction makes this the likeliest action.

xii. *In the past:* In 1911, the Humane Society claimed to have locked up 3,554 abusers to the SPCA's 2,293; the SPCA charged the Humane Society with making headline-catching arrests and doing little else ("Humane Societies in a Bitter Clash," *New York Times*, February 9, 1912).

xiii. *The officers frog-marched:* "Arrest Bullfight Men," *New York Times*, September 10, 1913, 20.

xiii. *The police eventually:* *New York World*, January 17, 1914, 10; "Bull Fighter Fined $25," *Brooklyn Daily Eagle*, November 19, 1913, 7.

PART I

CHAPTER 1: THE ADVENTURERS' CLUB

2. *Santa has a new scheme:* Janet Barry, "Christmas Opens Purse Lest Poor Children Plead in Vain," *Evening Telegraph*, December 10, 1913.

2. *But more than:* "Weather Forecast," *Sun*, December 8, 1913, 13.

2. *It would be two hours:* "Mitchel Gets Home, but Avoids Politics," *New York Times*, December 9, 1913.

3. *. . . 250 miles per hour:* H. Addington Bruce, *Above the Clouds and Old New York* (New York: 1913), 25.

3. *. . . lightning-deflection:* Karen Plunkett-Powell, *Remembering Woolworth's* (New York: St. Martin's Press, 1999), 91.

3. *The winds rushed:* "High Wind Blows Young Woman into Path of Automobile," *Sun*, December 9, 1913, 5.

3. *Eleven blocks north:* Advertisement, *Evening Mail*, December 10, 1913, 18.

3. *For fifty-one years:* Jeremy Seal, *Nicholas: the Epic Journey from Saint to Santa Claus* (New York: Bloomsbury USA, 2005), 193.

4. *"Paul Henkel knows:* Advertisement, *New York Times*, August 15, 1913, 9.

4. *No, Henkel's Café:* "The third dinner of the Adventurers' Club was given at Paul Henkel's Chop House, 58 West Thirty-sixth street, Manhattan, last evening," from "In the Social World," *Daily Standard Union: Brooklyn*, February 16, 1913, 8.

4. *I claim to be:* "Adventurers at Dinner," *New York Times*, March 16, 1913.

4. *Wooden chairs were:* Barry, "Christmas Opens Purse Lest Poor Children Plead in Vain," *Evening Telegraph*.

5. *My dear Santa:* "Santa Claus Will Answer His Mail," *New York Times*, December 7, 1913.

5. *A week earlier:* "Bomb Wrecks Shop, Alarm on Heights," *New York Times*, November 28, 1913.

6. *Dear Santa Claus:* "Santa Claus Will Answer His Mail," *New York Times*.

6. *The 1910s were:* Alan M. Kraut, *The Huddled Masses: The Immigrant in American Society* (Arlington Heights, Ill.: Harlan Davidson, 1982), 8.

6. *A day like:* Jacob A. Riis, *Children of the Tenements* (New York: MacMillan, 1904), 185–86.

7. *About a dozen:* "Form Santa Claus Body," *New York Times*, December 6, 1913; the article notes that Gluck had a "staff of from twenty to thirty stenographers," and Zoe Beckley, "Girls and Boy Scouts Work Day and Night Sorting Santa's Mail," *Evening Mail*, December 19, 1913; this article refers to "Not so numerous, but equally enthusiastic [as the Boy Scouts] are a bunch of pretty girls and young matrons who have volunteered their services and are working, thirty strong."

7. *. . . Flatbush Theatre:* Four months later, a wall would collapse during construction, killing four laborers. Rasmussen would be arrested, though released on $5,000 bail, and go on to construct the Bay Ridge Theatre on 72nd St. and Third Avenue in Brooklyn.

("Three Men Killed When Wall Falls," *New York Times*, April 3, 1914; *Architecture and Building* 50, 1918, plates 18, 19).

7. *Dr. William Edward Fitch:* "A Santa Claus' Will Answer Gotham's Kids," *Tampa Morning Tribune*, December 7, 1913, 10.

8. *Editor of the journal:* William Stevens Powell, ed., *Dictionary of North Carolina Biography: D–G* (Chapel Hill: University of North Carolina Press, 1986), 203.

9. *Though a member:* "Would Preserve Tots' Xmas Faith," *Telegram*, December 13, 1915.

9. *He described it:* "Former Westfield Boy Now Plays Santa Claus," *Standard*, December 24, 1915.

9. . . . *produce nautical charts:* "History of Coast Survey," *Office of Coast Survey*, www.nauticalcharts.noaa.gov/staff/hist.html.

11. *When John Sr. died: Westfield Leader*, November 6, 1907.

11. . . . *antique machine gun:* "A Trophy from Manila," *Evening Times Washington*, October 21, 1898, 2.

11. . . . *American-Asiatio Steamship:* "New Line to China," *Minneapolis Journal*, September 9, 1902, 8.

11. *When a wealthy British executive:* "Father's Cabled Ire Didn't Stop Elopers," *New York Times*, April 25, 1904.

11. . . . *bylines in:* John D. Gluck Jr., "John D. Gluck Jr., on Matting Customs," *American Carpet and Upholstery Journal* 25 (February 1907): 57–59.

11. *At the turn:* Richard L. Kaplan, "Transformation in the American Press, 1880–1940," in *A History of the Book in America*, vol. 4: *The Expansion of Publishing and Reading, 1880–1940*, edited by Janice Radway and Carl Kaestle, 116–39 (Chapel Hill: University of North Carolina Press, 2008).

11. *As mass media grew:* Scott Cutlip, *The Unseen Power: Public Relations: A History* (Hillsdale, NJ: Lawrence Erlbaum, 1994), 10.

11. *The field provided:* Public relations pioneer Edward Bernays would write in 1923: "there is probably no single profession which within the last ten years has extended its field of usefulness more remarkably and touched upon intimate and important aspects of the everyday life of the world more significantly than the profession of public relations counsel." Edward Bernays, *Crystallizing Public Opinion*, reprint (New York: Ig, 2011), 49.

11. . . . *Republican League:* "Will Erect Building Here for Santa Claus," *Evening Telegram*, December 26, 1915.

11. . . . *Merchant Marine:* "Voters League Meets To-Night," *New-York Tribune*, August 31, 1909, 2.

12. . . . *Good Fellows:* "Former Westfield Boy Now Plays Santa Claus," *Standard*, December 24, 1915.

12. *The successful years:* "Santa Claus Has Latchstring Out," *New-York Tribune*, December 7, 1913, 2; *New York City Directory* 1912.

12. *These traditional agencies:* Edward Marshall, "Played Santa Claus and Solved an Economic Problem," *New York Times*, January 18, 1914.

12. *"There are people:* Marshall, "Played Santa Claus," *New York Times*.

14. *A colleague who:* O. O. McIntyre, "New York Day by Day," *Reading Eagle*, February 10, 1938, 10.

14. *"Well, the boys:* Barry, "Christmas Opens Purse Lest Poor Children Plead in Vain," *Evening Telegraph.*

14. *Another asked for a new suit:* "Many Strange Requests Reach Modern Santa Claus," *New-York Tribune,* December 25, 1913, 9.

14. *Several writers:* Beckley, "Kiddies' Notes Full of Smiles and Tears Fill Bag of Mr. Santa Gluck," *Evening Mail,* December 11, 1913.

14–15. *Gluck grabbed up:* Beckley, "Kiddies' Notes," *Evening Mail.*

16. *. . . Insufficient Address:* Elizabeth Smith, "Childhood's Belief in Santa Saved by Generous Purses of Benevolent Citizens," *Evening Telegraph,* November 17, 1920.

16. *The 1910 Census:* New York City Census, 1910.

18. *Tower Manufacturing and Novelty:* "Santa Claus Will Answer His Mail," *New York Times.*

18. *Hammerstein sent an usher:* "Well! Well! Here's a $616 Roll That Owner Won't Take," *Evening World,* June 7, 1912, 14.

18. *They had good reason:* "Drink Made Jadwin Kill," *New York Times,* January 15, 1913.

18. *Before the shocked Minna:* "Beautiful Young Woman Killed by Husband in Presence of Her Family," *San Francisco Call,* January 14, 1913, 1–2.

20. *This concerned John Pintard:* James Grant Wilson, "John Pintard, Founder of the New York Historical Society," delivered December 3, 1901 (New York: New York Historical Society, 1902), 17.

20. *In 1810:* Charles W. Jones, *Saint Nicholas of Myra, Bari, and Manhattan* (Chicago: University of Chicago Press, 1978), 341–42.

20. *. . . saved sailors from famine:* "Who Is St. Nicholas?" St. Nicholas Center. www .stnicholascenter.org/pages/who-is-st-nicholas. Accessed April 4, 2015.

20. *"To the memory of Saint Nicholas:* Jones, 341.

20. *Versions of the poem:* In 1811, the *New York Spectator* ran a verse that borrowed heavily from Pintard's, beginning, "Oh good holy man! whom we Sancte Claus name, / The Nursery forever your praise shall proclaim" (cited in Jones, *Saint Nicholas of Myra,* 347).

21. *As historian Stephen Nissenbaum:* Stephen Nissenbaum, *The Battle for Christmas* (New York: Vintage, 1997), 50.

21. *. . . puffs from the:* Advertisement, *New York Times,* August 19, 1913, 11.

21. *. . . J. P. Morgan:* "History of Keens," www.keens.com/AboutKeens/History (accessed January 24, 2015).

22. *The apartments included:* "Classified Real Estate: Furnished Rooms to Let," *New York Press,* January 8, 1913.

22. *. . . proliferated along:* "Bachelor Apartment Houses," *Real Estate Record & Builders Guide,* January 21, 1905, 131.

23. *. . . more than twenty:* Beckley, "Girls and Boy Scouts Work Day and Night Sorting Santa's Mail," *Evening Mail,* December 19, 1913.

24. *As one of the most:* "Health Department Appeals to Mothers," *New York Times,* July 27, 1910.

24. *. . . ruled by gangsters:* "Policeman Shoots Leader of a Gang," *New York Times,* September 10, 1911.

24. *Riots, gunfights:* "Negro Shot by Policeman," *New York Times,* July 3, 1911; "Eight

Killed in Fight Riots," *New York Times*, July 5, 1910.

24. *"It was a gathering:* "San Juan Hill Gets Fine Playground," *New York Times*, September 10, 1911.

24. *Each member of the class:* Beckley, "Girls and Boy Scouts Work Day and Night Sorting Santa's Mail," *The Evening Mail*.

25. *The first delivery:* Barry, "Christmas Opens Purse Lest Poor Children Plead in Vain," *Evening Telegraph*.

25. *As Christmas Day approached:* Marshall, "Played Santa Claus and Solved an Economic Problem," *New York Times*.

CHAPTER 2: APPOINTED ROUNDS

27. *To send these appeals:* Letter dated December 15, 1911, Charity Organizational Services files, "Christmas Giving (Santa Claus Letters)," Box 105, Columbia University Rare Book & Manuscript Library.

27. *He assured Gluck:* Letter dated December 8, 1913, in *The Santa Claus Association Inc.*, January 1, 1916, 14.

28. *The headquarters:* "Post-Office," *Appleton's Dictionary of Greater New York and Its Neighborhoods*, 26th ed. (New York: Appleton, 1940), 225.

28. *This inadequacy never:* "Move Record Mail with Extra Force," *New York Times*, December 25, 1913.

28. *Eleven months earlier:* Henry M. Gobie, *U. S. Parcel Post: A Postal History* (Miami: Postal Publications, 1979), 1–3.

28. *... this meant rural:* Richard B. Kielbowicz, "Government Goes into Business: Parcel Post in the Nation's Political Economy, 1880–1915," *Studies in American Political Development* (Spring 1994): 150–72.

28. *It meant his men:* James Middleton, "Uncle Sam, Expressman," *World's Work*, vol. 28 (New York: Doubleday, Paige, 1914), 171.

28. *Mail Xmas Parcels:* "'Mail Xmas Parcels Early,'" *New York Times*, November 9, 1913.

29. *The committee discovered:* "To Stop Speeding of Mail Trucks," *New York Times*, November 26, 1913.

29. *... first airmail delivery:* "Ovington Takes First U.S. Mail through Air," *New-York Tribune*, September 24, 1911, 1.

29. *It held ten rungs:* "Edward M. Morgan Made Postmaster," *New York Times*, August 15, 1907.

29. *A few months before:* "Postmaster Morgan," *New York Times*, February 23, 1913.

30. *It would be the third:* "New Post Office Is Ready to Open," *New York Times*, December 28, 1913.

30. *It was far larger:* "Morgan Moves into New Post Office," *New York Times*, September 6, 1914.

31. *"Without exception:* Sam Roberts, "100 Years of Grandeur," *New York Times*, January 18, 2013.

31. *"the greatest public:* "50,000 at the Dedication of City's Great Library," *Evening Sun*, May 23, 1911, 1.

31. *"the largest building:* "New Pennsylvania Station Is Opened," *New York Times*, August 28, 1910.

31. *Morgan and his staff:* "Post-Office Ready for Move to New Uptown Building," *Evening World*, December 18, 1913, 11.

31. *He had received the gift:* "Postmaster M. Morgan's Happy Return to His Office Monday, Dec. 14, '08," *Postal Clerk* (December 1908): 28.

32. *On November 9:* "Postmaster Morgan Shot by a Maniac," *New York Times*, November 10, 1908.

32. *The earliest reference:* Theodore Ledyard Cuyler, quoted in Phillip Snyder, *December 25th: The Joys of Christmas Past* (New York: Dodd, Mead, 1985), 228.

32. *Fanny Longfellow:* Edward Wagenknecht, ed., *Mrs. Longfellow: Selected Letters and Journals of Fanny Appleton Longfellow (1817–1861)* (New York: Longmans, Green, 1956), 196–98; also cited in Penne Restad, *Christmas in America: A History* (New York: Oxford University Press, 1995), 54.

32. . . . *letters on the fireplace: Chicago Daily Tribune*, December 22, 1901, 39.

33. *Having letters hand-delivered:* Free city delivery, uniform postage rates, railway mail service, and class designations of mail all began between 1863 and 1864. about.usps .com/publications/pub100/pub100_076.htm (accessed March 26, 2015).

33. *"Though we had:* "Our Letter Carriers: The New Method of Free Delivery, Routes, Boxes and Collectors, Advantages of the Plan," *Chicago Tribune*, December 28, 1864, 4.

33. *"The little folks:* "City Matters," *Daily Phoenix*, December 3, 1873, 2.

33. . . . *the following year:* The sudden rise of Santa letters dropped into the mail—rather than near chimneys—may partly be due to two widely read works. The first is Thomas Nast's illustration for the December 1871 issue of *Harper's Weekly* with Santa Claus, seated at his desk, opening his mail. One pile, stacked to the ceiling, reads "Letters from Naughty Children's Parents" while a smaller pile reads "Letters from Good Children's Parents." The following year saw the publication of Emily Huntington Miller's poem "A Letter to Santa Claus." Originally published in the popular juvenile magazine *The Little Corporal*, the poem is ostensibly a letter from a girl named "Kitty Clover" saying such things as "This year, at least, when you empty your pack, / Pray give a portion to all who may lack." It was widely reprinted in local papers.

33. *"There are at present:* "Letters for Santa Claus," *New York Times*, December 22, 1899.

33. *"So the letters:* "Want to Play Santa Claus," *New York Times*, December 10, 1906.

34. *The Silver Belt:* "Additions Made to Santa Claus Fund," *Daily Arizona Silver Belt*, December 17, 1908.

34. *In some cities:* "Uncle Sam's Santa Claus Bureau in the Dead Letter Office," *Brooklyn Daily Eagle*, December 18, 1910, 2; the article mentions how "such bitter jealousies over the handling of the letters arose among charitable organizations in certain cities that the whole scheme had to be abandoned."

34. *"That vicarious activity:* "Post Office Resigns as Santa Claus," *New York Times*, December 18, 1908, 2.

34. *The former schoolteacher:* William Waits, *The Modern Christmas in America: A Cultural History of Gift Giving* (New York: New York University Press, 1994).

35. *No one knows my suffering:* "'Miss Santa Claus' Suicide," *Boston Evening Transcript*, August 11, 1909.

35. *Finally, in 1911:* Frank H. Hitchcock, "Order No. 5874," *Daily Postal Bulletin,* November 1, 1911.

35. *Two years later:* A. S. Burleson, "Order No. 7670," *Daily Postal Bulletin,* November 20, 1913.

36. *mail men disown:* "Mail Men Disown Santa," *New-York Tribune,* December 2, 1912, 4.

36. *. . . the only New Yorker:* Though the coverage did not name which clothier, it may have been Phillips Turnbull of Rogers Peet & Co., who would offer his assistance in the 1913 season of the association, and a company that regularly incorporated Santa Claus in its print advertising.

36. *"If Santa Claus:* "Santa Claus Is Tardy Saint," *Sun,* December 17, 1912, 1.

CHAPTER 3: TO ALL A GOOD NIGHT

38. *And the Christ-Child:* Arthur Farwell and Jean Dwight Franklin, "The Christ Child's Christmas Tree," in *Patriotic Drama in Your Town,* edited by Constance D'Arcy Mackay, 125 (New York: Henry Holt, 1918).

38. *The businessman:* "Tobacco Trust Gets D. H. M'Alpin & Co.," *New York Times,* November 22, 1901.

38. *His father would not:* "Gen. E. A. McAlpin Dies at Ossining," *New York Times,* April 13, 1917.

39. *Luxuries like:* "Flock to Inspect the Biggest Hotel," *New York Times,* December 30, 1912.

39. *It not only included:* Tom Miller, "The 1912 McAlpin Hotel—Broadway and 34th Street," *Daytonian in Manhattan,* August 23, 2011, http://daytoninmanhattan.blogspot.com/2011/08/1912-mcalpin-hotel-broadway-and-34th.html (accessed November 15, 2014).

39. *With the extra manpower:* "Santa in Need of Stamps," *New York Times,* December 18, 1913, 18.

40. *Norman Rockwell:* Cover, *Boys' Life,* December 1913.

40. *The BSA leadership:* David I. Macleod, *Building Character in the American Boy: The Boy Scouts, YMCA, and Their Forerunners, 1870–1920* (Madison: University of Wisconsin Press, 1983), 148–50.

41. *At this point:* "Gen. McAlpin Chief Scout," *New York Times,* August 13, 1911.

41. *"They will be the pillar:* "Defends the Drill of U.S. Boy Scout," *New-York Tribune,* February 9, 1915, 3.

41. *He loved the trappings:* The BSA also added "reverent" to the Scout Law when adapting it from the British version.

41. *He summed up:* Keith Monroe, "When Scouting Battled a Rival," *Scouting* (October 1990): 62.

41. *On March 23:* "Scouts May Attend Slain Lad's Funeral," *New York Times,* March 25, 1912.

42. *"That was the way:* "Headquarters Warns Parents," *Boys' Life* (May 1912).

42. *Despite the bad press:* Roy Marcot, *The History of Remington Firearms* (Guilford, Conn.: Lyons Press, 2005), 62.

42. *Members of the US Boy Scout:* Beckley, "Girls and Boy Scouts Work Day and Night Sorting Santa's Mail," *The Evening Mail*, December 19, 1913.

43. *Don M. Parker:* Letter dated December 17, 1913, in *The Santa Claus Association Incorporated*, January 1, 1916, 16.

43. *One notable addition:* Beckley, "Real Old Santa Claus Replied to Many of Kiddies' 14,000 Letters," *Evening Mail*, December 24, 1913, 3.

44. *New Yorkers just wanted:* Barry, "Christmas Opens Purse Lest Poor Children Plead in Vain," *Evening Telegram*, December 10, 1913, 4.

44. *So Gluck went to:* "Santa in Need of Stamps," *New York Times*.

45. *By December 13:* "Christmas Mail Heavy," *New York Times*, December 13, 1913.

45. *So large was:* "No Christmas Mail Tie-Up," *New-York Tribune*, December 21, 1913, 6.

45. . . . *more men would:* "Xmas Too Much for Uncle Sam," *New-York Tribune*, December 20, 1913, 7.

45. *"Too many gifts:* "The Super-'Spugs,'" *New-York Tribune*, December 18, 1913, 6.

45. *They explained that:* "Santa Claus Will Answer His Mail," *New York Times*, December 7, 1913.

45. *"Everything is being cleaned:* "Postoffice Force Busy," *New-York Tribune*, December 21, 1913, 6; "Parcel Post Mail Handled on Time despite Big Rush," *Evening World*, December 23, 1913, 7.

46. *By December 24:* "Santa in Need of Stamps," *New York Times*.

46. *With the Christmas Eve mail:* J. North Conway, *The Big Policeman: The Rise and Fall of America's First, Most Ruthless, and Greatest Detective* (Guilford, CT: Lyons Press, 2010), 185.

46. *"Mr. Vanderbilt requests:* Letter dated December 23, 1913, in *The Santa Claus Association Incorporated*, January 1, 1916, 26.

46. *"I enclose letter:* Letter dated December 22, 1913, in *The Santa Claus Association Incorporated*, 43.

46. *"I feel sure:* Letter dated December 31, 1913, in *The Santa Claus Association Incorporated*, 44.

46. *E. C. Schoonmaker:* Letter dated December 31, 1913, in *The Santa Claus Association Incorporated*, 55.

47. *We business men:* Letter dated December 23, 1914, in *The Santa Claus Association Incorporated*, 13.

47. *"The job was done:* Marshall, "Played Santa Claus and Solved an Economic Problem," *New York Times*, January 18, 1914.

47. *Gluck reached out:* "Santa Claus Has Latchstring Out," *New-York Tribune*, December 7, 1913.

47. *On the late afternoon:* "Letters to Santa Really Answered," *New York Times*, December 25, 1913.

48. . . . *stylish bob:* Photo in Barry, "Christmas Opens Purse Lest Poor Children Plead in Vain," *The Evening Telegraph*.

49. *It was Christmas Eve:* "Hundreds to Sing at Christmas Tree," *New-York Tribune*, December 21, 1913, 6.

50. *As a squad:* "City's Christmas Begins Outdoors," *New York Times*, December 25, 1913.

50. *Come, gather:* Mackay, *Patriotic Drama*, 125.

50. *As attendees drank:* "Food for the Needy at Christmas Tree," *New York Times*, December 23, 1913.

50. *The* Times *noted:* "What They Will Do at Park Xmas Tree," *New York Times*, December 22, 1912, 7.

50. *No matter how many:* The shifts to public celebrations have related in part to safety concerns. Each Christmas season brought reports of homes burned down when candles used to illuminate the tree got out of control.

51. *"That the public:* "Celebrate All over the Country with Community Christmas Trees," *Chicago Tribune*, December 25, 1913, 5.

51. *Its lights:* "Santa's Electrician at Jersey City Tree," *New-York Tribune*, December 25, 1913, 4.

51. *"In all, fifty cities:* "Hundreds to Sing at Christmas Tree," *New-York Tribune*, December 21, 1913, 6.

51. *In 1923:* "Event History & Timeline," *National Christmas Tree Lighting*, http://the-nationaltree.org/event-history.

52. *But Monroe Kniskern:* "Boy Shot Dead by Pastor's Son," *New-York Tribune*, December 26, 1913, 1.

52. *The Christmas entertainment:* "Boy Scout Kills His Playmate at Outing," *Sun*, December 26, 1913, 5.

52. *It was about two weeks:* Marshall, "Played Santa Claus and Solved an Economic Problem," *New York Times*.

53. *. . . fueling the Bakeshop Act:* Barbara C. Steidle, "Lochner v. New York," in *The Oxford Guide to Supreme Court Decisions*, edited by Kermit L. Hall, 161 (New York: Oxford University Press, 1999).

53. *Gluck was thrilled:* He would refer to the article later in glowing terms and reprint it in the *Santa Claus Annual*.

CHAPTER 4: THE MOST PHOTOGRAPHED MAN IN THE WORLD

57. *Broadway, Fifth Avenue:* Theodore Dreiser, *The Color of a Great City* (New York: Boni and Liveright, 1923), 275.

58. *The fund-raisers for:* Letter to Mortimer Schiff, August 17, 1910, in USBS file, National Scouting Museum.

58. *"I am very glad:* Letter dated January 28, 1914, in *The Santa Claus Association Incorporated*, 60.

59. *"Gentlemen: I will be:* Letter dated January 28, 1914, in *The Santa Claus Association Incorporated*, 62.

59. *On March 13:* Letter dated March 13, 1914, in *The Santa Claus Association Incorporated*, 28.

59. *The same month:* A January 1, 1916, pamphlet for the group puts the incorporation date at March 10, 1913, but this seems to have been in error. "Santa Claus Association Incorporated," *New York Times*, March 26, 1914.

59. *Rather, "its primary:* Santa Claus Association mission statement, *Santa Claus Annual,* 1916.

59. . . . *renaming his brokerage office:* Correspondences dated as early as January 28, 1914, list this address as the Santa Claus Association mailing address in *The Santa Claus Association Incorporated*, 60.

60. *It was built:* "Hotel Astor Indian Hall," promotional brochure in "Hotel Astor," George B. Corsa Hotel Collection, New-York Historical Society.

60. *Gluck's eyes bulged:* "Hotel Astor," Museum of the City of New York collection.

60. *Gluck could already:* "Santa Claus's Home Address," *Sun*, December 8, 1914.

60. *Dozens, sometimes:* "Santa Claus Complains," *New York Times*, December 14, 1914, 3.

60. *The "Immediate Aid:* "Santa Claus Cave, Hotel Astor, NY," photo by Drucker & Co. (1915 Scrapbook).

61. *"Anyone visiting:* "Santa Claus has announced . . . ," *Tacoma Times*, December 12, 1914, 7.

61. *"Children who thought:* "Children's Letters Keep Santa Busy," *New-York Tribune*, December 14, 1914, 9.

62. *A member of:* "Boy Scouts Find Stolen Baby When All Others Fail," *New York Press*, February 15, 1915.

62. *Isabelle watched from:* "Santa Claus Finds Child," *New York Times*, February 15, 1915, 14.

63. *Gluck went through:* His scrapbooks contain a few versions of the letter.

63. *Gluck promised to muster:* "Santa Claus Finds Child," *New York Times*.

65. *On January 26:* "Business Troubles," *New York Times*, January 27, 1914, 11.

65. *At the end:* "Business Reverses," *New-York Tribune*, January 28, 1914, 9.

65. *Henkel's would become:* "Oscar and Billy," *New York Hotel Record*, April 28, 1914, 10.

65. *So he moved:* "Santa's Taxi Wrecked," *New-York Tribune*, December 24, 1914, 5.

65. . . . *Hoffman House would close:* "Three Out, All Out, Is Finale of Closing Tale of Hoffman," *New-York Tribune*, March 21, 1915, 1, 4.

66. . . . *"Central to All:* Mary Henderson, *The City and the Theatre: The History of New York Playhouses* (New York: Back Stage Books, 2004), 115.

66. *No wonder in 1914:* "44th Street Lease by Keen's," *New York Times*, May 13, 1914.

66. *This "helped make:* Lewis Erenberg, *Steppin' Out: New York Nightlife and the Transformation of American Culture* (Chicago: University of Chicago Press, 1984), 40–41.

66. *They could see:* Nasaw, *Children of the City: At Work and Play* (New York: Anchor Books, 2012), 115.

66. *Theodore Dreiser . . . called:* Dreiser, *The Color of a Great City*, 282–83.

66. *It drew in some:* "Cyril Maude Dines," *New York Times*, April 27, 1914, 11.

67. . . . *he'd opened five plays:* Internet Broadway Database. www.ibdb.com.

67. *But then Gluck:* "Christmas Fund," *New York Times*, December 15, 1914, 8.

67. *Just the week before:* "Santa Claus Complains," *New York Times*.

67. *But unaware of these:* "A. H. Woods Aids Santa Claus," *Sun*, December 20, 1914, 8.

67. *Tickets ranged from:* Henderson, *The City and the Theatre*, 183.

68. . . . *"The Most Photographed:* Darwin Porter, *The Secret Life of Humphrey Bogart: The Early Years (1899–1931)* (Georgia Literary Association, 2003), 239.

68. *A year earlier:* "Action and Interest of New Photoplays and the Newest Radiations of Film Stars," *Ogden Standard*, September 27, 1913, 2.

68. . . . *some 269 films:* "Santa Claus, by King Baggot," *New York Clipper*, January 2, 1915, 12.

68. *It was such a bravura:* "The Reel King," *Day Book*, November 27, 1914, 15.

68. . . . *"Monarch of Hearts:* "King Baggot—Monarch of Hearts and Arts," *El Paso Herald*, May 3, 1913, 4B.

69. . . . *"time honored sleigh:* "Baggot Plays Santa for Charity," *Moving Picture World*, January 2, 1915, 87.

69. *But the eyes:* "King Baggot Plays Santa Claus," *Motography*, January 2, 1915.

70. *One reviewer called:* Nathan Hurwitz, *A History of the American Musical Theater* (New York: Rutledge, 2014), 78.

70. . . . *133 new productions:* VR Macbeth, "The Great White Way," *Times Square*, last modified September 25, 2006./www.timessquare.com/component/k2/item/1493-the-great-white-way/1493-the-great-white-way.

70. . . . *by comparison:* Internet Broadway Database; this figure does not include repertory productions.

70. *To help pull theatergoers:* "Even Actors Must Pay," *New-York Tribune*, December 19, 1914.

70. *The play's star:* "Many Rally to Aid Santa Claus," *New-York Tribune*, December 21, 1914.

70. *Those who paid:* "Time Curtain Rises Today," *New-York Tribune*, December 21, 1914, 9.

70. . . . *lavish detail:* "'Good Little Devil' Gives Rare Delight," *New York Times*, January 9, 1913.

70. *He portrayed Chick Hewes:* "Illustrated Screen Report: Kick In," *Exhibitor's Trade Review*, December 30, 1922.

70. *The actor would later:* Michael A. Morrison, *John Barrymore, Shakespearean Actor* (New York: Cambridge University Press, 1997), 51.

71. *But on this night:* "Even Actors Must Pay," *New-York Tribune*.

CHAPTER 5: "ENEMY, DEATH, AND A CHRISTMAS TREE"

72. *I expect you:* "Fraternizing between the Lines," *New York Times*, December 31, 1914.

73. *Secretary of the Navy:* "Daniels at Odds with the Experts of General Board," *New-York Tribune*, December 11, 1914, 1.

73. *Organizations like the:* See, for example, an ad in bottom right-hand corner of the *New-York Tribune*, December 11, 1914, 2.

74. *"We cannot:* "Making Santa Real to Poor Children," *New York Times*, November 2, 1914, C4.

74. *After careful consideration:* Letter dated October 17, 1914, "Records of the Department of State Relating to World War I and Its Termination, 1914–29" *National Archives Microfilm Publications*, Roll 282, Microcopy No. 367.

75. *"We believe if:* "Making Santa Real to Poor Children," *New York Times*.

76. *"[T]here are some:* Washington Irving, *The Works of Washington Irving*, vol. 1:

Knickerbocker's New-York (New York: George P. Putnam, 1851), xv.

76. *A few days later:* Irving, *Knickerbocker's New-York.*

76. *As promised:* Irving, *Knickerbocker's New-York,* xvi.

76. . . . *strong sales:* Andrew Burstein, *The Original Knickerbocker: The Life of Washington Irving* (New York: Basic Books, 2007), 73.

77. *Without Irving:* Jones, *Saint Nicholas of Myra, Bari, and Manhattan* (Chicago: University of Chicago Press, 1978), 344–45.

77. *Or, as Irving:* Burstein, *The Original Knickerbocker,* 86.

77. *You are good enough:* "Santa to Direct Big Peace Prayer," *New-York Tribune,* December 7, 1914, 7.

78. *In an odd coincidence:* "Pope Urges Truce over the Holidays," *New-York Tribune,* December 8, 1914, 1.

78. *He appealed to:* "Hopes for Partial Christmas Truce," *New-York Tribune,* December 9, 1914, 2.

78. *The Germans responded:* "Germany Agrees to Truce for Holidays," *New-York Tribune,* December 11, 1914, 2.

78. *The same day:* "Works Urges Full Export Prohibition Bill—Kenyon Asks Christmas War Truce," *New-York Tribune,* December 11, 1914, 2.

78. *Andrew Carnegie:* "Carnegie Opposes Christmas Truce," *New-York Tribune,* December 12, 1914, 2.

78. *German captain Rudolph Binding:* Stanley Weintraub, *Silent Night: The Story of the World War I Christmas Truce* (New York: New York University Press, 1994), 40.

78. *"[O]ur good friends:* "London Paper Piqued Hits Our Unreadiness," *New York Times,* December 16, 1914.

78. *They called support:* "Friends of Trouble," *New York Times,* December 17, 1914.

79. *Nonetheless, just as:* "No Truce, Says Russia," *New York Times,* December 12, 1914.

79. . . . *imitating a strategy:* "The American Red Cross and the First Christmas Seals," *American Red Cross,* December 23, 2013, www.redcross.org/news/article/Early-Christmas-Seals-Join-the-Fight-Against-Tuberculosis.

79. *"Well-known American:* "Making Santa Real to Poor Children," *New York Times.*

79. *"Do you know:* St. Nicholas: An Illustrated Magazine for Young Folks, Vol. XLII, Part I (New York: The Century Co., 1915), 24.

79. . . . *Red Cross threatened:* "Gifts for 3,000 Children," *New-York Tribune,* December 6, 1915.

80. . . . *titled* Golly: This name was not an expression of the boy's excitement or surprise at his gifts, as the title would imply today, but a reference to a popular but crudely stereotypical toy from the period. "Golly" was short for "golliwogg," a cartoonish character of a black man who appeared in children's books and toys beginning with Florence Kate Upton's 1895 book *Two Dutch Girls and a Golliwog,* which coined the term. Mothers made "Golly dolls" from discarded black and white fabric, until they became widely available from toy manufacturers. In 1910, Robertson Jam Company adopted Golly as its mascot, putting the grinning image on its jars and ads (where it would remain until 2002). Although such racist imagery has led to the nearly complete discontinuation of the toys, in 1914, a Golly doll was as popular a Christmas gift as a toy truck or teddy bear.

80. *But in December 1914:* "Santa Thief Returns Loot," *New York Sun*, March 1, 1915, though other reports put the value at $4,500, including the *Philadelphia Press*.

80. *So excited about:* "Picture 'Golly!' Missing," *New York Times*, December 9, 1914.

81. *PAINTING taken:* "Santa Claus Robbed: Meanest Thief Wanted," *Washington Herald*, December 9, 1914.

81. *Under the headline:* Lorillard Spencer, "Headquarters Notices," *New-York Tribune*, December 10, 1914, 11.

82. *The blank check:* "Santa Claus Complains," *New York Times*, December 14, 1914, 3.

82. *The Madison Square Park:* "City Glows with Festal Day Joys," *New-York Tribune*, December 25, 1914.

83. *Come, rally round:* "Letters from the People: A Christmas Carol," *Hartford Courant*, September 22, 1914, 10.

83. *Gluck dubbed the song:* "A Christmas Carol Free," *Moderator-Topics*, November 12, 1914, 246.

83. *The reason for the accident:* "Santa's Taxi Wrecked," *New-York Tribune*, December 24, 1914, 5.

83. *Gluck spent Christmas Eve:* "Santa Claus Association Gave Aid to About 50,000," *New York Sun*, December 26, 1914.

84. *The 1914 season:* "Immortal Santa Claus," *Outlook* (January 12, 1916): 66.

84. *... Princess Mary's Fund:* Weintraub, *Silent Night*, 10.

84. *The Germans rolled it:* Weintraub, *Silent Night*, 82–85.

85. *They exchanged buttons:* Weintraub, *Silent Night*, 97.

85. *"Mr. Gluck ... :* "The Santa Claus Man," *Santa Claus Annual*, 1917, 18.

86. *It seemed too great:* "Fraternizing between the Lines," *New York Times*, December 31, 1914.

86. *Here is the:* "Thief Returns 'Golly!' the Santa Claus Picture," *New-York Tribune*, March 1, 1915.

87. *The note was signed:* "Santa Claus Robbed: Meanest Thief Wanted," *Washington Herald*.

88. *Caught by surprise:* "Santa Finds Her Boy," *New-York Tribune*, February 15, 1915.

88. *"My husband had:* "Boy Scouts Find Stolen Baby When All Others Fail," *New York Press*, February 15, 1915.

88. *He had studied under:* The Republican Club of the City of New York, 1911 pamphlet.

88. *Over his career:* "Joseph M. Kratina, 81, Sculptor, Rodin Pupil," *New York Times*, March 29, 1953, 95.

88. *He created limited-edition:* "Bust of Santa Claus Made from Children's Letters," *Geyer's Stationer*, April 8, 1915, 70–71.

89. *Upon further inspection:* "Santa's Aides Honored," *New-York Tribune*, March 19, 1915.

CHAPTER 6: CATHEDRALS OF COMMERCE

90. *This is our:* John Kennedy Winkler, *Five and Ten: The Fabulous Life of F. W. Woolworth* (New York: R. M. McBride, 1940), 109.

90. *Years had passed:* When he did wade into the details of customs work, it was in showier roles, such as organizing a gathering for the Merchant Marine Committee of One Hundred ("Japan Sole Reliance, Says John D. Gluck," *New York American*, August 1, 1914) or publishing articles about the weakness of the country's ocean fleet (John D. Gluck, "Huge Merchant Marine Great Need of U.S. To-Day," *New York American*, August 4, 1914).

90. *Whatever the reason:* "John D. Gluck (#122696)," Old German Files 1909–21, FBI Case Files, 23, hereafter referred to by the case number.

91. *This behavior upset:* "8 Directors Quit U.S. Boy Scouts," *Sun*, February 5, 1915, 6.

91. *All proceeds from:* Advertisement, *Sun*, February 7, 1915, 7.

91. *McAlpin had asked:* Keith Monroe, "When Scouting Battled a Rival," *Scouting* (October 1990): 12.

91. *Then came the:* "Benefit for Boy Scouts," *New York Times*, February 4, 1915.

91. *"Why could there:* "Defends the Drill of U.S. Boy Scout," *New-York Tribune*, February 9, 1915, 3.

92. *They were told:* Monroe, "When Scouting Battled," 12, 61–62.

92. *. . . guarding against English:* Daniel Shaw, "Tribeca: On Quiet Streets, the Ghosts of the Washington Market," *New York Magazine* (May 4, 1987): 96–98.

92. *By 1858:* Helen Tangires, *Public Markets* (New York: W. W. Norton, 2008), 249.

92. *Famous visitors:* "Celebration of the Reconstructed Washington Market," souvenir brochure, October 25, 1915.

92. *The shoppers:* Mark Kurlansky, *The Big Oyster: History on the Half Shell* (New York: Random House, 2006), 186–91.

93. *This made the market:* "Christmas Preludes," *New-York Daily Tribune*, December 25, 1876, 5.

93. *"Here you are:* Snyder, *December 25th: The Joys of Christmas Past* (New York: Dodd, Mead, 1985), 30.

93. *"Christmas pervaded:* "The Night before Christmas," *Sun*, December 25, 1873, 1.

94. *In 1851:* Alf Evers, *The Catskills: From Wilderness to Woodstock* (New York: Doubleday, 1972), 442–43.

94. *By 1880:* Restad, *Christmas in America: A History* (New York: Longmans, Green, 1956), 111.

94. *. . . Moore's estate:* Hilda Regier, "Chelsea," in *The Encyclopedia of New York City*, edited by Kenneth T. Jackson (New Haven, Conn.: Yale University Press, 1995), 209.

95. *. . . five slaves:* Nissenbaum, *The Battle for Christmas* (New York: Vintage, 1997), 67.

95. *He had published:* Benson John Lossing, *History of New York City* (New York: Perine Engraving, 1884), 445. There remains debate about whether Moore was in fact the author of "A Visit from St. Nicholas." Don Foster argues in his book *Author Unknown* (New York: Henry Holt & Company, 2000), that the real author was poet Henry Livingston Jr. whose family claims he had been reciting the poem for fifteen years prior to the date Moore claimed to have devised it. While Foster makes a compelling case, the evidence in favor of Moore's authorship appears stronger.

95. *Upon his marriage:* Gerald Del Re, *The Story of 'Twas the Night before Christmas* (Gretna, La.: Wynwood Press, 1991), 33.

95. *When satirizing:* Clement Clarke Moore, "The Water Drinker," in *The Poet of Christmas Eve: A Life of Clement Clarke Moore, 1779–1863*, edited by Samuel White Patterson, 85 (New York: Morehouse-Gorham, 1956).

95. *He also gathered:* Duncan Emrich, *Folklore on the American Land* (New York: Little, Brown, 1972); Restad, *Christmas in America*, 47–48; Washington Irving, *A History of New York*, 174. It would be changed to the German *Donner* and *Blitzen* in subsequent years.

95. . . . *neighbor of Moore's:* "Saint Nicholas and the Origin of Santa Claus," *St. Nicholas Center*, 2014, www.stnicholascenter.org/pages/origin-of-santa (accessed November 24).

95. *He no doubt:* Moore's father served as a founding member of the New-York Historical Society, so likely owned one of the original broadsheets.

95. *"A portly, rubicund:* Joseph Jackson, "'The Night before Christmas': Its Author and Legend," *World's Work* (December 1912): 158.

96. *As his wife prepared:* "'Twas the Night before Christmas, 190 years ago, that an iconic poem was written in Chelsea," *The Bowery Boys*, December 24, 2012, http://theboweryboys.blogspot.com/2012/12/twas-night-before-christmas-190-years.html.

96. . . . *could appreciate:* Patterson, *The Poet of Christmas Eve*, 1–7.

96. *This friend then:* Patterson, *The Poet of Christmas Eve*, 17–18.

96. *The poem exhibited:* Patterson, *The Poet of Christmas Eve*, 123.

96. *Less charitable:* Jones, *Saint Nicholas of Myra, Bari, and Manhattan* (Chicago: University of Chicago Press, 1978), 348–49.

97. *As New Yorkers:* "Our August Markets," *Sun*, August 7, 1878, 2.

97. *One story headlined:* "Ugly Spots in Gotham That Might Be Removed," *New-York Tribune*, June 16, 1907, 46.

97. . . . *"[T]here are few:* "Dirty and Costly Marketing," *New-York Tribune*, December 29, 1879, 4.

98. . . . *"filthy disgrace:* "Dirty and Costly Marketing," *New-York Tribune*.

98. . . . *"like a miniature:* "Celebration to Open New Washington Market," *Sun*, October 24, 1915, 6.

98. *Perhaps most transformative:* "Reopening of New York's Most Famous Market," *National Provisioner* (October 30, 1915): 40.

98. *Initially slated for:* "Merchants Rebel at Market Plans," *New York Times*, October 7, 1914, 6.

99. *As he strolled:* "Weather Forecast," *Sun*, November 25, 1913, 13.

99. *In full view:* "Murder Merchant and Escape in Auto," *New York Times*, November 25, 1914, 1.

99. *In December, authorities:* "Ten Men Caught in Baff Murder," *New York Times*, December 17, 1914, 1, 6.

100. *So Gluck looked on:* "Washington Market Ready," *New York Times*, October 4, 1915, 6.

100. *"Old Washington Market:* "Old Washington Market to Reopen This Week in New $116,000 Suit of Tiles and Concrete," *New-York Tribune*, October 4, 1915, 5.

101. *He mustered all:* "Reopening of New York's Most Famous Market," *National Provisioner*.

101. *Listen, listen, listen:* "Washington Market to Have a Rousing Opening," *Sun*,

October 18, 1915, 4.

103. *Gluck (or whomever:* Walter Thornbury, *Old and New London, A Narrative of Its History, Its People and Its Places*, vol. 1 (London: Cassell, Petter & Galpin, 1873). Tufts Digital Library, http://dl.tufts.edu/catalog/tei/tufts:UA069.005.DO.00062/chapter/c30.

104. *Mayor John Purroy Mitchel:* "Washington Mart, Rebuilt, Reopens," *New York Times*, October 26, 1915.

104. *But the sale:* Larry D. Griffin, "Christmas Decorations," in *The Guide to United States Popular Culture*, edited by Ray Broadus Browne and Pat Browne, 170 (Madison: University of Wisconsin Press, 2001).

104. *In 1880:* Plunkett-Powell, *Remembering Woolworth's* (New York: St. Martin's Press, 1999), 45–50.

105. *After a trip:* "Christmas Decorations for Seven Generations," *Woolworths Museum*, www.woolworthsmuseum.co.uk/xmasdecs.htm (accessed June 6, 2014); Restad, 126.

105. *"For good or ill:* Plunkett-Powell, *Remembering Woolworth's*, 2, 166–74.

105. *Gift giving began:* James D. McCabe, *Lights and Shadows of New York Life* (Philadelphia: National Publishing, 1872), 577.

105. *While the feasts:* Leigh Eric Schmidt, *Consumer Rites: The Buying and Selling of American Holidays* (Princeton, NJ: Princeton University Press, 1995), 129.

106. *Woolworth bought up:* Plunkett-Powell, *Remembering Woolworth's*, 87.

106. *"55-story building:* "55-Story Building Opens on a Flash," *New York Times*, April 25, 1913, 20.

106. *He had provided:* "Changes at the Top Following the Death of Frank Woolworth," Woolworths Museum, www.woolworthsmuseum.co.uk/1910s-changes_at_the_top.html (accessed February 2, 2015).

106. *The executive had: Santa Claus Annual*, 1927, 21.

CHAPTER 7: CHILD WONDERLAND

108. *Mr. Gluck bids:* "The Santa Claus Association . . . ," *New York American*, December 10, 1915.

108. *From here he:* "Santa's New York Office Is Like the North Pole," *Evening Post*, December 6, 1916.

108. *. . . Gluck borrowed the:* "Features of New York's Celebration of Christmas Season," *Philadelphia Press*, December 27, 1915. The following year it would be loaned to the Frederick Loeser & Co. department store in Brooklyn, which would promote the "Special Exhibit of a Bust of Santa Claus" in its holiday ads. Advertisement, *Brooklyn Daily Eagle*, December 15, 1916, 13.

108. *Some forty new:* "Women to Aid Santa," *Brooklyn Times*, December 12, 1915.

108. *These women oversaw: The Santa Claus Association Inc.*, January 1, 1916, 4–11.

109. *The group's volunteer leaders:* "No Giddy Broilers of Sixty Can Boss This Santa's Shop," *Evening Mail*, December 17, 1915.

110. *"Call and see:* Print ad, *St. Nicholas Magazine*, December 1915.

111. *In addition to:* "This Santa Wants Help," *Evening World*, December 13, 1915.

111. *On December 8:* "Santa Has Branch Here," *Brooklyn Daily Eagle*, December 9, 1915.

111. *The proprieto,r A. G. Wegge:* "Santa Claus to Be Busy in All Parts of Brooklyn." *New York World* (scrapbook).

111. *Gluck claimed:* "Former Westfield Boy Now Plays Santa Claus," *The Standard*, December 24, 1915.

111. *F. May Simpson:* "How Would You Like to Be a Santa Claus?" *Toronto Daily News*, November 18, 1915.

112. *Omaha introduced:* "'Puss Puss' Company at Gayety Is to Aid Santa Claus Association," *Omaha Daily News*, December 12, 1915.

112. *The Charleston, South Carolina:* "Santa Claus Assistants," *Charleston Post*, December 16, 1915 and December 21, 1915.

112. *Gluck announced:* "4,000 Children Write Santa Claus," *New York Press.* 29 Nov. 1915: 12.

112. *Although he asserted:* "Santa Claus Prepares Dead Letter Answers," *Brooklyn Standard Union*, December 9, 1915.

112. *Specifically, the group:* "Santa Claus Wants 50,000 2-Cent Stamps," *New York Globe*, December 10, 1915.

112. *"[W]hile no begging:* "Santa Claus $3,000 in Debt," *New-York Tribune*, December 19, 1915.

112. *"What are you going:* "Money Embargo on Santa's Mail," *Brooklyn Times*, December 15, 1915.

113. . . . *They would pay the postage:* "P.O. Men Aid Santa," *Brooklyn Times*, December 13, 1915.

113. *By Christmas Eve:* "Cheered Xmas for Many," *Brooklyn Daily Eagle*, December 25, 1915.

113. *A boy named:* "No Giddy Broilers of Sixty Can Boss This Santa's Shop," *Evening Mail*.

114. . . . *hotel's Grand Ballroom:* Henry C. Brown, *New York of To-Day* (New York: Old Colony Press, 1917), 241.

114. *Women filled the box:* Photo and caption, in *Santa Claus Annual*, 1918, 7–8.

114. *The attendees then:* "The Theatre Assembly . . . ," *New York American*, December 18, 1915.

114. *The daughter:* United States Census 1910.

114. *Eager to follow:* "Reflections," *New York Dramatic Mirror*, February 7, 1912, 10.

115. *Her statement in:* *The 1916 Vassarian* (Poughkeepsie, N.Y.: Vassar College, 1916). Ancestry.com, *U.S. School Yearbooks* database.

115. *After a few enthusiastic:* Florence O'Neil, "Educational Values at the Theatres," *Educational Foundations* (January 1916): 300.

115. *Over the next week:* "To Give 4 Plays for Santa Claus Benefit," *Evening Telegraph*, December 15, 1915.

116. . . . *managers of movie theaters:* "Stage Folks as 'Santa' for 250,000 Children," *New York Press*, December 20, 1915.

116. . . . *she passed the hat:* "Marguerite Namara . . . ," *New York Journal of Commerce*, December 22, 1915.

116. *The group together:* "The Santa Claus Association . . . ," *New York Commercial Advertiser*, December 22, 1915.

117. *Among them was Symona:* Photo of group outside post office, *Santa Claus Annual*, 1916, 30.

117. *Barry explained:* "Plum Pudding for Morgan," *New York Times*, December 24, 1915.

117. *Santa had touched:* "New York Joyous as Santa Beams into Every Nook," *Sun*, December 25, 1915, 12.

118. . . . *just two years:* "Immortal Santa Claus," *Outlook* (January 12, 1916): 66.

119. *Gluck had commissioned:* "Child Wonderland Building Planned," *New York Times*, December 26, 1915.

119. *A frieze about the base:* "Santa Claus Association Plans Memorial to Children's Saint," *Brooklyn Citizen*, January 2, 1916.

120. *He was an aggressive:* "Douglas Robinson Dies Suddenly at 63," *New York Times*, September 13, 1918, 11.

120. *"This department:* "Santa Claus Association Plans Memorial to Children's Saint," *Brooklyn Citizen*.

120. *There would be:* "Plans Home for Santa," *Brooklyn Daily Eagle*, December 26, 1915.

121. *Many printed:* "Santa Claus Building Right Here Is Planned," *Sun*, December 26, 1915.

121. *"Recognized at last!:* "Recognized at Last!" *Hartford Herald*, December 29, 1915.

121. *"All effort like:* "Temple to Santa Claus," unknown Portland, Oregon, paper, December 27, 1915.

121. *"The only building:* "Hearst-Selig News Pictorial No. 104 (Dec. 30)," *Moving Picture World*, January 15, 1916, 473.

121. . . . *this new project:* "For a Building to Santa Claus," *New York Herald*, December 26, 1915.

121. *Now Gluck announced:* $300,000 was about how much such a project would have cost at this time. "Business Expansion in Uptown Centre Shown in Broadway Building Movement," *New York Times*, June 13, 1915, 92. These included the twelve-story Moses Crystal building expected to cost $200,000 and the twelve-story building at 31st Street and Fifth Avenue for $350,000.

121. *"Everybody in the world:* "Santa Claus Building Right Here Is Planned," *Sun*.

122. . . . *proposed to Americanize:* "Temple to Santa Claus," Unknown Portland, Oregon, paper.

122. *"monument to movement":* Donald L. Miller, *Supreme City: How Jazz Age Manhattan Gave Birth to Modern America* (New York: Simon & Schuster, 2014), 164–66.

PART II

CHAPTER 8: DOORS TO DECEPTION

126. *Dear Santy:* "Letters to Santa Claus," *Perrysburg Journal*, December 7, 1916, quoting letters supplied by the Santa Claus Association.

127. . . . *no public announcement:* An exact date is difficult to determine. I could find no marriage license or newspaper report, and the two may have never been officially married. However, about this time, there are references to Gluck's "wife" in association reports and the Gluck family Bible lists her as his second spouse.

127. *Despite the dozens:* "Opens Wide Doors to Deception," *New York Times*, December 25, 1915.

127. *They had once assumed:* "Want to Play Santa Claus," *New York Times*, December 10, 1906. "Letters for Santa Claus," *New York Times*, December 22, 1899.

128. *The likeliest explanation:* "The Neediest Cases Fund: A Brief History," *New York Times*, www.nytimes.com/ref/nyregion/Neediest_BRIEFHISTORY.html (accessed December 4, 2014).

128. *The very first case:* "Santa Claus, Please Take Notice! Here Are New York's 100 Neediest Cases," *New York Times Magazine*, December 15, 1912, 1, 14.

128. *The* Times *put:* "Gifts for the Needy Continue to Arrive," *New York Times*, December 30, 1916, 5.

129. *The COS aimed:* John E. Hansan, "Charity Organization Societies: 1877–1893," The Social Welfare History Project, (accessed August 11, 2014). www.socialwelfarehistory.com.

129. *The "friendly visitors:* Edwin G. Burrows and Mike Wallace, *Gotham: A History of New York City to 1898* (Oxford: Oxford University Press, 2000), 1160.

129. *It created a:* Burrows and Wallace, *Gotham*.

129. *As emotional and ineffective:* Referred to in a letter from W. F. Persons dated October 22, 1908, COS files, "Christmas Giving (Santa Claus Letters)," Box 105, Columbia University Rare Book & Manuscript Library.

129. *"They had a very pleasant:* Letter dated December 27, 1912, Box 105, COS files.

130. *While the* Times: "Want to Play Santa Claus," *New York Times*, December 10, 1906, 1.

130. *"Children were represented:* Mary Willcox Glenn, "The Santa Claus Letters—A Departure in Post Office Regulations," *Charities and the Commons* (December 5, 1908): 384.

130. *A representative for:* Glenn, "The Santa Claus Letters," 385–86.

131. *"Dear Santa:* "Plead with Santa to Give Them Cheer," *New York World*, December, 1908, 12.

131. *The visitor was:* Letter dated December 24, 1908, COS files, "Christmas Giving (Santa Claus Letters)," Box 105, Columbia University Rare Book & Manuscript Library.

131. *Upon investigation:* Letter dated December 23, 1908, COS files.

131. *Looking into the Ross:* Letter dated January 4, 1908, COS files.

132. *Many of these letters:* Letter dated October 26, 1908, COS files.

132. *"Complaints having been:* "Order No. 1950," December 17, 1908, *Records of the Fourth Assistant Postmaster General and Successors, 1837–1970,* Records of the Post Office Department, 28.3, Library of Congress, Washington, DC.

133. *When the question:* Letter dated November 2, 1911, Records of the Post Office Department.

133. *The New York chapter's:* Letter dated December 11, 1911, COS files.

134. *"With many thousands:* Letter dated December 15, 1911, COS files.

134. *"Santa Claus is a part:* Quoted in letter dated October 22, 1908, COS files.

134. *Another executive:* Glenn, "The Santa Claus Letters," 284.

134. *"The point of our:* Letter dated January 2, 1912, COS files.

135. *These included that:* "Calculation in 'Santa Letters,'" *Greater New York: Bulletin of the Merchants' Association of New York,* December 22, 1913, 12.

135. *The same year:* Letter dated November 10, 1913, Records of the Post Office Department.

135. *"This is a material:* "Santa Claus Charity," *New York Times,* December 29, 1915.

136. *"According to the results:* "Santa Has 1,000 Less Appeals This Year," *Brooklyn Eagle,* December 18, 1916, 2.

136. *It was also a fraction:* Glenn, "The Santa Claus Letters," 386.

136. *To help raise awareness: Santa Claus Annual,* 1916.

137. *. . . only seventy-five:* "Plum Pudding for Morgan," *New York Times,* December 24, 1915.

137. *. . . "How Mary Katharine:* Mary Hamilton Talbott, "How Mary Katharine Became a Member of The Santa Claus Association," *Santa Claus Annual,* 1916, 19–25. Talbott was not involved with the association but was a professional writer, contributing to *Good Housekeeping* and publishing a book of popcorn recipes.

CHAPTER 9: NAUGHTY LIST

139. *This, then, broke:* Irving, "The Author's Apology," *A History of New-York,* 18.

139. *Gluck liked to say: Santa Claus Annual,* 1917, 17.

141. *At the time Gluck:* "Marine Scouts in Drive for Smokes," *Sun,* September 25, 1917, 3.

141. *This was hardly the only:* Scott Cutlip, *Fund Raising in the United States: Its Role in American Philanthropy* (New Brunswick, NJ: Transaction, 1990), 118–19, 149.

141. *Organizations popped up:* "War Relief Tested by Charity Society," *New York Times,* December 9, 1917, 43.

142. *The concerns were significant:* "War Relief Bazaar Opens at Brighton," *Brooklyn Daily Standard Union,* September 7, 1916, 12.

142. *. . . "Red Card System: Santa Claus Annual,* 1917, 18.

142. *Those who answered:* "Mars and Santa Claus Meet Here," *New York Times,* December 23, 1917, 55.

143. *"Knowing the liberality:* "The Santa Claus Man," *Santa Claus Annual,* 1917, 20–21.

144. *Julius Kruttschnitt:* "Ask U.S. Boy Scout to Drop Their Names," *New York Times,* August 10, 1917.

145. *Seeing that his friend:* Don L. Hofsommer, "Julius Kruttschnitt," *Encyclopedia of American Business History and Biography: Railroads in the Age of Regulation, 1900–1980,* edited by Kevin L. Bryant Jr., 253–55 (New York: Facts on File Publications, 1988).

146. *At the start of the war:* "Scouts Body Drops 'Seventh Regiment' as Part of Title," *New York Herald,* May 28, 1918, 2.

147. *The USBS would later:* United States Boy Scout, "Answer to the B.S.A.," 3, in Baden-Powell Collection, Box Number 63, National Scouting Museum Archive.

147. *. . . saw the boys' mock battles:* "Malverne Sham Battles May Solve Modern War Problems," *Nassau Post,* August 27, 1915, 3.

147. *And he had died:* "Gen. E. A. McAlpin Dies at Ossining," *New York Times,* April 13, 1917, 13.

147. *. . . drew commissions of at least:* Canvasser Arthur Camp was promised a 40 percent commission, while Francis W. Winch pulled in 35 percent, according to a report from Supreme Court referee Adam Wiener.

147. *The USBS would claim:* "Very large commissions were paid to the officers and soliciting agents for collecting voluntary contributions, and that, except for the payment of commissions, there appears to be no indication of the manner of the outlay of $42,000 collected and $9,000 expenses incurred in 1917," Wiener would write.

147. *These boys would pay:* "Rival Boy Scout Societies Renew Battle in Court," *New-York Tribune,* March 26, 1918, 6.

148. *At least one:* United States Senate, Committee on Military Affairs, *Hearing, Regulating Collection of Money,* 65th Congress, 3rd session (Washington: GPO, 1919).

148. *Collector Edwin Southard:* "Urges Accounting for U.S. Boy Scout," *New York Times,* July 21, 1918.

148. *On July 31, 1917:* "Scouts in Court Fight," *Sun,* August 1, 1917, 3.

149. *"At first little:* Barry C. Smith, "Charities Control Needed in New York," *New York Times,* July 29, 1917, 29.

149. *The bureau was figuring:* Barry C. Smith, "Lessons from Indorsement Work in Relation to War Charities," *Social Welfare Forum: Proceedings of the National Conference of Social Work* (Chicago: Rogers & Hall Co., 1919), 705.

150. *"I believe that Mr. Smith's:* John Duval Gluck, "Plans for a Charity Service League," *New York Times,* August 5, 1917, 61.

151. *"Our records are absolutely:* "The Santa Claus Man," 19–20.

151. *. . . a clear, beautiful:* "The Weather," *Sun,* November 10, 1917, 16.

151. *Hundreds of uniformed:* "Girl Wins Medal as a Bond Seller," *Sun,* November 11, 1917, 16.

151. *As its name implied:* "The 'Recruit'—Our Only Land Battleship," *Popular Science* (August 1917): 212–13.

152. *Civilians could come:* "Landship Recruit Sails," *New York Times,* March 17, 1920.

152. *Amerman pinned the medal:* "Pictorial Section," *Evening Public Ledger,* November 13, 1917, 22.

152. *No doubt her father:* "New Liberty Bonds Are Sold below Par," *New York Times,* November 11, 1917.

152. *"You must be:* "Girl Wins Medal as a Bond Seller," *Sun,* 16.

152. *In an article:* "Champion Liberty Bond Seller Is a Little Girl," *Evening Independent*, November 19, 1917, 5.

153. . . . *two leadership qualifications:* "The Santa Claus Man," 27–28.

153. *It gave Boniface:* "Plays and Players," *New-York Tribune*, December 22, 1917, 9.

154. *Several members quit:* "John D. Gluck (#122696)," 30.

155. *Habicht paid twenty-five dollars:* "7th Regiment U.S. Boy Scout Probed," *Sun*, May 22, 1918, 8.

155. *He demanded that:* Letter dated May 20, 1918, Official Letters of NYC District Attorney, Roll 85, New York City Municipal Archives.

155. *"They said they:* Unfortunately, the New York City Department of Records' Municipal Archives only holds records of cases for individuals who were formally indicted, so more detailed information on the Swann/Kilroe investigation is not available.

156. *Swann asked Korn how:* "Investigation of U.S. Boy Scout Begun by Swann," *New-York Tribune*, May 22, 1918.

156. *But when Gluck:* "Scouts Body Drops 'Seventh Regiment' as Part of Title," *New York Herald*.

156. *The officer scouts grossly:* United States Senate, *Hearing, Regulating* (accessed August 17, 2012).

156. *Another barrier:* Smith, "Charities Control Needed in New York," *New York Times*, 29.

156. *"In failing to:* United States Senate, *Hearing, Regulating Collection*, 32.

157. . . . *"pitiless publicity":* United States Senate, *Hearing, Regulating Collection*, 28.

157. *It was a miniscule:* United States Senate, *Hearing, Regulating Collection*, 28.

157. *Indeed, Kilroe:* United States Senate, *Hearing, Regulating Collection*, 35.

157. *Despite consulting:* Smith, "Lessons from Indorsement Work," 707.

CHAPTER 10: GERMAN INTRIGUE

159. *We want:* Charles Loring Brace, *Home-Life in Germany* (New York: Charles Scribner, 1853), 225–26.

159. *"I have just a few:* "John D. Gluck (#122696)," 21–22.

160. *Woodrow Wilson accused:* Woodrow Wilson, Address during Flag Day exercises in Washington, DC, June 14, 1917, *Supplement to the Messages and Papers of the Presidents Covering the Second Term of Woodrow Wilson* (New York: Bureau of National Literature, 1921), 8276–77.

160. *Incidents such as:* Carmela Karnoutsos, "Black Tom Explosion," *Jersey City Past and Present*, www.njcu.edu/programs/jchistory/pages/b_pages/black_tom_explosion.htm (accessed October 31, 2014).

160. *These concerns led:* David Greenberg, "The Hidden History of the Espionage Act," *Slate* (December 27, 2010).

160. *This organization would:* American Protective League, Correspondence with Field Offices, 1917–1919, Entry 12, Box 5, Record Group 65, FBI Files, Library of Congress.

161. . . . *cousin Ferdinand:* American Protective League, Register of Members,

1918–1919, Entry 13, Record Group 65, FBI Files, Library of Congress.

161. *The Justice Department:* Joan Jensen, "Civil Liberties: A WWI Horror Story Ripped from the History Books," *History News Network,* http://hnn.us/article/960.

161. *When the bureau:* "John D. Gluck (#122696)," 15–18.

161. *The young Miss Adams:* United States Senate, *Hearing, Regulating* (accessed August 17, 2012), 37, 46, 58.

161. *Not surprisingly:* United States Senate, *Hearing, Regulating,* 14.

161. *The State Board:* New York State Board of Charities, *52nd Annual Report* (New York: J.B. Lyon Company), 27.

161. . . . *"a very affected:* "Helen Murray Adams (#2589760)," Old German Files 1909–21, FBI Case Files, 15.

162. *The agent concluded:* "Helen Murray Adams (#2589760)," 16.

162. *The only way to prove:* "Scouts Body Drops 'Seventh Regiment' as Part of Title," *New York Herald,* May 28, 1918, 2.

162. *"He's out for the money:* "John D. Gluck (#122696)," 33.

163. *A 1916 article:* "Citizenry Secret Service Calls for 1,000 More Men," *Evening Telegram,* May 26, 1916.

163. *The secretary of state:* The cabinet member, however, might have been familiar with the Santa Claus Association. The secretary of state, Robert Lansing, was the same man who had declined Gluck's appeal for a Christmas truce a few years earlier.

163. *But Kemp would learn:* "John D. Gluck (#122696)," 30.

164. . . . *never missed any:* "Fountain at Dinner Spouts Champagne." *New York Times,* June 3, 1914.

164. *Whitehead & Hoag:* Whitehead & Hoag was acquired by Bastian Company in the early 1950s. Shortly thereafter, all historical records were destroyed in a fire, according to the company. The bill was finally paid months later. "Satisfied Judgments," *Sun,* October 12, 1918, 14.

165. *As wartime set in:* "Take 200 Germans in Round-up Here," *New York Times,* September 27, 1917, 1.

165. *The Metropolitan Opera:* "German Opera Is Sung in Italian," *Sun,* November 22, 1917, 9.

165. *Schools cancelled:* "Historical Note," City University of New York, City College, Department of Germanic and Slavic Languages, Archival Collection Finding Aid, 81. http://digital-archives.ccny.cuny.edu/archival-collections/wp-content/uploads/2012/03/Archival-Finding-Aid.pdf.

165. *The German Hospital:* "Our History," Lenox Hill Hospital, www.lenoxhillhospital.org/about.aspx?id=102 (accessed November 2, 2014).

166. *"Let us do:* "Women Open Fight to Bar German Toys," *New York Times,* October 26, 1918, 14.

166. *When it became:* Plunkett-Powell, *Remembering Woolworth's* (New York: St. Martin's Press, 1999), 117.

166. *By 1918, the* Times: "Santa Claus Is Now in New York," *New York Times,* February 7, 1918, 14.

166. *In 1853, social reformer:* Charles Loring Brace, *Home Life in Germany,* 225–226.

166. *Upon observing:* Julius Froeres, "Emigration from Germany," *New-York Daily Tribune,* February 22, 1859, 5.

166. *In fact, it was a German:* Albert Bigelow Paine, *Th. Nast: His Period and His Pictures* (New York: Macmillan, 1904), 9–16.

166. *Nast filled Santa's:* Philip B. Meggs and Alston W. Purvis, *Meggs' History of Graphic Design* (Hoboken, NJ: Wiley, 2011), 162. Halloran, *Thomas Nast*, 192–193. Paine, *Th. Nast*, 319–320.

167. *Through the high-circulation:* Meggs and Purvis, *Meggs History*, 162. Halloran, *Thomas Nast*, 45–46.

167. *. . . Oval Office gatekeeper:* William Keylor, "Tumulty, Joseph Patrick (1879–1954)," in *The United States in the First World War: An Encyclopedia*, edited by Anne Cipriano Venzon, 600 (New York: Routledge, 1995).

168. *If trouble breaks out:* Letter dated January 5, 1918, "John D. Gluck (#122696)," 2–11.

168. *While Gluck's claims:* Keylor, "Tumulty, Joseph Patrick," 600.

168. *. . . "a sinister purpose:* Joseph Patrick Tumulty, *Woodrow Wilson as I Know Him* (New York: Doubleday, Page & Company, 1921), 202.

168. *Tumulty forwarded:* "Lamar Arrested at the Waldorf," *New York Times*, November 7, 1914; the article gives Offley's title.

169. *"At this time it seems:* "John D. Gluck (#122696)," 23–24.

CHAPTER 11: POOR BOY GETS NOTHING

170. *So many tears:* M.R.P., "A Toast," *Boys' Life* (December 1917): 37.

170. *In a few short:* Macleod, *Building Character in the American Boy: The Boy Scouts, YMCA, and Their Forerunners, 1870–1920* (Madison: University of Wisconsin Press, 1983), 150–57.

171. *"I, John Duval:* "John D. Gluck (#122696)," 47.

171. *[T]here has been a palpable:* Ibid.

172. *While he shied:* "James Edward West," biography in Finding Aid, James West Papers, National Scouting Museum Archive.

172. *Determined to help:* Macleod, *Building Character*, 148.

173. *Under Gluck's direction:* "John D. Gluck (#122696)," 32; the case file includes a report that A. F. Troescher wrote a $100 check to the "Boy Scouts of America" and sent it in to the USBS's Amerman, who endorsed and cashed it.

173. *The group secured:* "Complaint," *Boy Scouts of America v. The United States Boy Scout*, Supreme Court, New York County, 1918.

173. *All of these:* "Scouts in Court Fight," *Sun*, August 1, 1917, 3.

173. *The prosecution quickly:* "Address delivered by Sir Robert Baden-Powell," USBS file in Baden-Powell Collection, Box Number 63, National Scouting Museum Archive.

173. *He submitted an editorial:* John Gluck, "Boy Scouts: Suggestion That the Rival Bodies End Their Quarrel and Get to Work," Letter to the Editor, *New York Times*, August 19, 1917.

173. *Gluck and the USBS:* Edward L. Rowan, *To Do My Best: James E. West and the History of the Boy Scouts of America* (Las Vegas: Edward Rowan, 2005), 68.

174. *West accused Gluck:* "Head of U.S. Boy Scout Is Accused," *Sun*, February 16, 1918, 16.

175. *He threatened:* "Boy Scout Officials Deny West's Charge," *New-York Tribune*, February 17, 1918, 6.

174. . . . *pointing out that:* "'U.S. Boy Scouts' Offer to Unite with Rival Body," *New-York Tribune*, February 21, 1918, 13.

175. *"I only hope:* "Boy Scout Head Replies," *Evening State Journal and Lincoln Daily News*, March 26, 1918.

175. *He added that:* "Seeks Investigation of Boy Scouts of America," *Evening Star*, March 26, 1918, 4.

175. *Attorney General:* "Department of Justice Kills Effort to Discredit American Boy Scouts," *United Press*, April 22, 1918.

175. *"Any person can:* "Upholds Officials of the Boy Scouts," *Sun*, April 22, 1918, 12.

175. *Charles Evan Hughes:* "Investigate Boys' Society," *New York Times*, May 22, 1918.

176. *The legal and public-relations:* "The United States Boy Scout," *Ninth Annual Report of the Boy Scouts of America* (New York: Boy Scouts of America, 1919), 57.

176. *In March 1919:* "Scouts of America Win Sole Right to Use of Scout Name," *Brooklyn Daily Eagle*, May 13, 1919, 2.

176. *"Some of the most:* Susan Waggoner, *Christmas Memories: Gifts, Activities, Fads, and Fancies, 1920s–1960s* (New York: Stewart, Tabori, and Chang, 2009), 23.

176. *By 1926:* William R. Leach, *Land of Desire: Merchants, Power, and the Rise of a New American Culture* (New York: Vintage Books, 1993), 328.

177. *She joined the:* "Signs with Yonkers," *New York Clipper*, January, 29, 1919, 12.

177. *Later that year:* "Playhouse," *Brooklyn Standard Union*, October 19, 1919, 9.

177. *Like her father:* "Plays Title Role on Short Notice," *Billboard*, December 30, 1922, 26.

177. *One critic:* "Warburton Player Gives Fine Example of Ability," *Yonkers Statesman*, 1922.

177. *"Naturally she was:* Wood Soanes, "Curtain Calls," *Oakland Tribune*, September 20, 1923, 22.

178. *Whatever the reason:* The 1920 U.S. Census states Gluck was again living as a bachelor tenant.

178. *Beginning in 1935:* Peter Seely, "Dames, Babes, Battleaxes, and Tomatoes: Women and the Three Stooges," in *Stoogeology: Essays on the Three Stooges*, edited by Peter Seely and Gail W. Piper, 239 (Jefferson, NC: McFarland, 2007).

178. *Playing dowagers:* Tom Kuntz, "Thoughts on the Social Significance of Getting Hit with a Pie. Seriously." *New York Times*, July 10, 1994; Bill Cappello, "Supporting Player Symona Boniface: A Brief Biography," *Three Stooges Journal* (Summer 1993): 6–7.

178. *Though her grave:* "Fan Club Honors Supporting Player Symona Boniface with Installation of Grave Marker," *Three Stooges Journal* (Summer 2005): 3.

178. *Visitors to Symona:* FindAGrave.com. Memorial #5924280, added November 2, 2001.

178. *More than even:* Leigh Eric Schmidt, *Consumer Rites*, 136.

178. *Publicly Gluck stated:* "City Briefs," *New-York Tribune*, December 20, 1918.

179. *"The immediate success:* Financial Committee, "Report of 1918 Santa Claus Association," *Santa Claus Annual*, 1918, 11–12.

179. *On November 7:* *Santa Claus Annual*, 1919, 1.

PART III

CHAPTER 12: "SANTA CLAUS AS A BUSINESS MAN AND ADVERTISER"

182. *The disillusions that: Boys' Life* (December 1917): 11.

182. *Hollywood's original celebrity:* Richard Corliss, "The King of Hollywood," *Time Magazine*, June 17, 1996.

182. *The stars had just cancelled:* "Doug and Mary Leave for Home in California," *Exhibitors Trade Review*, December 9, 1922, 71.

182. *Fairbanks wore: Santa Claus Annual*, 1923, inside cover; Mary B. Mullett, "Mary Pickford Describes Her Most Thrilling Experience," *American Magazine* (May 1923): 34.

183. *It was reportedly:* Later reports would put it under the million-dollar mark. According to Jeffrey Vance, *Douglas Fairbanks* (Berkeley: University of California Press, 2008), 146, its budget was $930,000, making it less than Erich von Stroheim's *Foolish Wives*. Gary Carey, *Doug and Mary* (New York: E. P. Dutton, 1977), 129, puts its budget closer to $750,000.

183. *Refusing to rest:* Vance, *Douglas Fairbanks*, 153.

183. . . . *"the most universally:* Mullett, "Mary Pickford Describes," 34.

183. *Exiting their car:* Vance, *Douglas Fairbanks*, 111.

183. *The year before:* "Mary Pickford Plays Santa Claus," *Holly Leaves*, December 29, 1922, 6.

184. *The same year:* "Mary Pickford, Partner of Santa Claus," *Holly Leaves*, July 8, 1922, 14.

184. *Pickford would later:* Gregory Paul Williams, *The Story of Hollywood: An Illustrated History* (Los Angeles: BL Press, 2005), 279. Carey, *Doug and Mary*, 199.

184. *On any given day:* Mullett, "Mary Pickford Describes," 34.

184. *The twenty-six-inch:* "Shot with an Arrow in Fifth Avenue," *New York Times*, October 4, 1922.

184. *Fairbanks settled:* Carey, *Doug and Mary*, 130.

185. *Set on three wooden:* K. G. Beauchamp, *History of Telegraphy: Its Technology and Application* (Edison, NJ: Institution of Engineering and Technology, 2001).

185. *Not wanting to keep: Santa Claus Annual*, 1923, 1.

185. *As Gluck moved:* "Doug and Mary Leave for Home in California," *Exhibitors Trade Review*, 71.

186. *He moved to:* 1920 U.S. Census.

186. . . . *"a pianist of international:* Elizabeth Smith, "Childhood's Belief in Santa Saved by Generous Purses of Benevolent Citizens," *Evening Telegram*, November 17, 1920.

186. *The American Red Cross: Santa Claus Annual*, 1922, 6.

187. *"You have a splendid: Santa Claus Annual*, 1918, 17.

187. *Like Mary Pickford:* "Samuel Brill Dies; Clothing Merchant," *New York Times*, May 14, 1931, 22.

187. *The illusions of childhood:* Samuel Brill, "Santa Claus Association," *New York Times*, December 15, 1923.

187. *Brill's comments:* "Santa Claus to the Poor," *New York Times*, December 20, 1924, 14; this time the author is published as "Santa Claus Association."

188. . . . *lambasted such refusals:* "Now They'd Blacken Santa," *New-York Tribune*, January 31, 1921.

188. *By Christmas:* "Christmas Gifts in 1921," *New York Times*, December 25, 1921.

188. *The Knickerbocker would: Santa Claus Annual*, 1922, 12.

188. . . . *more than two thousand:* "Letters to Santa Show Faith He'll Brighten Dreary Poverty," *New-York Tribune*, December 17, 1922.

188. *Miniature Christmas trees: Santa Claus Annual*, 1922, 6.

190. *"Guided by a happy:* "Eighth Annual Report of the S.C.A.," *Santa Claus Annual*, 1920, 7.

190. *To glance at them:* Beyond the stylistic similarity of his writing, Frances Gluck confirmed "he wrote all that."

190. *Actress Margarita Fisher: Santa Claus Annual*, 1922, 4. "Artgravure Section," *Washington Post*, December 25, 1921, 5. An image of the group standing around a pile of letters reads, "All These Are Assistants of Santa Claus: Members of the Santa Claus Association, they receive all the kiddie letters to St. Nick and make sure that the writers are not disappointed. You will recognize William Faversham in the picture."

190. *The group tapped:* "Sgt. Mike Donaldson, the 'Fighting Irishman,' World War I hero," *Los Angeles Daily News* negatives collection, Islandora Repository.

190. *"I don't believe:* Smith, "Childhood's Belief in Santa," *Evening Telegram*.

190. *When the New-York:* "Santa Claus Association Prepares to Aid Children," *New-York Tribune*, December 5, 1921.

191. *Business leaders were:* "Store Executives Attend Funeral of Samuel Brill," *New York Herald Tribune*, May 16, 1931. While Brill's connection to the Santa Claus Association would not be remembered many months after his obituary ran, his name would become synonymous with New York City's songwriting industry. The Brill Building, a bronze art deco structure on Broadway at Forty-Ninth Street owned by the Brill Brothers, evolved into the hub of New York's music industry as songwriters, music publishers, and talent agents moved in as tenants. It was here where Johnny Marks set up his office for St. Nicholas Music, which published his hit Christmas songs "Rockin' around the Christmas Tree," "A Holly Jolly Christmas," and of course "Rudolph, the Red-Nosed Reindeer," based on the poem by Robert L. May, Marks's brother-in-law. See Mike Brocken, "Brill Building Pop," in *Continuum Encyclopedia of Popular Music of the World*, vol. 8, edited by John Shepherd and David Horn, 91–94 (New York: Continuum, 2012).

192. *Gluck described businessmen:* Kathleen Read, "What Becomes of Letters to Kriss Kringle?" *Utica NY Observer*, 1929.

192. *In an unsigned letter: Santa Claus Annual*, 1922, 12.

192. *Christ was a:* Norman K. Risjord, *Giants in Their Times: Representative Americans from the Jazz Age to the Cold War* (Lanham, Md.: Rowman & Littlefield, 2006), 51.

192. *[C]onsider the change:* Roy Dickinson, "Santa Claus as a Business Man and Advertiser," *Printers' Ink* (December 28, 1922): 105–8.

193. *"Despite the charitable:* Stanley W. Todd, "Help for Santa," *GRIT* (December 24, 1922).

193. *Instead of:* Santa Claus Annual, 1917, 1.

193. *Gluck bought space:* Advertisement, *Sun,* December 17, 1922, 130.

193. *Though Coca-Cola:* Karal Ann Marling, *Merry Christmas! Celebrating America's Greatest Holiday* (Cambridge, MA: Harvard University Press, 2001), 39, 213.

193. *These advertisements:* "By 1926 the United States was the greatest producer of toys and playthings in the world," according to Leach, *Land of Desire: Merchants, Power, and the Rise of a New American Culture* (New York: Vintage Books, 1993), 328.

193. *Following the sudden:* Calvin Coolidge, "Address to the American Society of Newspaper Editors," January 25, 1925.

194. *Rejecting the federal:* Donald T. Critchlow and Charles H. Parker, eds., *With Us Always: A History of Private Charity and Public Welfare* (Lanham, Md.: Rowman & Littlefield, 1998), 5–9.

194. *"Through the Santa:* "President Coolidge Wishes All Children Merry Christmas," *Brooklyn Standard Union,* December 21, 1923, 3.

Millionaires were sprouting: Some sixty-seven individuals would report an annual income of over $1 million for 1922, according to Larry Samuel, *Rich: The Rise and Fall of American Wealth Culture* (New York: AMACOM, 2009), 12.

195. *The massive fund-raising:* Cutlip, *Fund Raising in the United States: Its Role in American Philanthropy* (New Brunswick, NJ: Transactions, 1990), 159–60.

195. *. . . Radio Department:* Santa Claus Annual, 1923, 4.

195. *Newspaperman-turned-publicist:* Quoted in Cutlip, *Fund Raising,* 169.

195. *Fund-raiser John Price Jones:* Cutlip, *Fund Raising,* 296.

196. *Remember this, and then:* Santa Claus Annual, 1922, 23.

196. *Though A. M.'s judgment:* "J. C. Rabiner Fails; May Owe $1,000,000," *New York Times,* September 14, 1922, 31.

196. *"A large part:* Santa Claus Annual, 1922, 2.

197. *Attendees included:* "Some Party!" *Santa Claus Annual,* 1924, 14–18.

197. *Three months earlier:* "New Standards Set in Sport during 1923," *New York Times,* December 30, 1923, 16.

198. *He would pay:* Miller, *Supreme City: How Jazz Age Manhattan Gave Birth to Modern America* (New York: Simon & Schuster, 2014) 377, 405–6.

198. *Rickard and boxing:* Santa Claus Annual, 1924, 18.

199. *The project would:* "$1,000,000 Sought for Big Samaritan Hospital Addition," *Brooklyn Daily Eagle,* December 23, 1923, 3.

199. *Gluck spoke with:* "Samaritan Hospital Ladies Meet Elect," *Brooklyn Daily Eagle,* February 27, 1923, 9.

199. *The "Streets of Paris:* "H. M. Rynehart to Head Samaritan Hospital Drive," *Brooklyn Daily Eagle,* July 30, 1923, 13.

199. *Prizes included trips:* "Big Features for Samaritan Drive," *Brooklyn Daily Eagle,* August 28, 1923, 4.

200. *The campaign's director:* "Gluck Dismissed as Publicity Head of Samaritan Hospital Campaign," *Brooklyn Daily Times,* September 12, 1923.

200. *"This is to inform:* Ibid.

201. *"I have seen:* "Nortons Charge Hospital Paid Big Fees to Get Funds," *Brooklyn Daily Eagle*, September 15, 1923.

201. *"We welcome any:* "Coler Indorses Samaritan Drive," *Brooklyn Daily Eagle*, September 17, 1923.

202. *Gluck responded:* "Gluck Defies Rynegart," *Brooklyn Daily Eagle*, September 18, 1923 (not published, per Brooklyn Public Library collection).

CHAPTER 13: ORDER OUT OF CHAOS

203. *. . . unfailingly responded:* "Fake Solicitors Overrun the City," *New York Times*, February 24, 1924.

203. *. . . five questionable:* "5 'Charity' Funds to Be Investigated," *New York Times*, December 18, 1923; "Soldiers' Sale Dropped," *New York Times*, December 27, 1923, 14.

203. *Tuesday he requested:* "Two More 'Drives' Are Investigated," *New York Times*, December 19, 1923.

203. *He initiated:* "Charity Society Closes," *New York Times*, December 25, 1923, 7.

204. *By Thursday:* "Charity Lottery Barred," *New York Times*, December 21, 1923.

204. *Since the summer:* "Block Parties Hurt Morals, Says Coler," *New York Times*, June 27, 1923, 21.

204. *Throughout the week:* "To Guard Dinner Baskets," *New York Times*, November 6, 1923, 14.

204. *Coler and his team:* See correspondences of December 1923, COS files, Catalogued Correspondence, Bird S. Coler, Box 2, Columbia University Rare Book & Manuscript Library.

204. *He offered a one-hundred-dollar:* "Coler Would Check Selling of Tickets," *Brooklyn Daily Eagle*, December 16, 1923, 24.

204. *"If you women:* "Bird Coler Attacks Charities Society," *New York Times*, March 26, 1918, 5.

205. *"He brought order:* "Dinner to Bird S. Coler," *New York Times*, February 6, 1902.

205. *His investigation:* "Big Fight against the Ramapo Company," *New York Times*, January 18, 1901, 2.

205. *Coler lost:* "Odell Wins," *New York Times*, November 5, 1902.

206. *On the first:* "Named by Hylan for Big City Posts," *New York Times*, January 2, 1918.

206. *The responsibilities were: Directory of Activities of Public and Private Welfare Agencies* (New York: Department of Public Welfare, 1920).

206. *Coler had been interested:* Comments made at testimonial dinner for Bird S. Coler, Hotel Commodore, December 14, 1928.

206. *Early in his tenure:* "City Officials War on Fake Charities," *New York Times*, October 28, 1921, 36.

207. *"We sent a man:* "City Gives Full Aid to Poor, Says Coler," *New York Times*, February 7, 1922.

207. *"The first idea:* "The 'Block Party' in Trouble," *New York Times*, June 28, 1923, 14.

207. *Coler followed:* "Block Parties Hurt Morals, Says Coler," *New York Times*, 21.

207. *Coler earned headlines:* "Coler Says Charity Drives in City Are Robbing Orphans,"

New-York Tribune, November 24, 1920, 17. "Coler Rebukes Evangeline Booth," *New York Times,* April 9, 1922, 4.

207. *At the start:* See correspondences of January 1918, COS files, Catalogued Correspondence, Bird S. Coler, Box 2, Columbia University Rare Book & Manuscript Library.

207. *When they complained:* "Bird Coler Attacks Charities Society," *New York Times.*

207. *"Mr. Bird S. Coler: Santa Claus Annual,* 1921, 5.

208. *Fatigued from going:* "Fake Solicitors Overrun the City," *New York Times.*

208. *In New York:* Schmidt, *Consumer Rites: The Buying and Selling of American Holidays* (Princeton, NJ: Princeton University Press, 1995), 110.

208. . . . *"customs of outlawry:* Restad, *Christmas in America: A History* (New York: Oxford University Press, 1995), 35.

208. *But growth in:* Raymond A. Mohl, "Humanitarianism in the Preindustrial City: The New York Society for the Prevention of Pauperism, 1817–1823," *Journal of American History* (December 1970).

208. *The noisy revelers:* Pintard, I, 359. Quoted in Nissenbaum, *The Battle for Christmas,* (New York: Vintage, 1997), 50.

210. *In devising his version:* Nissenbaum, *The Battle for Christmas,* 84–85.

210. . . . *rebranded as "crime":* Nissenbaum, *The Battle for Christmas,* 99.

210. *"More than any:* Nissenbaum, *The Battle for Christmas,* 108.

211. *While he published a tract:* "The Reason Why the National Prohibition Law Is Not Enforced" (New York: John Duvall Gluck, 1924).

211. *Just as with the USBS:* "Forbids Use of His Name," *New York Times,* February 7, 1925.

211. *He created a society: Santa Claus Annual,* 1916, 12.

213. *An ad for the group: Santa Claus Annual,* 1927, 21.

213. *The complexity:* Jack Kenny, "Cash Taking Santa Stirs Coler Quiz," *New York Daily News,* December 23, 1928.

214. *In the 1923:* William Herringshaw, *Herringshaw's American Blue Book of Biography* (New York: American Publishers' Association, 1923), 253.

214. *In the 1924:* Lewis Randolph Hamersly, *Who's Who in New York City and State,* vol. 8 (New York: Who's Who, 1924), 512.

214. *In the 1925:* "Santa Claus!" *Santa Claus Annual,* 1925, 9.

216. *Gluck replenished:* Letter dated October 16, 1925, J. E. Watson (Santa Claus Association), Miscellaneous *Early Correspondence:* Through 1940, Series XII General Correspondence, Sheldon Glueck Papers, Harvard Law School Library.

216. *When Harvard social:* Letter dated October 21, 1925, J. E. Watson (Santa Claus Association), Sheldon Glueck Papers, Harvard Law School Library.

216. *As one newspaper:* "Santa Claus Marries on Friday the 13th," *San Antonio Express,* August 14, 1926.

217. *J. D. Gluck:* "Forty-Four Wed Here on Friday, the 13th," *New York Times,* August 14, 1926, 20.

217. *He instituted citywide:* Comments made at testimonial dinner for Bird S. Coler, Hotel Commodore, December 14, 1928.

217. *Two years after:* "City Hospital Standards Raised, Coler Reports," *New-York Tribune,* June 19, 1921, 10.

218. *Walker confronted Coler:* "Coler Is Rebuked Publicly by Mayor; May Get Out Soon," *New York Times*, May 17, 1927, 1, 8.

218. *In the end:* "Reaction for Coler Seen by His Friends," *New York Times*, May 21, 1927, 23.

218. *"If the Mayor:* "City Plans to Unify All Its Hospitals," *New York Times*, July 23, 1927, 15.

219. *The* Brooklyn Eagle: "Fate of Welfare Dept. Uncertain in Merger Plan," *Brooklyn Daily Eagle*, December 28, 1928, 3.

219. *"Business people throughout:* "Bill to Regulate Raising of Charity Funds Goes Over," *Brooklyn Daily Eagle*, April 1, 1926, 24.

CHAPTER 14: SPECTACLE ON 34TH STREET

220. *Are we living: Santa Claus Annual*, 1928.

220. *Though his assistants: Santa Claus Annual*, 1927.

220. *. . . six hundred clerks:* "Now the Santa Claus Letters Are Falling into the Mail," *New York Times*, December 4, 1927.

220. *This season:* "Santa Claus Group under Coler's Fire," *New York Times*, December 23, 1927.

221. *A few decades:* Robert M. Grippo, *Macy's: The Store. The Star. The Story* (Garden City Park, N.Y.: Square One, 2009), 61. While Macy's pioneered the outdoor parade, it was only one of many department stores throughout New York City to create elaborate "children's Christmas spectacles" in store. For example, in 1916, Wanamaker's New York introduced an in-store parade where every day at 10:30 a.m. a procession of costumed characters and Santa Claus trooped through the store. Leach, *Land of Desire*, 88–89.

221. *But by 1927:* Robert M. Grippo and Christopher Hoskins, *Macy's Thanksgiving Day Parade* (Charleston, SC: Arcadia, 2004), 39.

221. *Gluck could see:* Leach, *Land of Desire: Merchants, Power, and the Rise of a New American Culture* (New York: Vinage Books, 1993), 336.

222. *. . . begin filling:* "Store to Present Holiday Pageant," *New York Times*, November 27, 1928, 20.

222. *Towering over:* "Christmas Parade Staged in Broadway," *New York Times*, November 25, 1927, 13.

223. *While the Macy's parade:* Grippo, *Macy's: The Store*, 138–39.

223. *But through Coler's work:* "Santa Claus Group under Coler's Fire," *New York Times*, December 23, 1927.

224. *His 1927 holiday:* "Give Rules for Christmas," *New York Times*, December 20, 1927, 20.

224. *Its high profile:* "Santa Claus Group in Postal Inquiry," *New York Times*. December 24, 1927, 16.

224. *The year before: Santa Claus Annual*, 1927.

225. *But in 1927:* Coler would later acknowledge that he had never received a formal complaint about the Association's letter, making it unlikely that it came from one of the thousands of recipients on Gluck's mailing list. That would also mean no formal complaint came from any of the "honorary" officials listed on the Santa Claus Association

letterhead—a contrast to what set off the backlash to the USBS, Crusade Against Illicit Traffic in Narcotics, and others. The likely explanation is that Coler got it through the Welfare Council, created to combat just this type of unchecked solicitation, particularly around Christmas. It is also likely that from within the Welfare Council, it came from the Charity Organization Society, the most outspoken critic of the Association's work.

226. *So Gluck donned:* "The Weather," *New York Times*, December 22, 1927, 1.

226. *He wore round:* Jack Kenny, "Cash Taking Santa Stirs Coler Quiz," *New York Daily News*, December 23, 1927.

226. *Coler invited Gluck:* Jack Kenny, "Postal Inspector Asks Santa Report," *New York Daily News*, December 25, 1927, 14.

227. *"It would interfere:* "Santa Claus Group under Coler's Fire," *New York Times.*

227. *Irritated, the commissioner:* "Coler Aid Can't See Gluck's Books," *New York Sun*, December 23, 1927, 15.

227. *The day after:* Jack Kenny, "'Santa Claus' Closes Accounts to Prober," *New York Daily News*, December 24, 1927, 3.

228. *Gluck provided:* "'Santa' Inquiry Turned Over to Postal Officers," *New York Herald-Tribune*, December 24, 1927.

228. *Gluck and Forscher pushed:* "Santa Claus Group in Postal Inquiry," *New York Times*, 16.

229. *"The scope of many:* Jack Kenny, "'Santa Claus' Closes Accounts to Prober," *New York Daily News.*

229. *"We would like to know:* "Santa Claus, Inc. Now Offers Books," *New York Times.*

230. *. . . the letters were turned:* "Santa Claus Group under Coler's Fire," *New York Times.*

230. *"[T]he inquiry:* "Postoffice Refuses to Open Santa Claus Association Inquiry," *New York Herald-Tribune*, December 25, 1927.

230. *On Christmas Eve: Santa Claus Annual*, 1928.

CHAPTER 15: DEAD LETTERS

232. *Now I must:* "Trusting Children Flood 'Dere Santy' with Mail," *New York Evening Post*, December 18, 1928, 5.

232. *Coler's third deputy:* "Records of 'Santa' Demanded in Quiz," *New York Evening Post*, January 10, 1928.

232. *"I have never:* "Santa Claus Report," *Sun*, January 10, 1928, 5.

232. *Gluck invited:* "Submits Accounting of Santa Claus Fund," *New York Times*, January 11, 1928.

233. *The total spent:* "U.S. Mail Bars Letters Addressed to 'Santa' in City," *Brooklyn Daily Eagle*, December 10, 1928, 3.

233. *The total receipts:* "Santa Claus, Inc." *Sun*, January 11, 1928, 13.

233. *Every season:* Jack Kenny, "$20,000 in 'Santa Claus' Roll," *New York Daily News*, December 26, 1927, 8.

234. *A $10,000 fund:* Jack Kenny, "Cash Taking Santa Stirs Coler Quiz," *New York Daily News*, December 23, 1927.

234. *While Coler expected:* "Santa Letters to Aid Writers Guarded by U.S.," *Brooklyn Standard Union,* December 10, 1928, 8.

234. *The* Bridgeport Telegram*:* "New York Probe Proves Gluck Waxes Mustache," *Bridgeport Telegram,* February 17, 1928, 16.

234. *He spent much:* See, for example, "Some Smith Supporters," *New York Times,* September 25, 1928, 30.

235. . . . *starting February 1:* "Walker to 'Clean House' for Mayoralty Campaign," *New York Times,* December 23, 1928, 1, 2; "Schroeder Heads New Department of City Hospitals," *Brooklyn Daily Eagle,* December 24, 1928, 1. The bill would pass on November 9, 1928.

235. *The bureaucracy:* "Coler Considers Quitting City Post," *New York Times,* November 3, 1928.

235. . . . *typically cheery story:* "Dead Mail Keeps Post Office Busy," *New York Times,* March 18, 1928, 149.

235. . . . *Convention of the:* "New York City Federation of Women's Clubs Conduct Seventy-Seventh Convention," *Long Island Daily Press,* October 29, 1928, 4.

236. . . . *three thousand:* "Postoffice Awaits Record Yule Mail," *New York Times,* December 13, 1928, 23.

238. . . . *asked that his name:* "Ban on Santa, Inc. Due to Old Probe," *New York Evening Post,* December 10, 1928, 5.

238. *Clarahan contacted Gluck:* "U.S. Mail Bars Letters Addressed to 'Santa' in City," *Brooklyn Daily Eagle.*

239. *As a result:* John H. Bartlett, "Santa Claus Letters," *Postal Bulletin,* December 8, 1928.

239. *On December 9:* "Santa Letters to Aid Writers Guarded by U.S.," *Brooklyn Standard Union.*

239. *"We will stop:* "Santa Claus Inc. Letters Halted by Postoffice," *New York Herald-Tribune,* December 10, 1928.

240. *The board severed:* "'Santa Claus' Gluck Ignores His Critics," *New York Times,* December 11, 1928, 33. The story did note that the Board of Welfare workers "reported that poor families were well taken care of by the Gluck organization."

240. *Reverend S. Parkes:* "Dr. Cadman Quits as Head of Santa Claus Association," *Brooklyn Daily Eagle,* December 12, 1928, 3.

241. *The newspapers continued:* "Letters to Santa Pile Up in Mails," *New York Times,* December 21, 1932, 22.

241. . . . *destroyed—unanswered:* "Letters Indicate Santa Claus Has Shifted Home to Toyland," *Brooklyn Daily Eagle,* December 19, 1928, 11.

241. *"Your Excellency:* Letter from John Duvall Gluck, dated December 16, 1931, "Santa Claus Association," Box 277, Subject File, Presidential Period 1929–33, The Papers of Herbert Hoover, Herbert Hoover Presidential Library and Museum.

242. . . . *out of former COS executive:* "National Investigation Bureau to Aid Charity," *Greater New York,* July 21, 1919, 19.

242. *"When he first:* Letter from May H. Harding, dated December 17, 1931, Box 277, Subject File, Presidential Period 1929–33, the Papers of Herbert Hoover, Herbert Hoover Presidential Library and Museum.

243. . . . *what the Brooklyn:* "Mr. Coler's Retirement," *Brooklyn Daily Eagle*, December 16, 1928, 28.

244. *"After breaking:* "Kings Hospital Rated Class I by the State," *New York Times*, July 28, 1928, 24.

244. *Over the next two hours:* Comments made at testimonial dinner for Bird S. Coler, Hotel Commodore, December 14, 1928; "500 Doctors Dine Bird S. Coler on His Retirement," *Brooklyn Daily Eagle*, December 15, 1928, 10.

245. . . . *helped organize events:* "Cancer Institute Party," *New York Times*, December 23, 1928, 22. "City in Holiday Mood Aids Unfortunates," *New York Times*, December 25, 1928, 3.

245. . . . *businessman S. S. Rosen:* "Tribune Fresh Air Fund," *New-York Tribune*, August 23, 1919, 7.

246. *When the time came:* "Child Convalescents Have Christmas Fete," *New York Times*, December 19, 1928, 29; photo spread, *New York Daily News*, December 19, 1928, 25.

EPILOGUE: OPERATION SANTA CLAUS

247. . . . *found steady work:* "John Duvall Gluck," *Miami News*, February 18, 1951, 6A.

247. *The hospital named:* In 1996 it was merged with the Goldwater Memorial Hospital and is now the Coler-Goldwater Specialty Hospital.

248. . . . *on an informal basis:* "Letters to Santa Flood Post Office," *New York Times*, December 13, 1936, 46.

248. . . . *clerks in the money-order:* "'Deer santa plees bring us . . .' Underprivileged Children Put in Their Requests," *New York Times*, December 10, 1970, 53.

248. . . . *from Johnny Carson:* "Santa's Helpers in New York Answer Letters," *New York Times*, December 22, 1985.

BIBLIOGRAPHY

1815–1915 Official Souvenir Celebration of the Reconstructed Washington Market. New York: Washington Market Merchants' Association, Inc., 1915.

Appleton's Dictionary of Greater New York and Its Neighborhoods, 26th ed. New York: D. Appleton, 1904.

Boy Scouts of America Annual Reports. New York: Boy Scouts of America, 1911–1919.

Boy Scouts of America v. The United States Boy Scout. Supreme Court. New York County, 1917–1918.

"Constitution & By-Laws of the New-York Historical Society." New York: Grattan's Office, 1829.

Santa Claus and Jenny Lind. New York: John R. M'Gown, 1850.

Santa Claus Association Annual Reports. New York: Santa Claus Association, 1916–1928.

St. Nicholas: An Illustrated Magazine for Young Folks. Vol. XLII, Part I. New York: The Century Co., 1915.

"The Social Welfare Forum: Proceedings of the National Conference of Social Work." Chicago: Rogers & Hall, 1919.

"The Woolworth Building (Highest in the World) Illustrated with Details from the Architects Drawings and with Floor Plans." New York: Edward J. Hogan, 1912.

Anonymous. *The Children's Friend.* New York: William B. Gilley, 1821.

Armstrong, Nancy. *The Rockefeller Center Christmas Tree: The History & Lore of the World's Most Famous Evergren.* Kennebunkport, ME: Cider Mill Press, 2010.

Barton, Bruce. *The Man Nobody Knows.* Lanham, MD: Ivan R. Dee, 2000.

Bernays, Edward. *Crystallizing Public Opinion.* New York: Ig Publishing, 2011 reprint.

Boorstin, Daniel J. *The Americans: The Democratic Experience.* New York: Vintage Books, 1974.

Bowler, Gerry. *Santa Claus: A Biography.* New York: McClelland & Stewart, 2005.

———. *The World Encyclopedia of Christmas.* New York: McClelland & Stewart, 2004.

Brace, Charles Loring. *Home-Life in Germany.* New York: Charles Scribner, 1853.

Brace, Emma, ed. *The Life of Charles Loring Brace.* London: Sampson Low, Marston, 1894.

Brandes, Joseph. *Herbert Hoover and Economic Diplomacy.* Pittsburgh: University of Pittsburgh Press, 1962.

Brandt, Lilian. *The Charity Organization Society of the City of New York, 1882–1907.* New York: B. H. Tyrrel, 1907.

Brown, Henry C. *New York of To-Day.* New York: Old Colony Press, 1917.

Brown, Malcolm, and Shirley Seaton. *Christmas Truce*, 3rd ed. London: Pan Books, 2001.

Browne, Ray Broadus, and Pat Browne, eds. *The Guide to United States Popular Culture.* Madison: University of Wisconsin Press, 2001.

Bruce, H. Addington. *Above the Clouds and Old New York.* New York,1913.

Burrows, Edwin G., and Mike Wallace. *Gotham: A History of New York City to 1898.* Oxford: Oxford University Press, 2000.

Burstein, Andrew. *The Original Knickerbocker: The Life of Washington Irving.* New York: Basic Books, 2007.

Campbell, Robert D. *Reminiscences of a Birdman.* Uxbridge, MA: Living History Press, 2009.

Carey, Gary. *Doug and Mary.* New York: E. P. Dutton, 1977.

Cartwright, Otho G. *The Middle West Side: A Historical Sketch.* New York: Survey Associates, 1914.

Chudacoff, Howard P. *The Age of the Bachelor.* Princeton, NJ: Princeton University Press, 2000.

Churchwell, Sarah. *Careless People: Murder, Mayhem, and the Invention of The Great Gatsby.* New York: Penguin Press, 2014.

Coler, Bird Sim. *Directory of Activities of Public and Private Welfare Agencies.* New York: Department of Public Welfare, 1920.

———. *Socialism in the Schools.* New York: Devinne Press, 1911.

———. *Two and Two Make Four.* New York: Devinne Press, 1912.

Collins, Paul. *The Murder of the Century: The Gilded Age Crime That Scandalized a City and Sparked the Tabloid Wars.* New York: Broadway Books, 2012.

Conway, J. North. *The Big Policeman: The Rise and Fall of America's First, Most Ruthless, and Greatest Detective.* Guilford, CT: Lyons Press, 2010.

Critchlow, Donald T., and Charles H. Parker, eds. *With Us Always: A History of Private Charity and Public Welfare.* Lanham, MD: Rowman & Littlefield, 1998.

Crump, William D. *The Christmas Encyclopedia,* 3rd ed. Jefferson, NC: McFarland, 2013.

Cutlip, Scott. *Fund Raising in the United States: Its Role in American Philanthropy.* New Brunswick, NJ: Transaction, 1990.

———. *The Unseen Power: Public Relations: A History.* Hillsdale, NJ: Lawrence Erlbaum, 1994.

Dash, Mike. *Satan's Circus: Murder, Vice, Police Corruption, and New York's Trial of the Century.* New York: Broadway Books, 2008.

Del Re, Gerard. *The Story of 'Twas the Night before Christmas.* Gretna, LA: Wynwood Press, 1991.

Dreiser, Theodore. *The Color of a Great City.* New York: Boni and Liveright, 1923.

Eisner, Marc Allen. *From Warfare State to Welfare State.* University Park: Pennsylvania State University Press, 2000.

Emrich, Duncan. *Folklore on the American Land.* New York: Little, Brown, 1972.

Evers, Alf. *The Catskills: From Wilderness to Woodstock.* New York: Doubleday, 1972.

Erenberg, Lewis. *Steppin' Out: New York Nightlife and the Transformation of American Culture.* Chicago: University of Chicago Press, 1984.

Ferrell, Robert H. *The Presidency of Calvin Coolidge.* Lawrence: University Press of Kansas, 1998.

Fischer, Roger. *Them Damned Pictures: Explorations in American Political Cartoon Art.* Hamden, CT: Archon Books, 1995.

Foster, Don. *Author Unknown: Tales of a Literary Detective*. New York: Henry Holt & Co., 2000.

Fowler, Gene. *Beau James*. New York: American Ltd, 1976.

Funk, Elizabeth Paling. "From Amsterdam to New Amsterdam: Washington Irving, the Dutch St. Nicholas, and the American Santa Claus." Martha Dickinson Shattuck, ed. *Explorers, Fortunes & Love Letters: A Window on New Netherland*. Albany, NY: Mount Ida Press, 2009. 102–115.

Gilje, Paul A. *The Road to Mobocracy: Popular Disorder in New York City, 1763–1834*. Chapel Hill, NC: University of North Carolina Press, 1987.

Gluck, John Duvall. *The Reason Why the National Prohibition Law Is Not Enforced*. New York: John Duvall Gluck, 1924.

Gobie, Henry M. *U.S. Parcel Post: A Postal History*. Miami: Postal Publications, 1979.

Grippo, Robert M. *Macy's: The Store. The Star. The Story*. Garden City Park, NY: Square One, 2009.

Grippo, Robert M., and Christopher Hoskins. *Macy's Thanksgiving Day Parade*. Charleston, SC: Arcadia, 2004.

Harris, Bill. *One Thousand New York Buildings*. New York: Black Dog & Leventhal, 2005.

Hurwitz, Nathan. *A History of the American Musical Theater*. New York: Routledge, 2014.

Irving, Washington. *A History of New-York from the Beginning of the World to the End of the Dutch Dynasty*. New York: George P. Putnam, 1864.

Jackson, Kenneth T., ed. *The Encyclopedia of New York City*. New Haven, CT: Yale University Press, 1995.

Jones, Charles W. *Saint Nicholas of Myra, Bari, and Manhattan*. Chicago: University of Chicago Press, 1978.

Kantor, Michael. *Broadway: The American Musical*. New York: Bulfinch Press, 2004.

Kasson, John F. *Amusing the Millions: Coney Island at the Turn of the Century*. New York: Hill and Wang, 1978.

Kent, Zachary. *World War I: From the* Lusitania *to Versailles*. Melrose Park, IL: Lake Book Manufacturing, 2011.

Kraut, Alan M. *The Huddled Masses: The Immigrant in American Society*. Arlington Heights, IL: Harlan Davidson, 1982.

Kurlansky, Mark. *The Big Oyster: History on the Half Shell*. New York: Random House, 2006.

Leach, William R. *Land of Desire: Merchants, Power, and the Rise of a New American Culture*. New York: Vintage Books, 1993.

Leuchtenburg, William. *The Perils of Prosperity 1914–32*. Chicago: University of Chicago Press, 1958.

Halloran, Fiona Deans. *Thomas Nast: The Father of Modern Political Cartoons*. Chapel Hill: University of North Carolina Press, 2012.

Harris, Bill. *One Thousand New York Buildings*. New York: Black Dog & Leventhal, 2005.

Henderson, Mary. *The City and the Theatre: The History of New York Playhouses*. New York: Back Stage Books, 2004.

Herwig, Holger H. *The First World War: Germany and Austria-Hungary 1914–1918*, 2nd ed. New York: Bloomsbury Academic, 2014.

Hobsbawm, Eric. *The Age of Extremes: A History of the World, 1914–1991*. New York: Vintage, 1996.

Hunt, Tamara Robin. *Tony Sarg: Puppeteer in America, 1915–1942*. Vancouver: Charlemagne Press, 1988.

Jackson, Kenneth T., ed. *The Encyclopedia of New York City*. New Haven, CT: Yale University Press, 1995.

Jacobson, Gerald F., ed., *History of the 107th Infantry U.S.A.* New York: Seventh Regiment Armory, 1920.

Jonnes, Jill. *Conquering Gotham: Building Penn Station and Its Tunnels*. New York: Penguin Books, 2008.

Lerner, Michael. *Dry Manhattan: Prohibition in New York City*. Cambridge, MA: Harvard University Press, 2009.

Lossing, Benson John. *History of New York City*. New York: Perine Engraving, 1884.

Mackay, Constance D'Arcy, ed. *Patriotic Drama in Your Town*. New York: Henry Holt, 1918.

Macleod, David I. *Building Character in the American Boy: The Boy Scouts, YMCA, and Their Forerunners, 1870–1920*. Madison: University of Wisconsin Press, 1983.

Marcot, Roy. *The History of Remington Firearms*. Guilford, CT: Lyons Press, 2005.

Marling, Karal Ann. *Merry Christmas!: Celebrating America's Greatest Holiday*. Cambridge, MA: Harvard University Press, 2001.

Marshall, David Edward. *The Story of the Rough Riders*. New York: G. W. Dillingham, 1899.

McCabe, James D. *Lights and Shadows of New York Life*. Philadelphia: National Publishing, 1872.

Meggs, Philip B. and Alston W. Purvis. *Meggs' History of Graphic Design*. Hoboken, NJ: Wiley, 2011.

Miles, Clement A. *Christmas in Ritual and Tradition, Christian and Pagan*. London: T. Fisher Unwin, 1912.

Miller, Donald L. *Supreme City: How Jazz Age Manhattan Gave Birth to Modern America*. New York: Simon & Schuster, 2014.

Moore, Clement Clarke. *A Plain Statement, Addressed to the Proprietors of Real Estate, in the City and County of New-York*. New York: J. Eastburn, 1818.

Morrison, Michael A. *John Barrymore, Shakespearean Actor*. New York: Cambridge University Press, 1997.

Murray, William D. *The History of the Boy Scouts of America*. New York: Boy Scouts of America, 1937.

Nasaw, David. *Children of the City: At Work and Play*. New York: Anchor Books, 2012.

Nast, Thomas. *Christmas Drawings for the Human Race*. New York: Harper & Brothers, 1890.

Nissenbaum, Stephen. *The Battle for Christmas*. New York: Vintage, 1997.

Paine, Albert Bigelow. *Th. Nast: His Period and His Pictures*. New York: Macmillan, 1904.

Patterson, Samuel White. *The Poet of Christmas Eve: A Life of Clement Clarke Moore, 1779–1863*. New York: Morehouse-Gorham, 1956.

Paulding, James K. *The New Mirror for Travellers and Guide to the Springs*. New York: G. & C. Carvill, 1828.

Peterson, Robert. *The Boy Scouts: An American Adventure*. New York: American Heritage, 1984.

Pintard, John. *Letters from John Pintard to His Daughter Eliza Noel Pintard Davidson*, 4 vols. New York: New-York Historical Society, 1940.

Piven, Frances Fox. *Regulating the Poor: The Functions of Public Welfare*. New York: Vintage Books, 1993.

Plunkett-Powell, Karen. *Remembering Woolworth's*. New York: St. Martin's Press, 1999.

Radway, Janice, and Carl Kaestle, eds. *A History of the Book in America*, vol. 4: *The Expansion of Publishing and Reading, 1880–1940*. Chapel Hill: University of North Carolina Press, 2008.

Restad, Penne. *Christmas in America: A History*. New York: Oxford University Press, 1995.

Riis, Jacob A. *Children of the Tenements*. New York: MacMillan, 1904.

———. *How the Other Half Lives: Studies Among the Tenements of New York*. New York: Charles Scribner's Sons, 1890.

———. *Is There A Santa Claus?* New York: Macmillan, 1904.

———. *Nibsy's Christmas*. New York: Charles Scribner's Sons, 1893.

Risjord, Norman K. *Giants in Their Times: Representative Americans from the Jazz Age to the Cold War*. Lanham, MD: Rowman & Littlefield, 2006.

Rohe, William, and Harry Watson, eds. *Chasing the American Dream: New Perspectives on Affordable Homeownership*. Ithaca, NY: Cornell University Press, 2007.

Rowan, Edward L. *To Do My Best: James E. West and the History of the Boy Scouts of America*. Las Vegas: Edward Rowan, 2005.

Samuel, Larry. *Rich: The Rise and Fall of American Wealth Culture*. New York: AMACOM, 2009.

Schmidt, Leigh Eric. *Consumer Rites: The Buying and Selling of American Holidays*. Princeton, NJ: Princeton University Press, 1995.

Seal, Jeremy. *Nicholas: The Epic Journey from Saint to Santa Claus*. New York: Bloomsbury USA, 2005.

Seely, Peter, and Gail W. Pieper, eds. *Stoogeology: Essays on the Three Stooges*. Jefferson, NC: McFarland, 2007.

Segrave, Kerry. *Begging in America: 1850–1940*. Jefferson, NC: McFarland, 2011.

Skocpol, Theda. *Protecting Soldiers and Mothers*. Cambridge, MA: Belknap Press of Harvard University Press, 1992.

Snyder, Phillip. *December 25th: The Joys of Christmas Past*. New York: Dodd, Mead, 1985.

Society for the Prevention of Pauperism. "Report of a Committee on the Subject of Pauperism." New York: Samuel Wood & Sons, 1818.

Tangires, Helen. *Public Markets*. New York: W. W. Norton, 2008.

Taylor, William R., ed. *Inventing Times Square: Commerce and Culture at the Crossroads of the World*. Baltimore, MD: Johns Hopkins University Press, 1996.

Trager, James. *The New York Chronology: The Ultimate Compendium of Events, People, and Anecdotes from the Dutch to the Present*. New York: Collins Reference, 2003.

Tumulty, Joseph Patrick. *Woodrow Wilson as I Know Him*. New York: Doubleday, Page, 1921.

United States Senate, Committee on Military Affairs, *Hearing, Regulating Collection of Money*. 65th Congress, 3rd session. Washington, DC: Government Printing Office, 1919.

Vance, Jeffrey. *Douglas Fairbanks*. Berkeley: University of California Press, 2008.

Venzon, Anne Cipriano, ed. *The United States in the First World War: An Encyclopedia*. New York: Routledge, 1995.

Wagenknecht, Edward, ed., *Mrs. Longfellow: Selected Letters and Journals of Fanny Appleton Longfellow (1817–1861)*. New York: Longmans, Green, 1956.

Waggoner, Susan. *Christmas Memories: Gifts, Activities, Fads, and Fancies, 1920s–1960s*. New York: Stewart, Tabori & Chang, 2009.

Waits, William. *The Modern Christmas in America: A Cultural History of Gift Giving*. New York: New York University Press, 1994.

Weintraub, Stanley. *Silent Night: The Story of the World War I Christmas Truce*. New York: Free Press, 2001.

Wiebe, Robert H. *The Search for Order, 1877–1920*. New York: Hill and Wang, 1967.

Williams, Gregory Paul. *The Story of Hollywood: An Illustrated History*. Los Angeles: BL Press, 2005.

Wilson, James Grant. "John Pintard, Founder of the New York Historical Society." New York: New-York Historical Society. 1902.

Winkler, John Kennedy. *Five and Ten: The Fabulous Life of F. W. Woolworth*. New York: R. M. McBride, 1940.

Index

Note: Abbreviations BSA, NYC, SCA, USBS stand for Boy Scouts of America, New York City, Santa Claus Association, and United States Boy Scouts, respectively. Page numbers for photographs are shown in *italics*.